RACINET'S HISTORIC ORNAMENT

in Full Color

All 100 Plates from "L'Ornement Polychrome," Series I

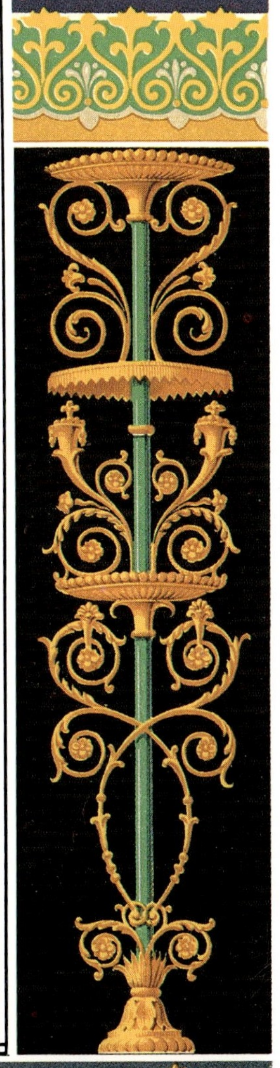

AUGUSTE RACINET

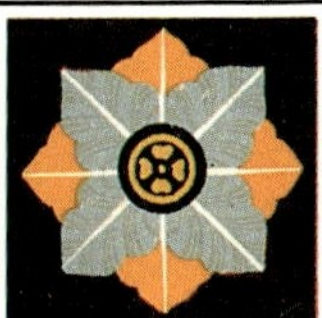

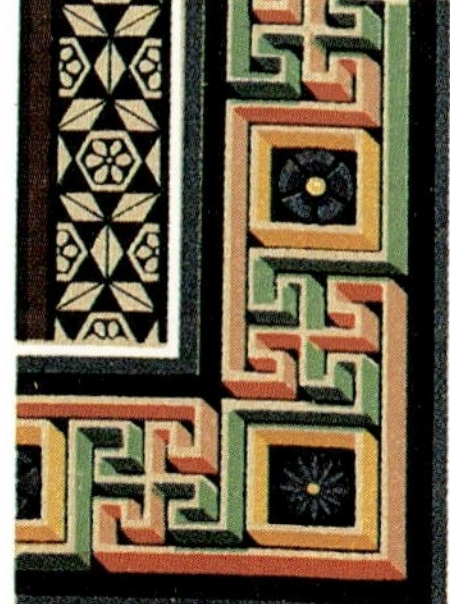

DOVER PUBLICATIONS, INC.
NEW YORK

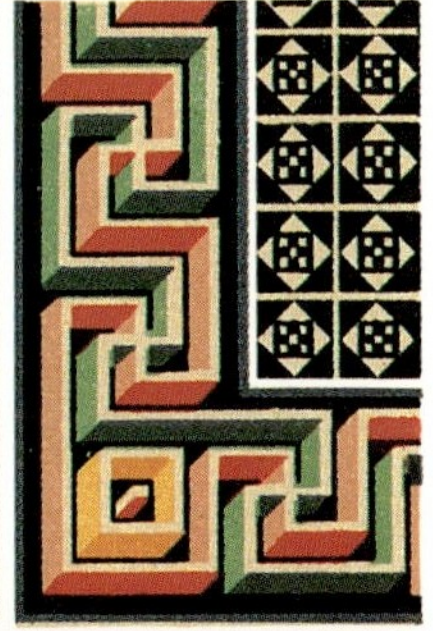

Published in Canada by General Publishing Company, Ltd., 30 Lesmill Road, Don Mills, Toronto, Ontario.
Published in the United Kingdom by Constable and Company, Ltd., 10 Orange Street, London WC2H 7EG.

This Dover edition, first published in 1988, contains all 100 color plates from the third edition (n.d.) of Racinet's *L'Ornement Polychrome*, originally published by the Librairie de Firmin-Didot et C[ie], Paris (see Publisher's Note for longer title and further bibliographical details). The original French text is here omitted, being replaced by new captions, Publisher's Note and List of Illustrations in English, all prepared specially for the present edition.

Manufactured in the United States of America
Dover Publications, Inc., 31 East 2nd Street, Mineola, N.Y. 11501

Library of Congress Cataloging-in-Publication Data

Racinet's historic ornament in full color : all 100 plates from "L'ornement polychrome," Series I [edited by] Auguste Racinet.
p. cm.
"The original French text is here omitted, being replaced by new captions, publisher's note, and list of illustrations in English"—T.p. verso.
ISBN 0-486-25787-8 (pbk.)
1. Color decoration and ornament—Themes, motives. I. Racinet, A. (Auguste), 1825–1893. II. L'ornament polychrome.
NK1548.R34 1988
745.4'4—dc19 88-20225
CIP

PUBLISHER'S NOTE

Though he himself was a distinguished painter and illustrator, Albert-Charles-Auguste Racinet (1825–1893) is best remembered for two monumental color-plate publications he edited: *Le Costume historique* (Historic Costume)[1] and *L'Ornement polychrome* (Color Ornament).

L'Ornement polychrome, a visual record in color of ornament and decorative arts from all over the world and throughout history to the end of the eighteenth century, eventually included 220 plates. The first 100 plates (referred to for convenience in the present Dover volume as Series I, although they were not so called until the publication of the second series mentioned below) appeared in ten installments between 1869 and 1873. A first edition of 5000 copies in volume form was published shortly after the completion of the installments, a second edition appearing as early as 1875.[2]

The original subtitle of "Series I" was: "Cent planches en couleurs or et argent contenant environ 2,000 motifs de tous les styles / art ancien et asiatique / Moyen Age / Renaissance, XVIIe et XVIIIe siècles / Recueil historique et pratique publié sous la direction de M. A. Racinet / l'un des dessinateurs du Moyen Age et la Renaissance, des Arts somptuaires, de la Collection Soltikoff, etc. / avec des notices explicatives et une introduction générale" (100 plates in color, including gold and silver, containing about 2,000 motifs in all styles: art of antiquity, Asia, Middle Ages, Renaissance and the 17th and 18th centuries / Historical and practical collection published under the direction of Mr. A. Racinet, one of the draftsmen of [the books] *Le Moyen Age et la Renaissance, Les Arts somptuaires, La Collection Soltikoff,* etc. / With explanatory text and a general introduction).[3]

The first 100 plates of *L'Ornement polychrome* ("Series I"), in their various editions, were so successful that Racinet later (1885–1887) issued another 120 plates specifically designated as "Deuxième série" (with a reference to the first 100 plates as "1re série").

The present Dover edition contains all the plates from Series I, with brief new

---

[1]*Le Costume historique*, with 500 plates (300 in full color), was issued in parts from 1876 to 1886 and published in volumes in 1888. In 1987 Dover published 92 of the color plates in its volume *Racinet's Full-Color Pictorial History of Western Costume* (ISBN 0-486-25464-X).

[2]The third edition, used for this Dover volume, bears no date. As Racinet himself pointed out, no loss of plate quality could occur from one edition to another because of the chromolithographic technology employed: the proofs were pulled by a transfer method that caused no wear and tear to the original lithographic stones.

[3]In the present Dover edition, all the French text has been omitted. In its place are new English captions, a new list of illustrations and this Publisher's Note. In addition, Arabic numerals here replace the Roman numerals of the original in the plate numbers.

English captions that summarize the French text. The copious material, ranging from Europe to Oceania and from ancient Egypt to just before 1800, is derived from architecture, painting, woodwork, metalwork, leatherwork, textiles and many other art forms. Racinet's often-repeated purpose in publishing these decorative masterpieces was the encouragement and improvement of the arts of his own day, not only the so-called fine arts but also the commercial arts involved in the designing and selling of manufactured goods. Dover's reissue of the plates, recognizing their perennial value and appeal, naturally is meant to serve the same purpose. Racinet's breadth of insight and catholicity of taste, truly enlightened for his day, give his selection a welcome variety and a consistently high standard of excellence; while the consummate skill of his artistic fellow workers and of his printer/publisher, the celebrated Firmin-Didot company, make these plates true works of art in their own right.

Racinet's color plates were prepared on the basis of old works of art by a number of capable commercial artists, identified in the original editions at the lower left-hand corner of each plate. The following artists are represented in Series I of *L'Ornement polychrome:*

Bauer: 10, 17, 32, 39, 52, 63, 84, 88.
Daumont: 16, 37, 40, 43, 83.
Dufour & Bauer: 26.
Dufour & F. Durin: 1, 28, 73, 78, 86.
Dufour & Jeanningros: 82.
Dufour & Launay: 45.
Dufour & Laval: 65.
Dufour & Lebreton: 4, 44.
Dufour & Mathieu: 5.
Dufour & Picard: 79.
Dufour & Pralon: 90.
Dufour & Sanier: 6, 29.
Durin, F.: 7, 11, 14, 18, 19, 20, 25, 27, 33, 35, 41, 48, 49, 50, 51, 54, 62, 64, 67, 81, 91, 94, 96.
Gandon & Durin: 3.
Jetot: 9, 13, 15, 31, 59.
Kraatz (Krautz?) & Durin: 58.
Kraatz & Sanier: 72.
Laugier: 21.
Launay: 76, 87, 92, 93, 97, 98, 99, 100.
Lebreton (Le Breton?): 23.
Lebreton & Bailly: 22.
Lemoine: 68.
Leveil: 85.
Ligogue & Pralon: 57.
Painlevé: 12, 38, 42, 47, 53, 95.
Picard: 24, 70.
Pralon: 2, 34, 55, 56, 60, 61, 69, 71, 80.
Sanier, G.: 36, 66, 74, 75, 77, 89.
Sulpis & F. Durin: 8.
Wolfart: 46.

LIST OF ILLUSTRATIONS

36. Byzantine/Early Medieval: Mosaics from Palermo and Salerno.
37. Medieval: Designs from ivory and wood inlays, France and Italy, 14th and 15th centuries.
38. Medieval: "Celtic" ornament from manuscripts, British Isles, 7th–9th centuries.
39. Medieval: "Celtic" ornament from British and continental manuscripts, 7th–11th centuries.
40. Medieval: Romanesque manuscript ornaments, 11th and 12th centuries.
41. Medieval: Designs from embroideries, murals, manuscript illuminations and enamels.
42. Medieval: Ornaments from a 14th-century Italian manuscript.
43. Medieval: Ornaments from 14th- and 15th-century Italian manuscripts.
44. Medieval: Stained glass, 12th–14th centuries (various French and German cathedrals).
45. Medieval: Stained glass, 13th–15th centuries (Cologne, Bourges, Chartres, Strasbourg, Tournai).
46. Medieval: Designs from wall and floor tiles, 13th and 14th centuries.
47. Medieval: Designs from textiles depicted in 16th-century manuscript illuminations.
48. Medieval: Floral ornament from 15th-century manuscripts.
49. Medieval: Flowers and jewels from 15th-century manuscripts.
50. Medieval: Ornaments from 15th-century French and Flemish manuscripts.
51. Renaissance: Ornaments from a printed (but hand-colored) French book of hours, 1508.
52. Renaissance: Ornaments from a late 15th-century Italian manuscript.
53. Renaissance: From Raphael's frescoes in the Vatican, early 16th century.
54. Renaissance: From 16th-century frescoes in Milan and in the Vatican (by Raphael and others).
55. Renaissance: Miniatures from Italianate manuscripts of the early 16th century.
56. Renaissance: Designs from engraved ivories, including furniture inlays.
57. Renaissance: From Italian frescoes and manuscripts, 15th and 16th centuries.
58. Renaissance: Cartouches, Italianate, 15th and early 16th centuries.
59. Renaissance: From Limoges enamels and Italian faience, 16th century.
60. Renaissance: Glazed tiles.
61. Renaissance: Painting on vellum, on the election of Pope Gregory XIII, 1573.
62. 16th & 17th Centuries: Enameled metalwork and jewelry.
63. Renaissance: From Spanish illuminated manuscripts, late 16th century.
64. Renaissance: From French and Italian illuminated manuscripts.
65. Renaissance: Ceiling from the Palais de Justice, Rouen, ca. 1500.
66. Renaissance: Stone and wood carvings, and manuscript illuminations, France, 16th century.
67. Renaissance: Glazed earthenware by Bernard Palissy, France, 16th century.
68. Renaissance: From Venetian book covers and marquetry.
69. 16th & 17th Centuries: From French and Italian book covers.
70. Renaissance: Painted and typographic book ornament, France, 16th century.
71. Renaissance: Ornament from books and architectural painting, France, 16th century.
72. 16th & 17th Centuries: Cartouches from French and Flemish manuscripts and maps.
73. 16th & 17th Centuries: From embroidered wall hangings.

74. 17th Century: Louis XIII ornament from furniture and architecture.
75. 17th Century: Louis XIII ornament from a gilt leather hanging.
76. Early 17th Century: From murals, manuscripts and metalwork.
77. Early 17th Century: Cartouches from French and Flemish architectural maps.
78. Early 17th Century: From embroideries, leatherwork, woodwork and book décor.
79. 17th Century: From murals in the Louvre designed by Jean Bérain.
80. Later 17th Century: From a ceiling in a Parisian mansion.
81. 17th Century: From architectural paintings at Versailles and a furniture marble inlay.
82. 17th & 18th Centuries: From Rouen, Lille and Moustiers faience.
83. Late 17th Century: From French tapestries.
84. 17th & 18th Centuries: From inlaid furniture in the style of A.-C. Boulle.
85. Late 17th Century: Silk fabric and stamped book endpaper.
86. 17th & 18th Centuries: From gilt and color-printed leatherwork.
87. 17th/18th Century: Painted Louis XIV carpet design by Robert de Cotte.
88. 17th/18th Century: Painted tapestry designs by Robert de Cotte and others.
89. 17th & 18th Centuries: From Gobelin tapestries.
90. Early 18th Century: From a ceiling in a Versailles mansion.
91. Early 18th Century: From a painted French harpsichord.
92. 18th Century: From French tapestries, woodwork and a book cover.
93. 18th Century: Cartouches from various sources, France and Germany.
94. 17th and 18th Centuries: French chatelaines.
95. 18th Century: French silk fabrics.
96. 18th Century: Designs from snuffboxes and a fan, and borders (all French).
97. 18th Century: From French tapestries.
98. 18th Century: From painted Sèvres porcelain.
99. 18th Century: Designs from French lacquered woodwork and furniture.
100. 18th Century: Wall painting, from a French mansion, by van Spaendonck.

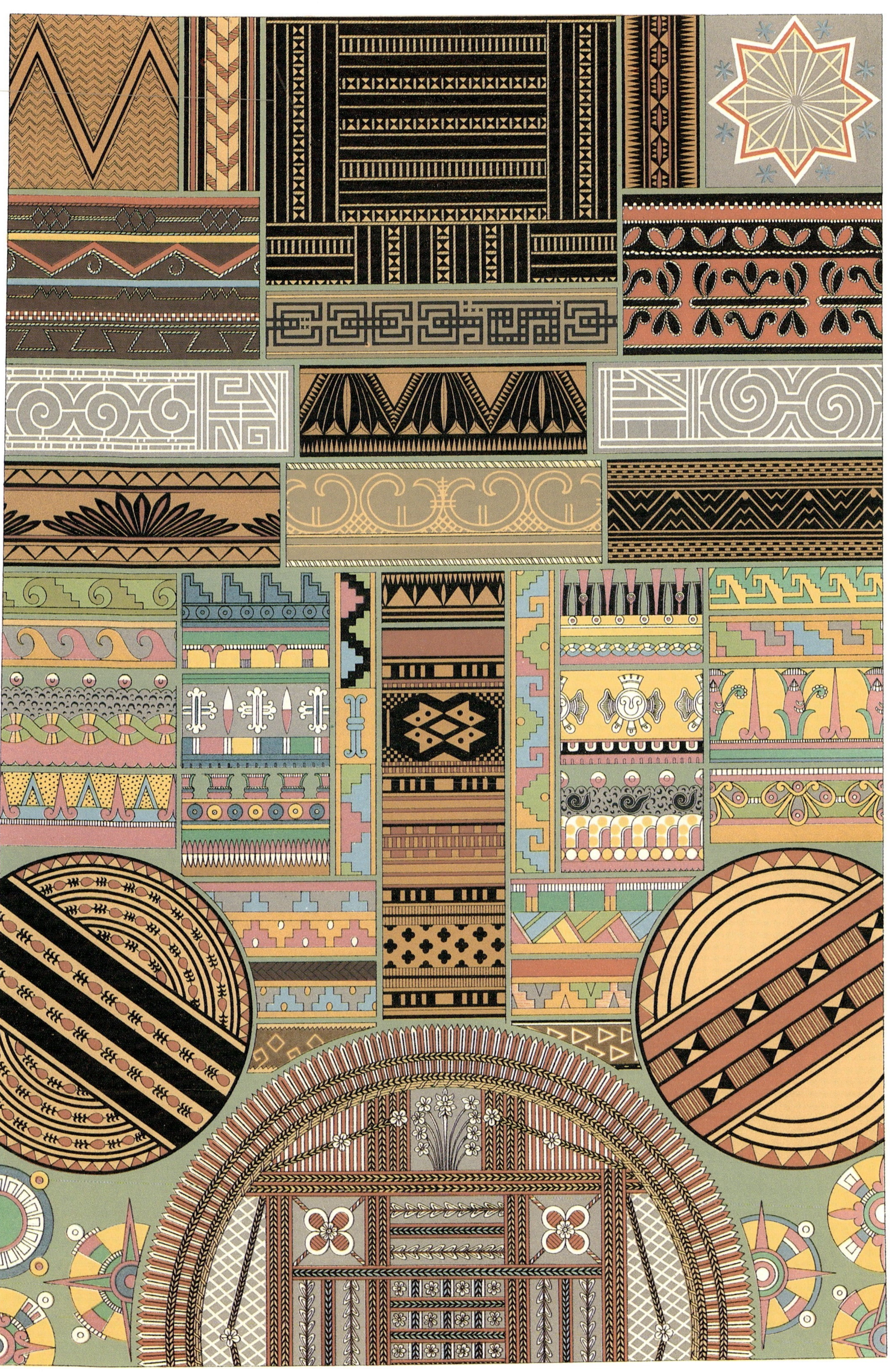

1. Oceania, Africa and Pre-Columbian Peru and Mexico: Painted decor and designs from various crafts.

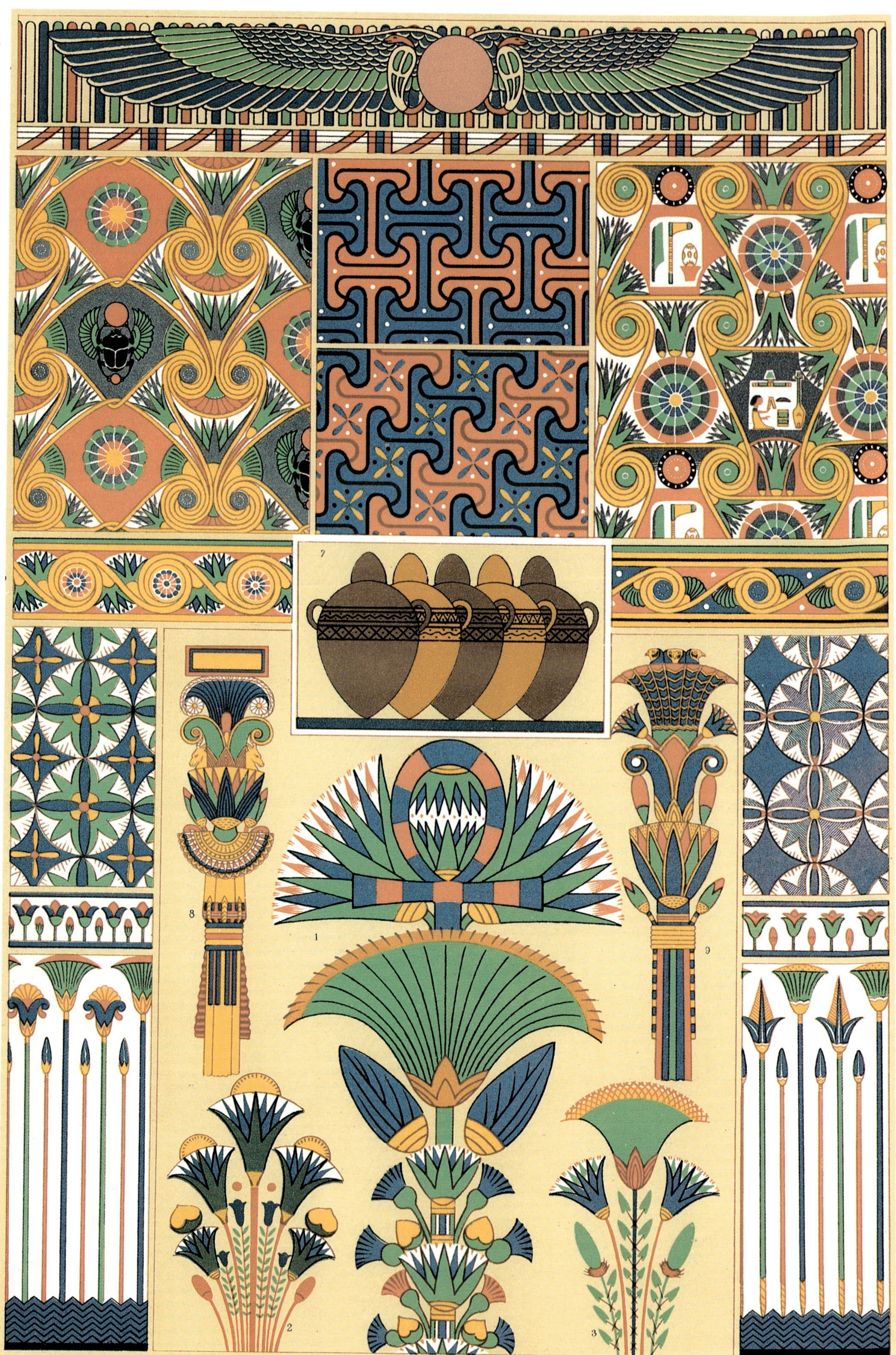

2. Ancient Egypt: Architectural and sculptural painted ornament.

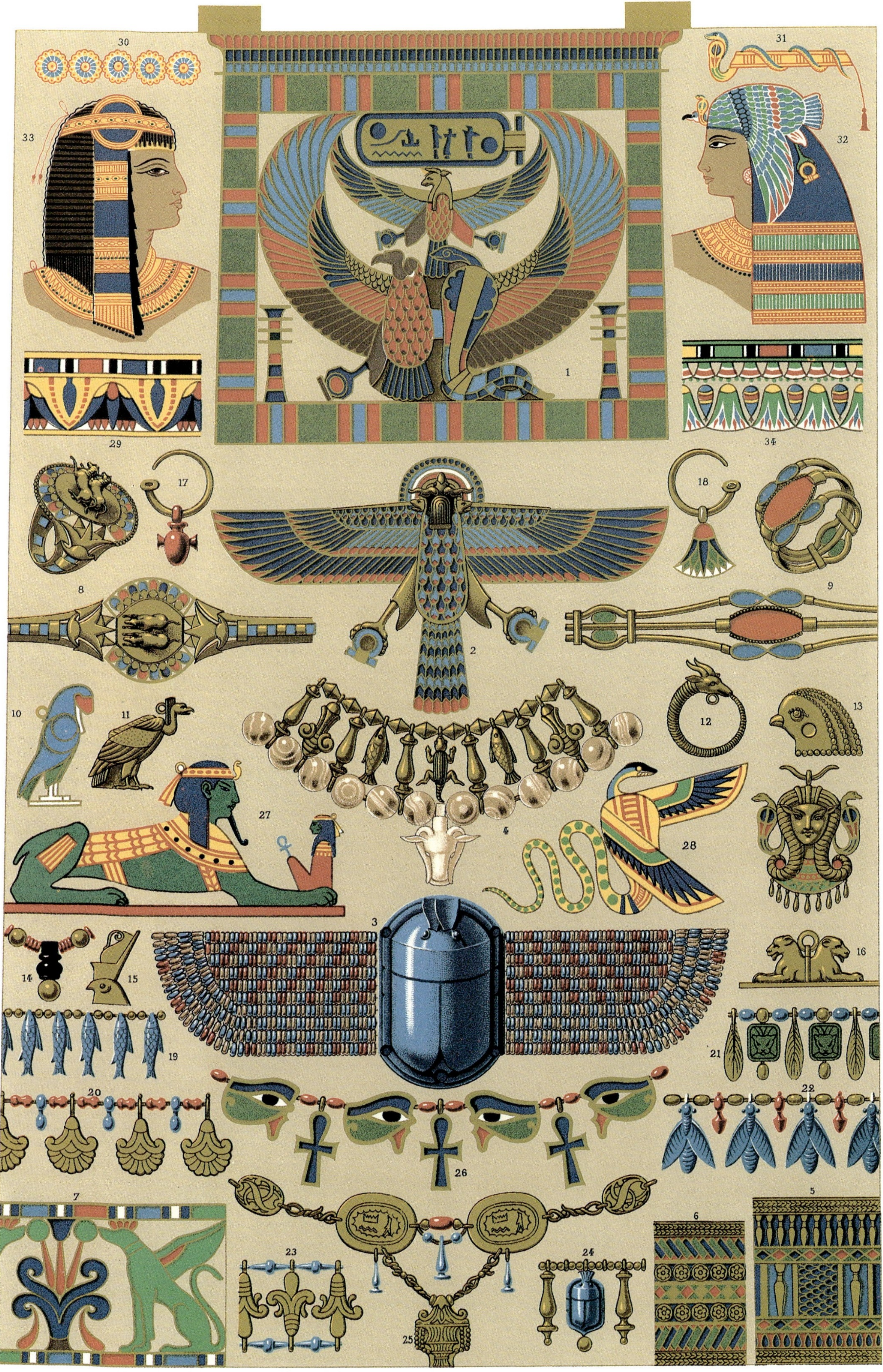

3. Ancient Egypt: Jewelry.

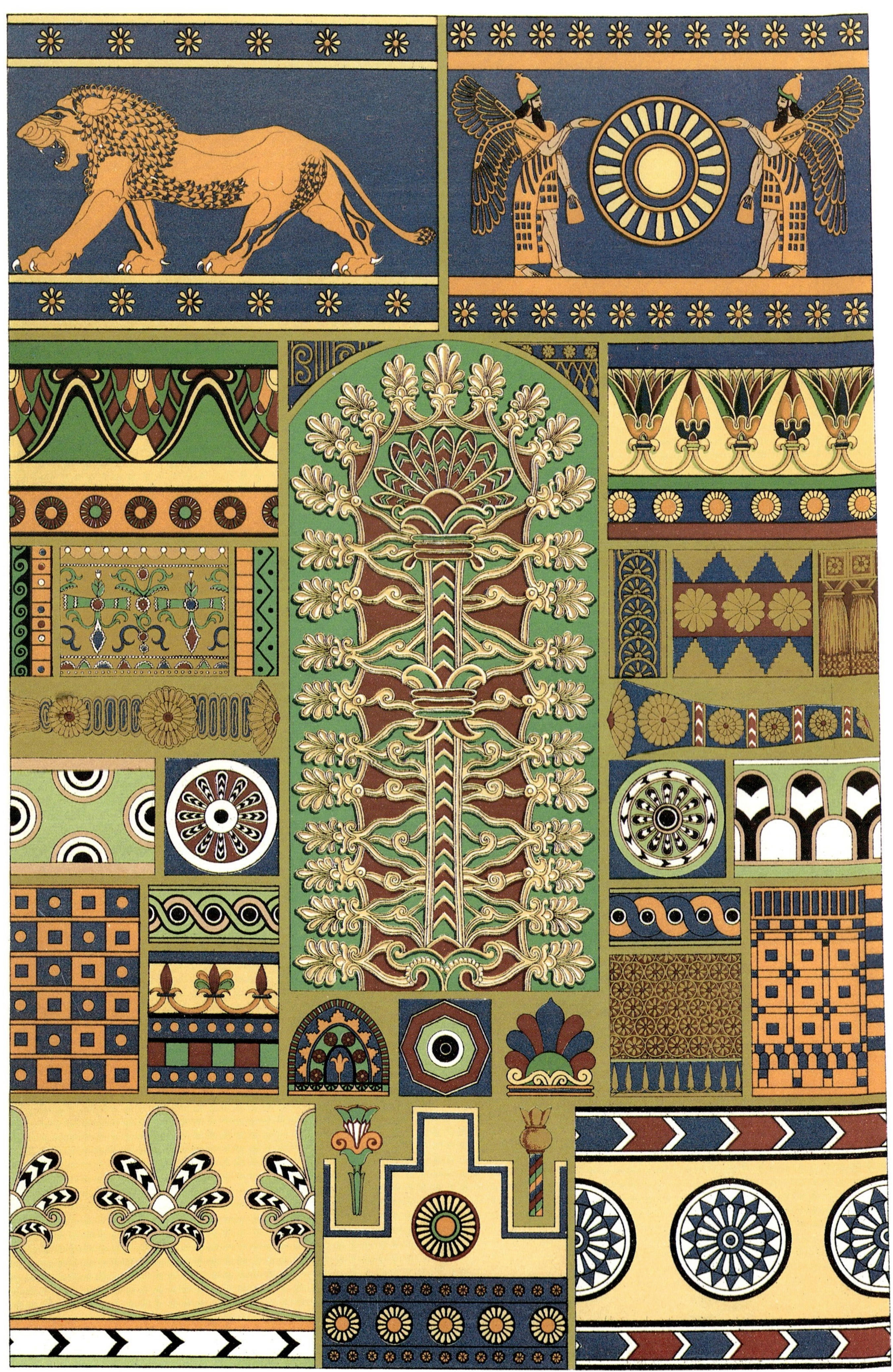

4. Assyria and Ancient Persia: Architectural ornament from Nineveh and Persepolis.

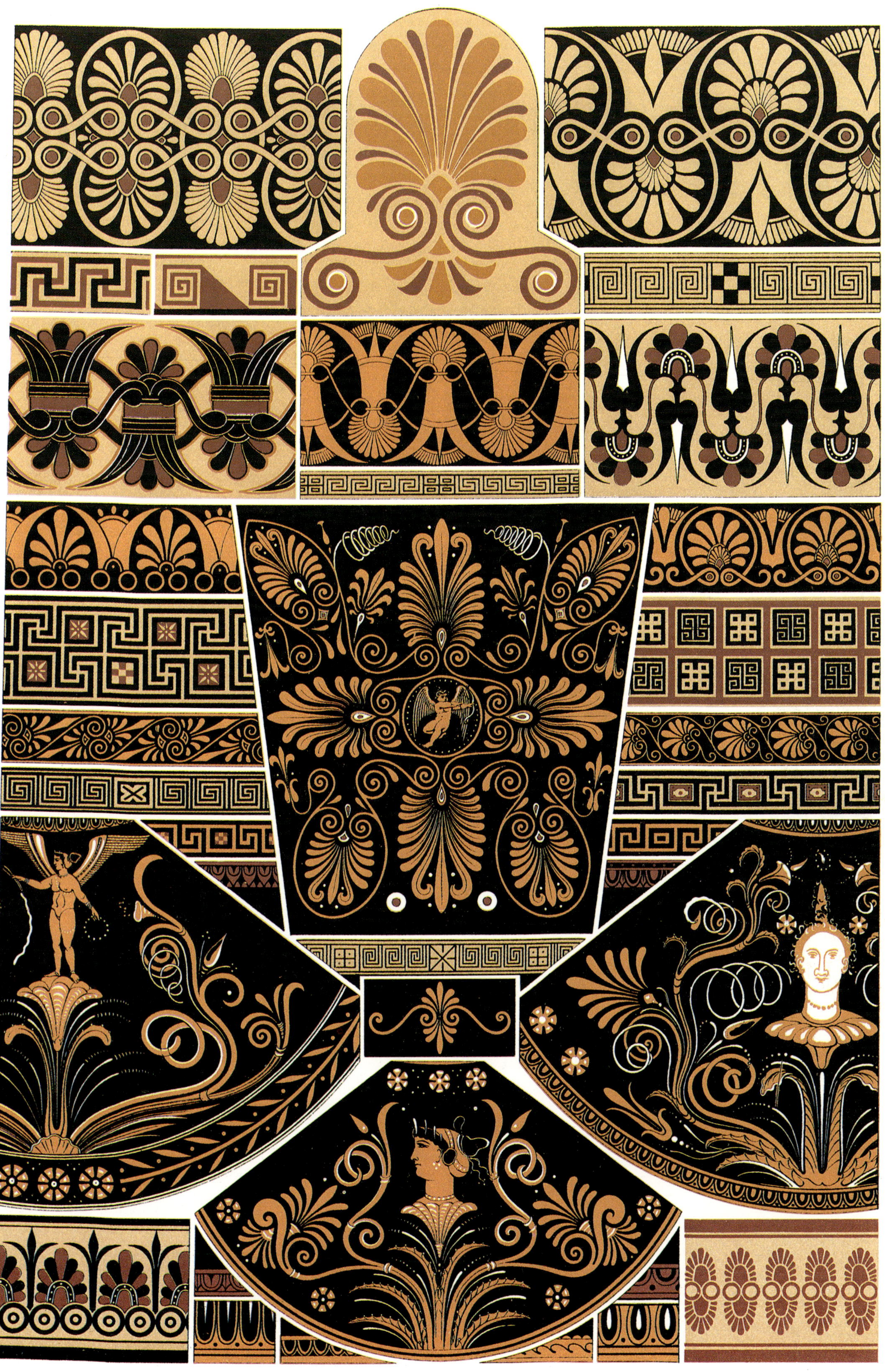

5. Ancient Greece: Floral ornament and frets from terra-cottas and vases.

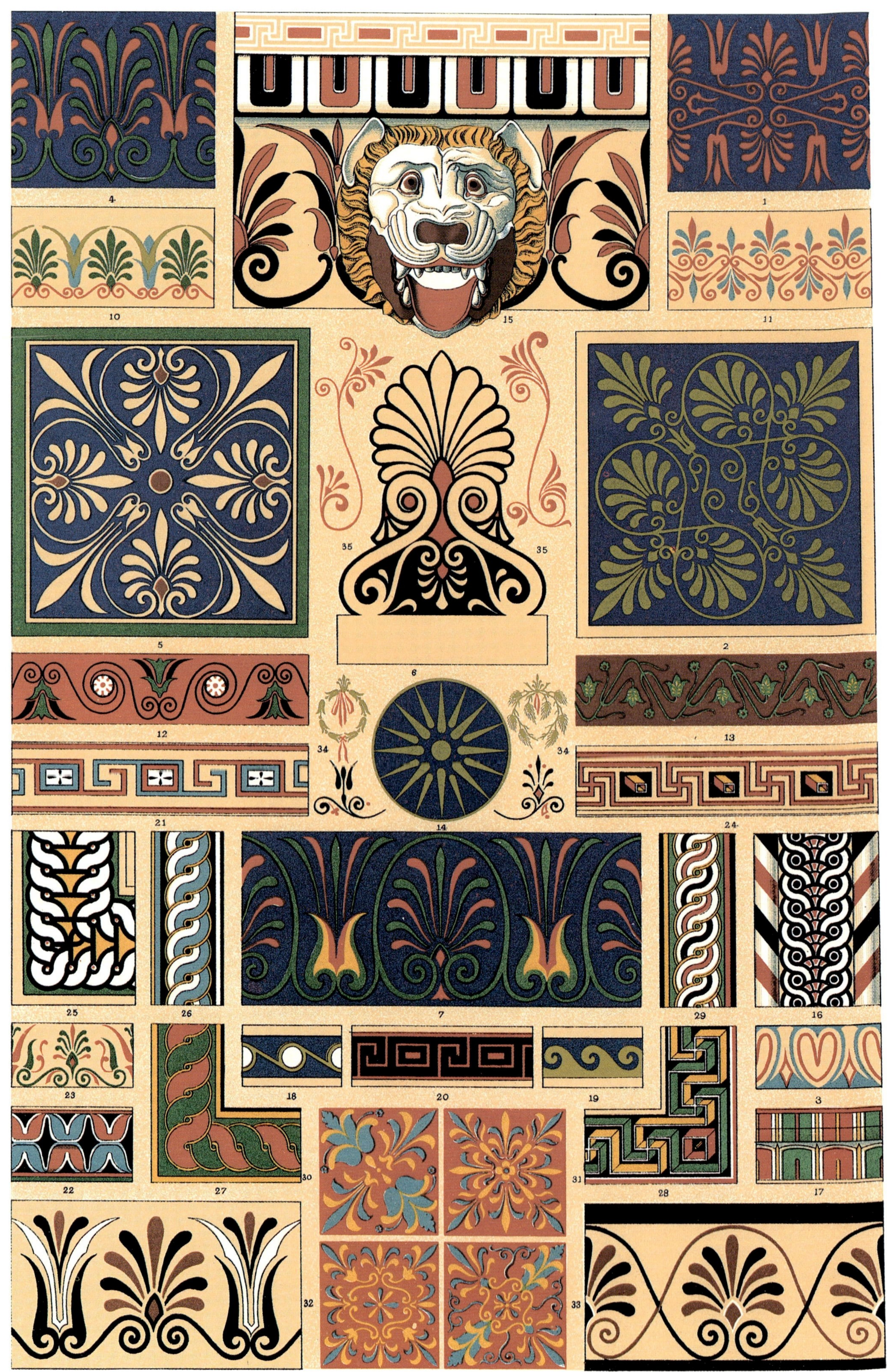

6. Ancient Greece: Ornament, chiefly architectural.

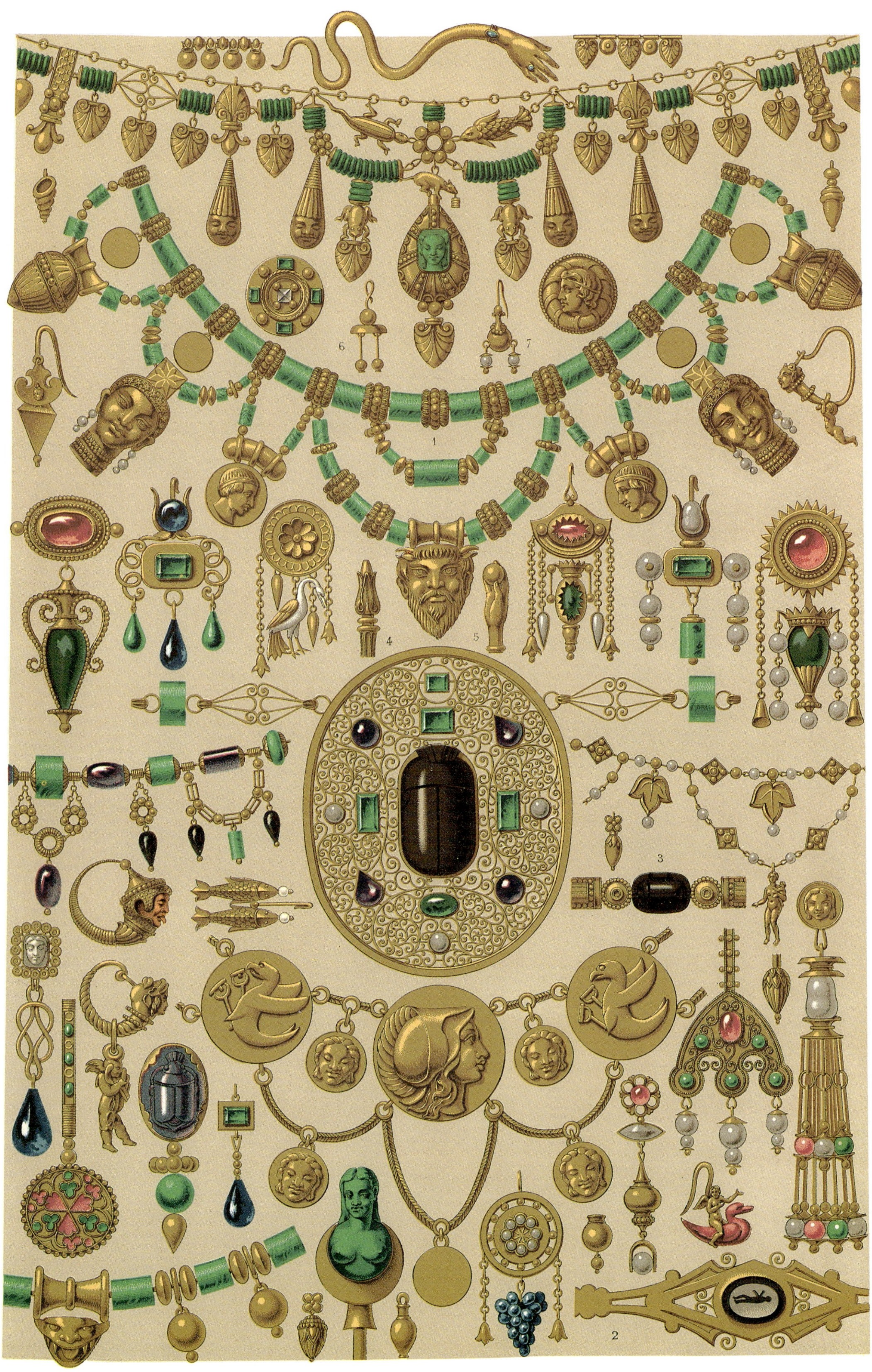

7. Ancient Italy: Etruscan jewelry.

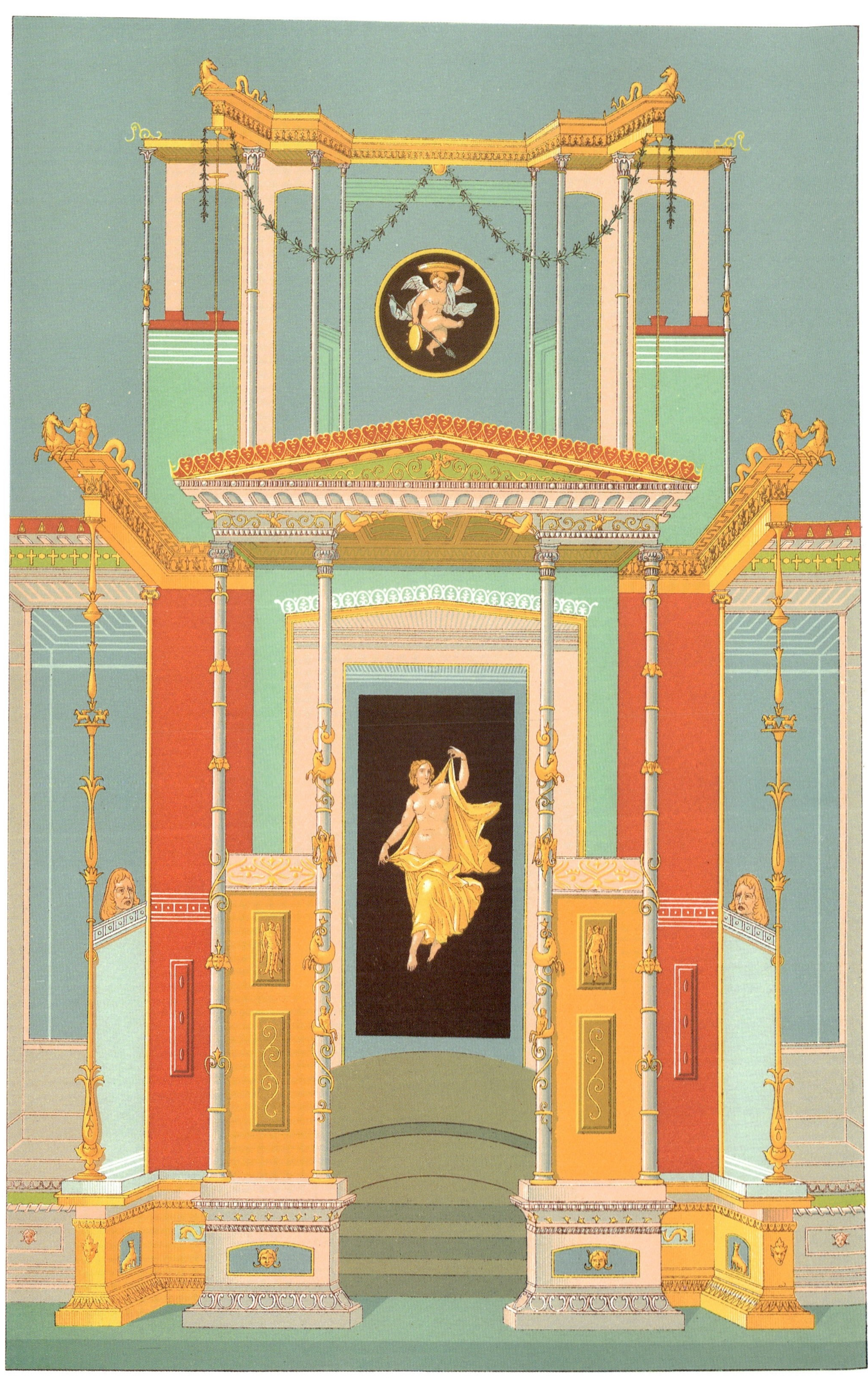

8. Ancient Italy: Wall painting from Pompeii.

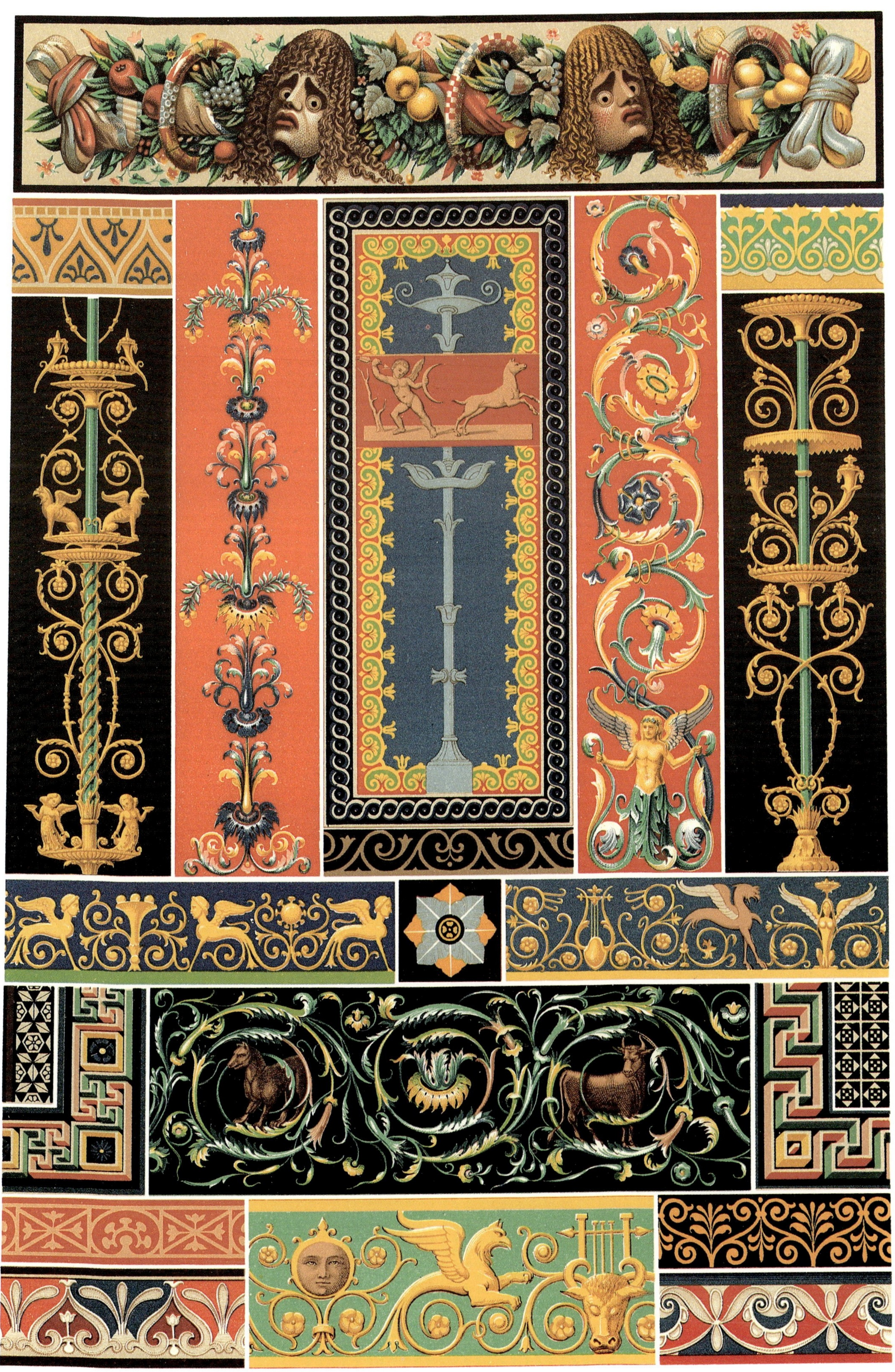

9. Ancient Italy: Mosaics and murals from Pompeii and Herculaneum.

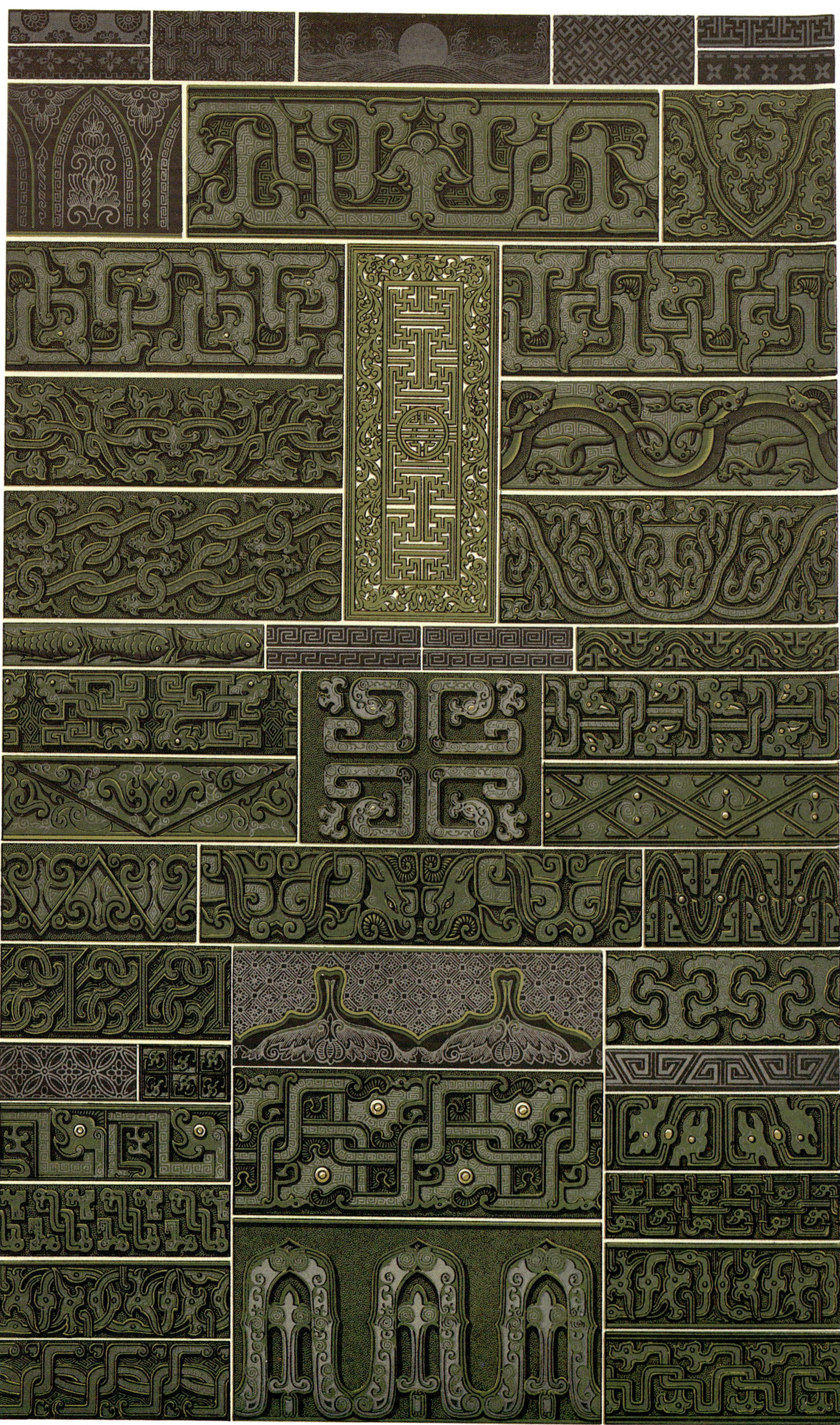

10. China: Designs from metal vessels.

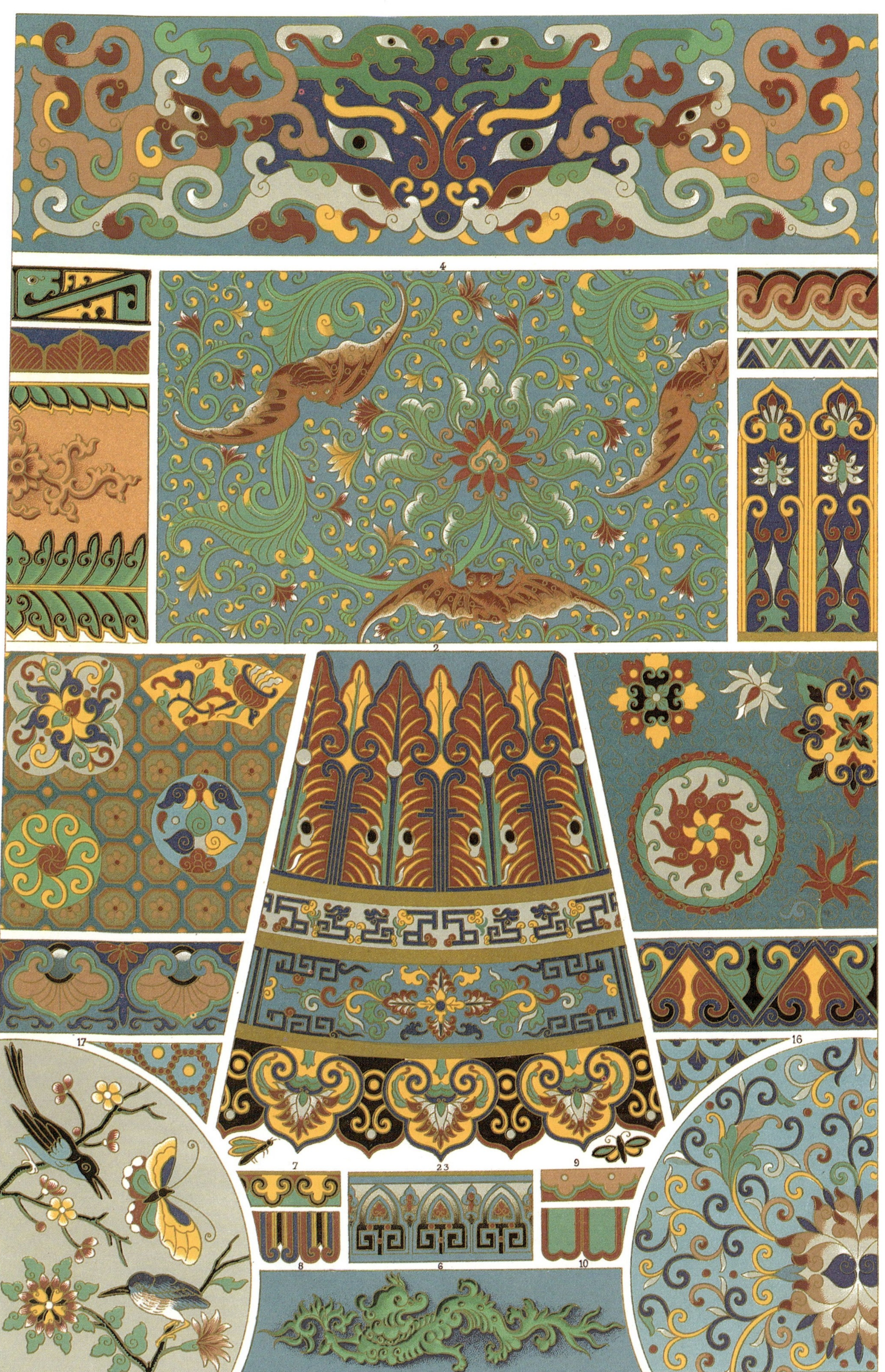

11. China and Japan: Designs from cloisonné enamels.

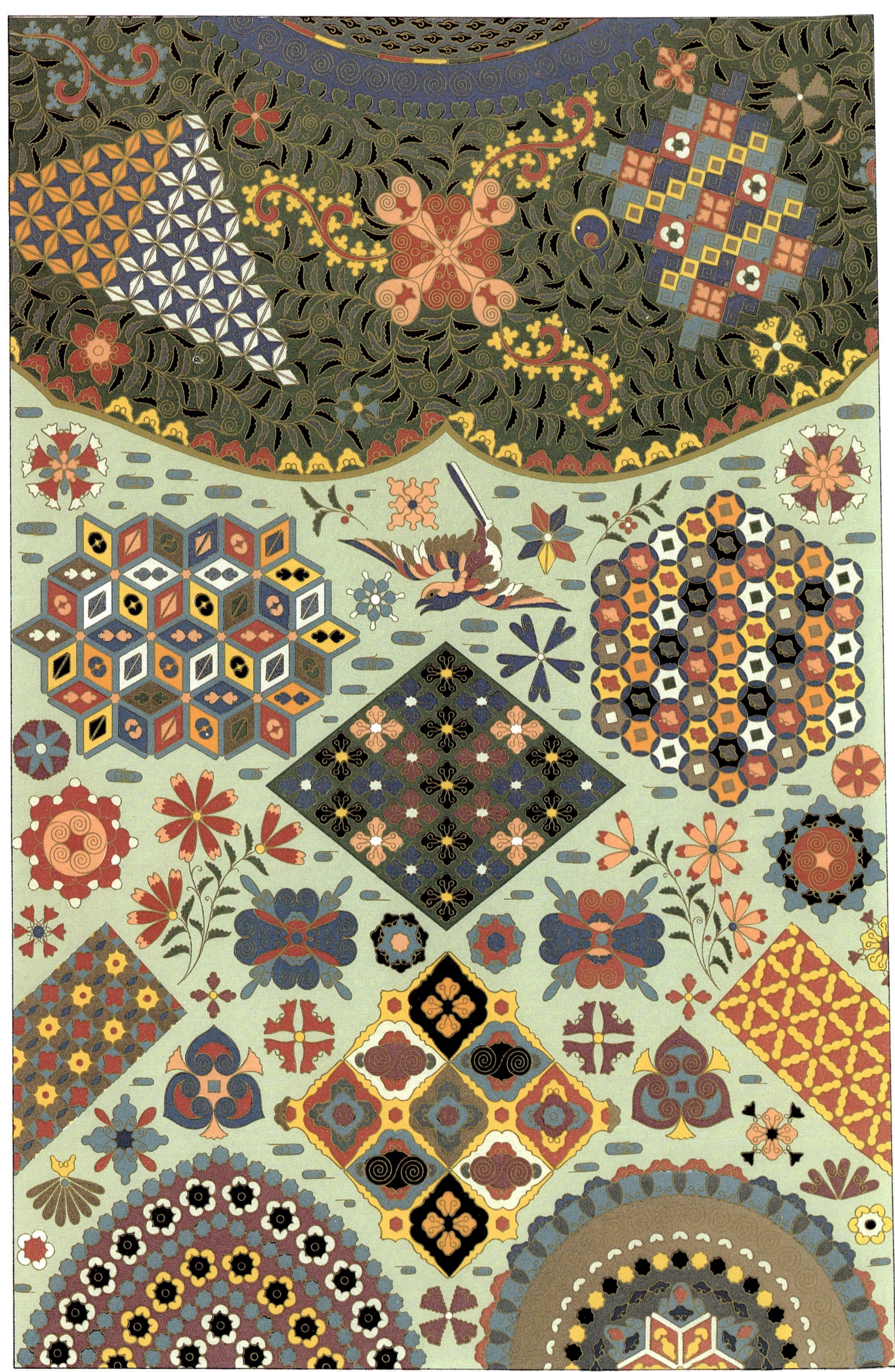

12. Japan: Designs from cloisonné enamels.

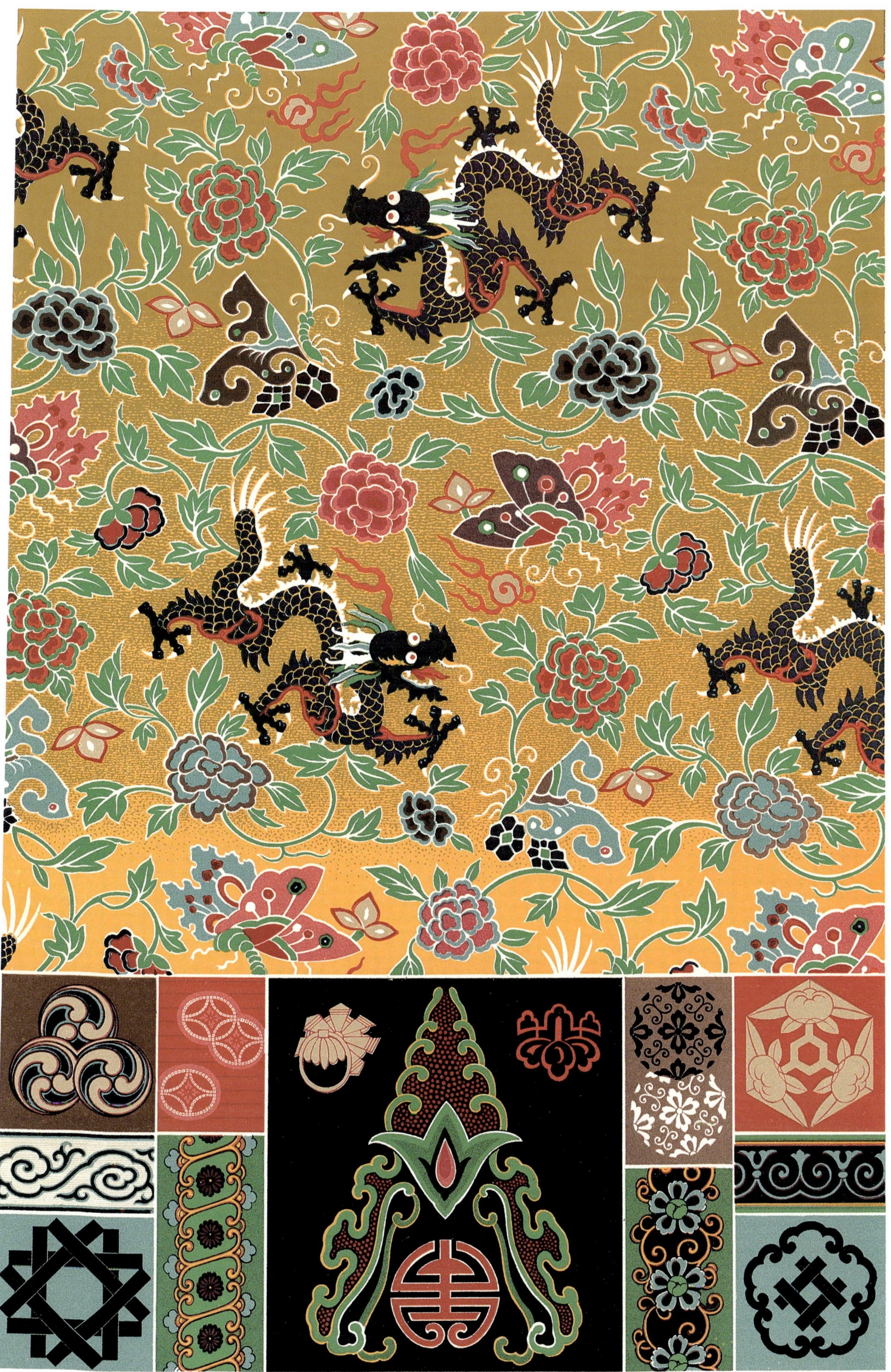

13. China and Japan: Design from a silk fabric and various motifs.

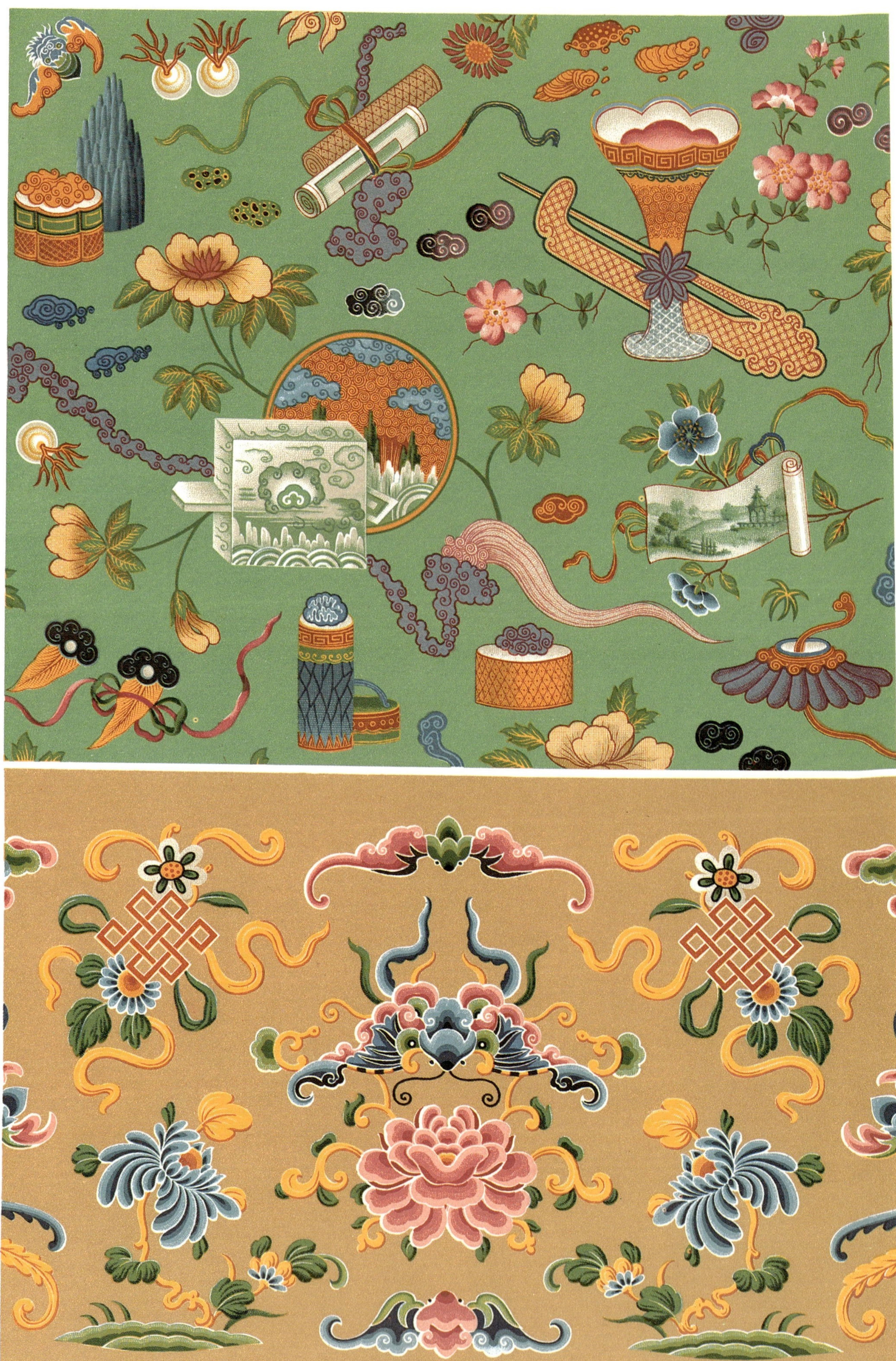

14. China: Free and symmetrical continuous patterns.

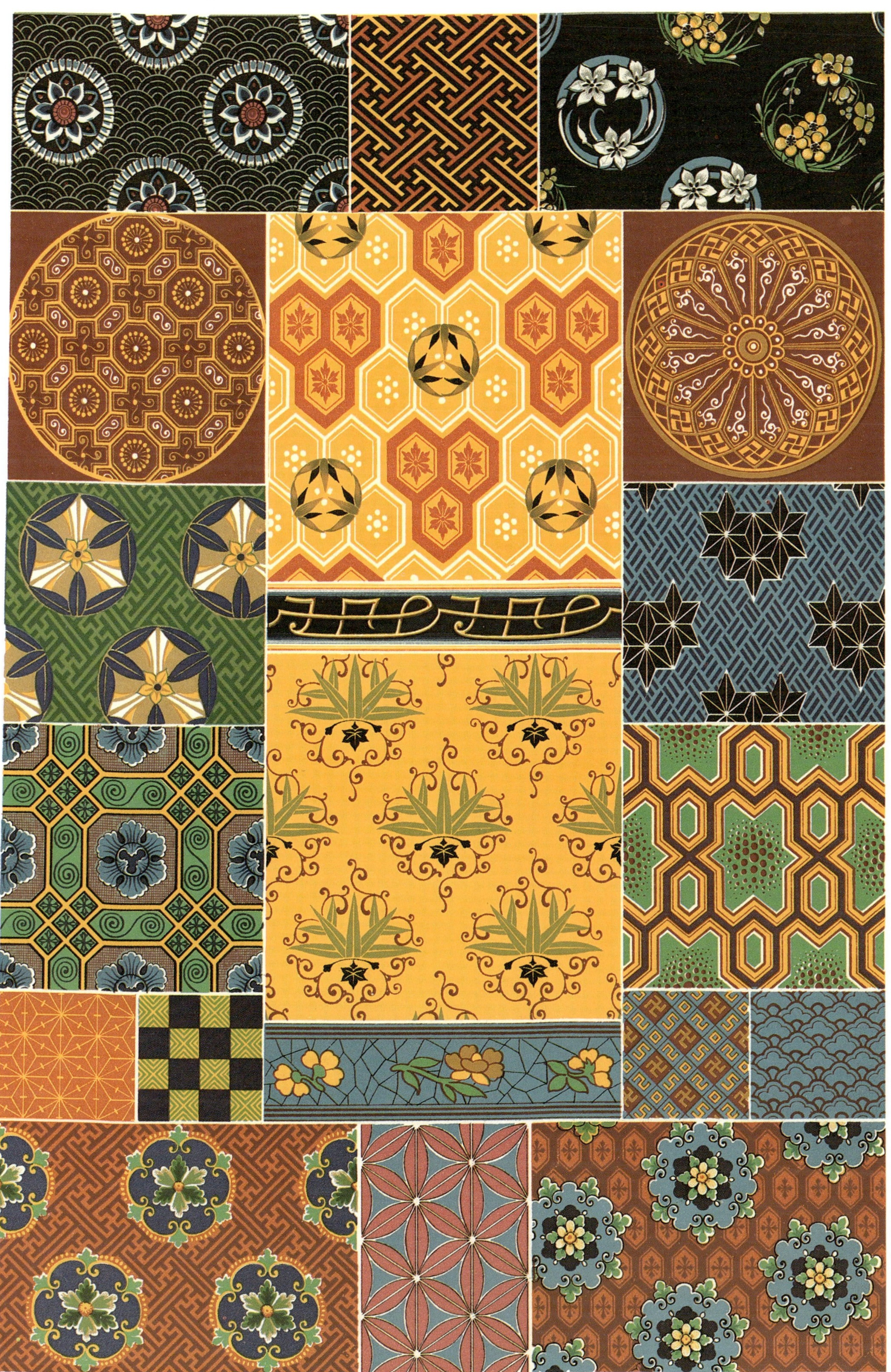

15. China and Japan: Fragments of allover designs.

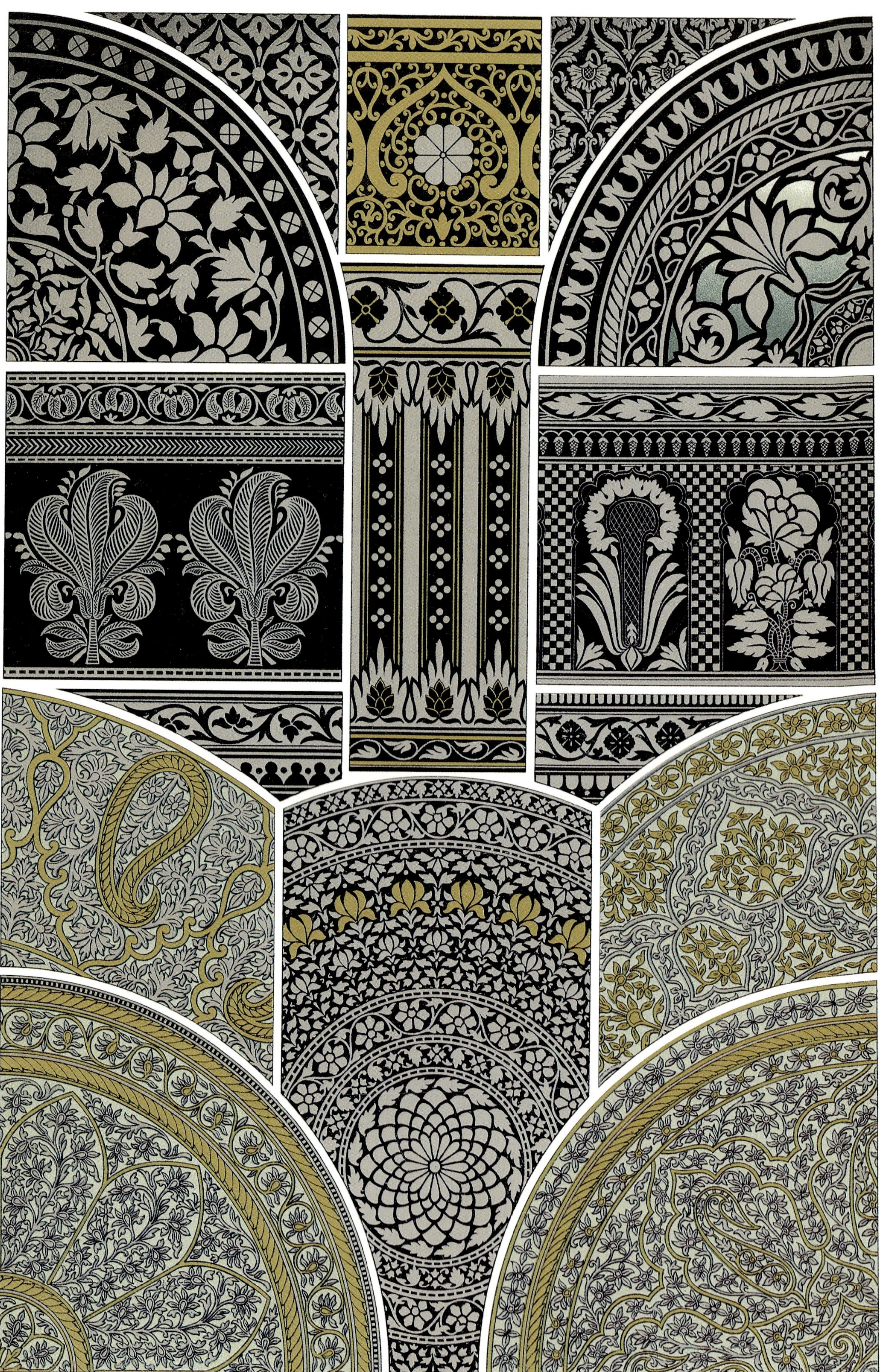

16. India: Designs from engraved and inlaid metal.

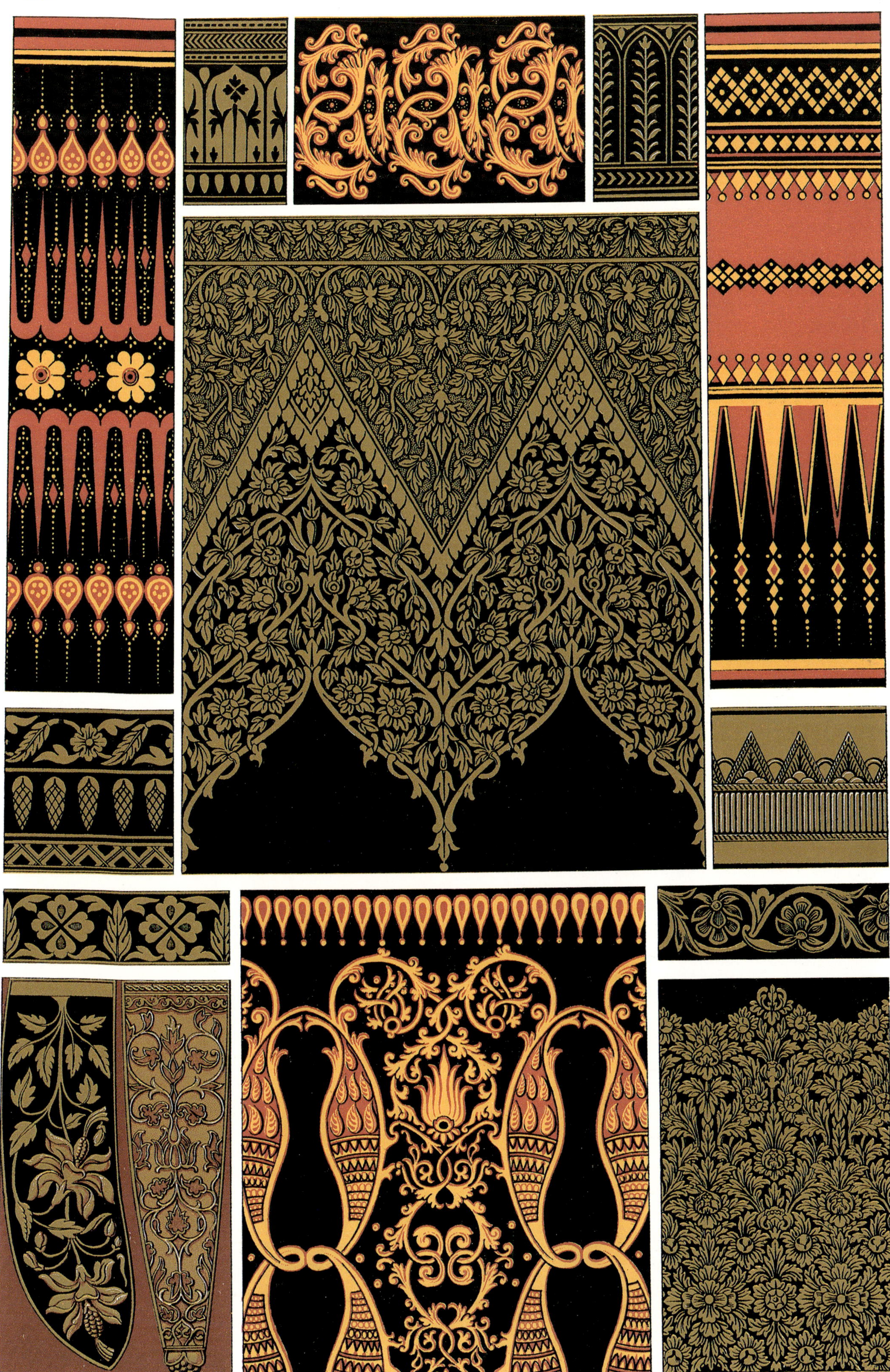

17. India: Designs from painting and metalwork.

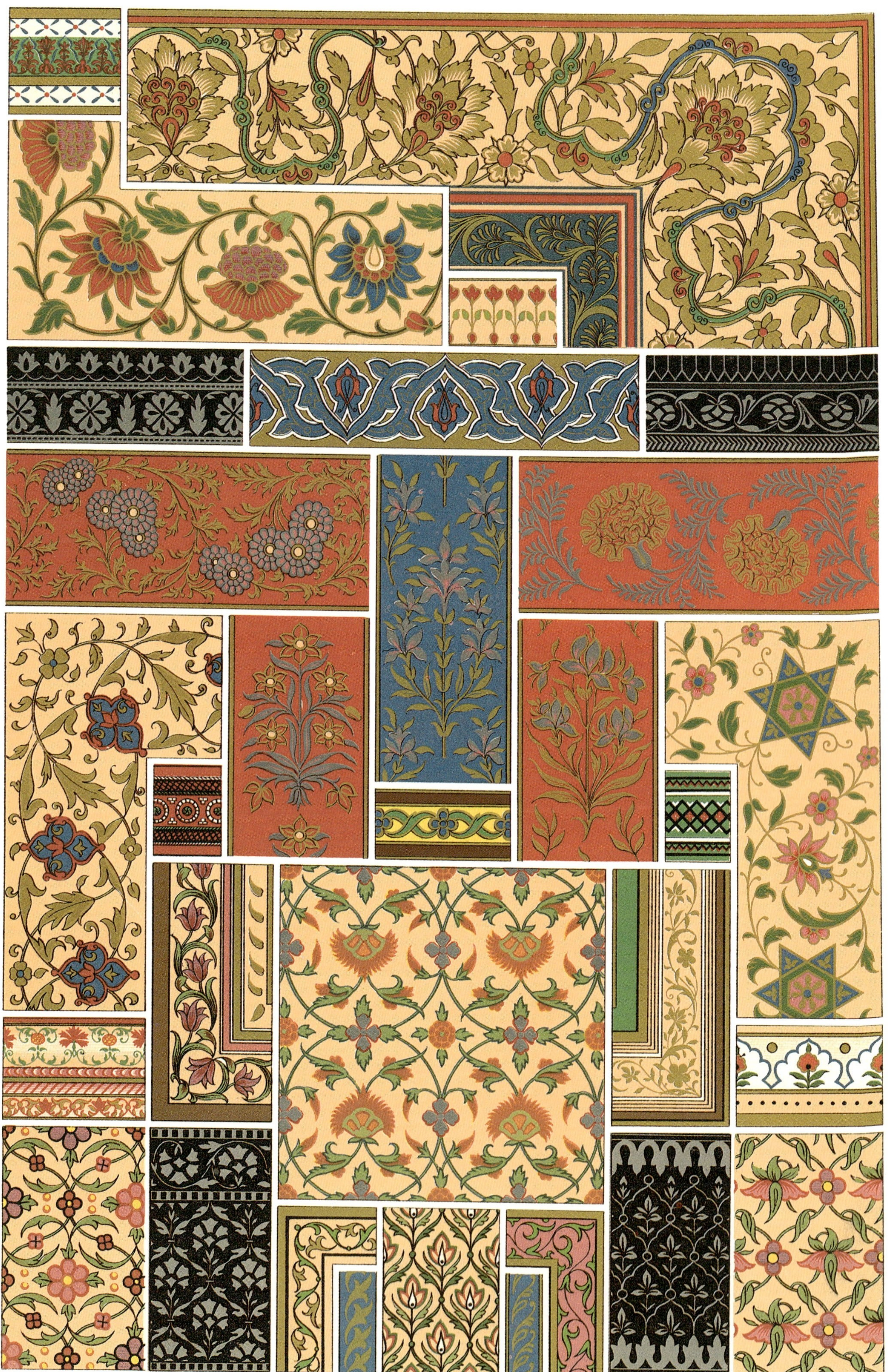

18. India: Florals and scrollwork from textiles, manuscripts and metalwork.

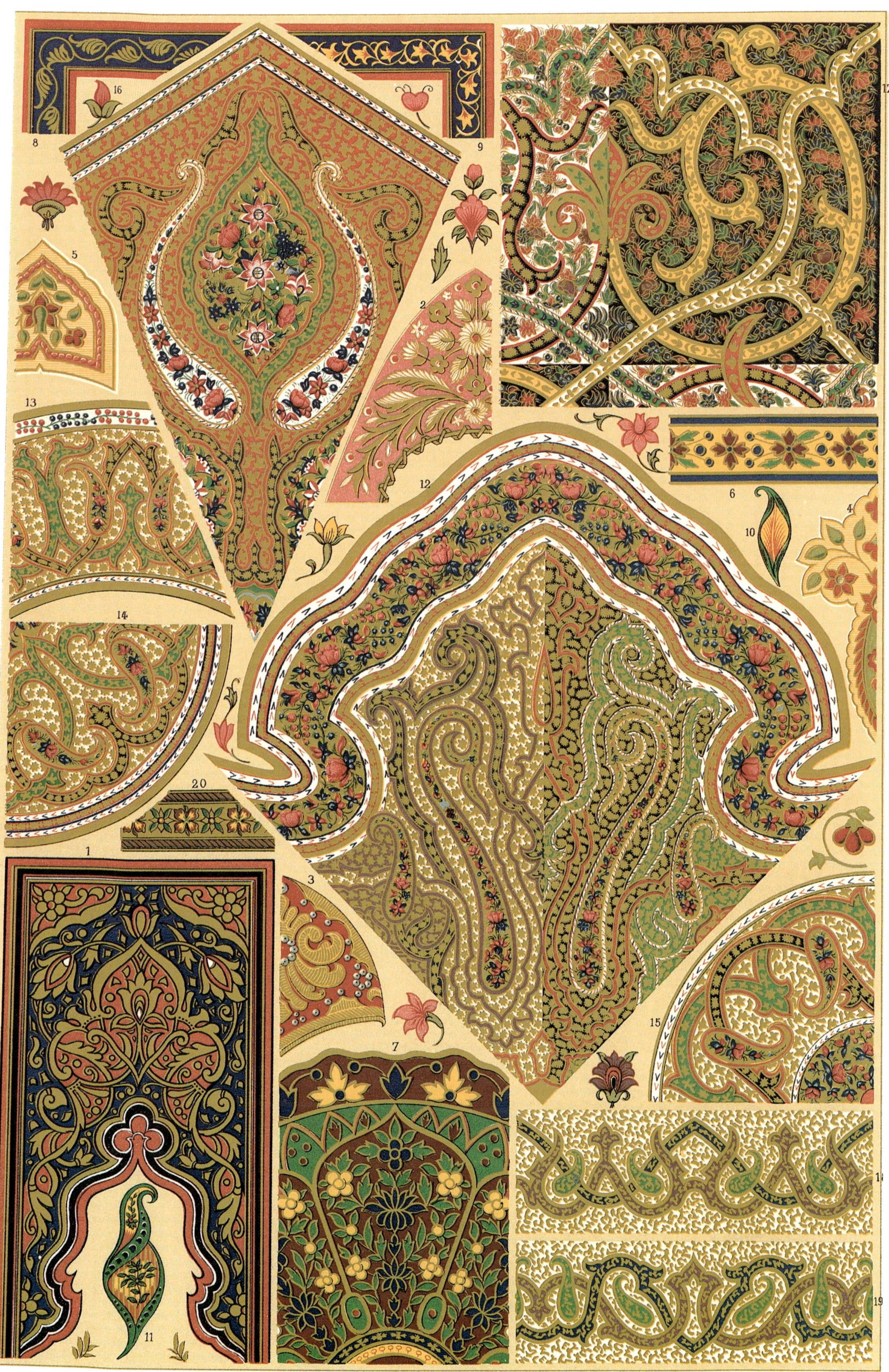

19. India: Designs from various artifacts.

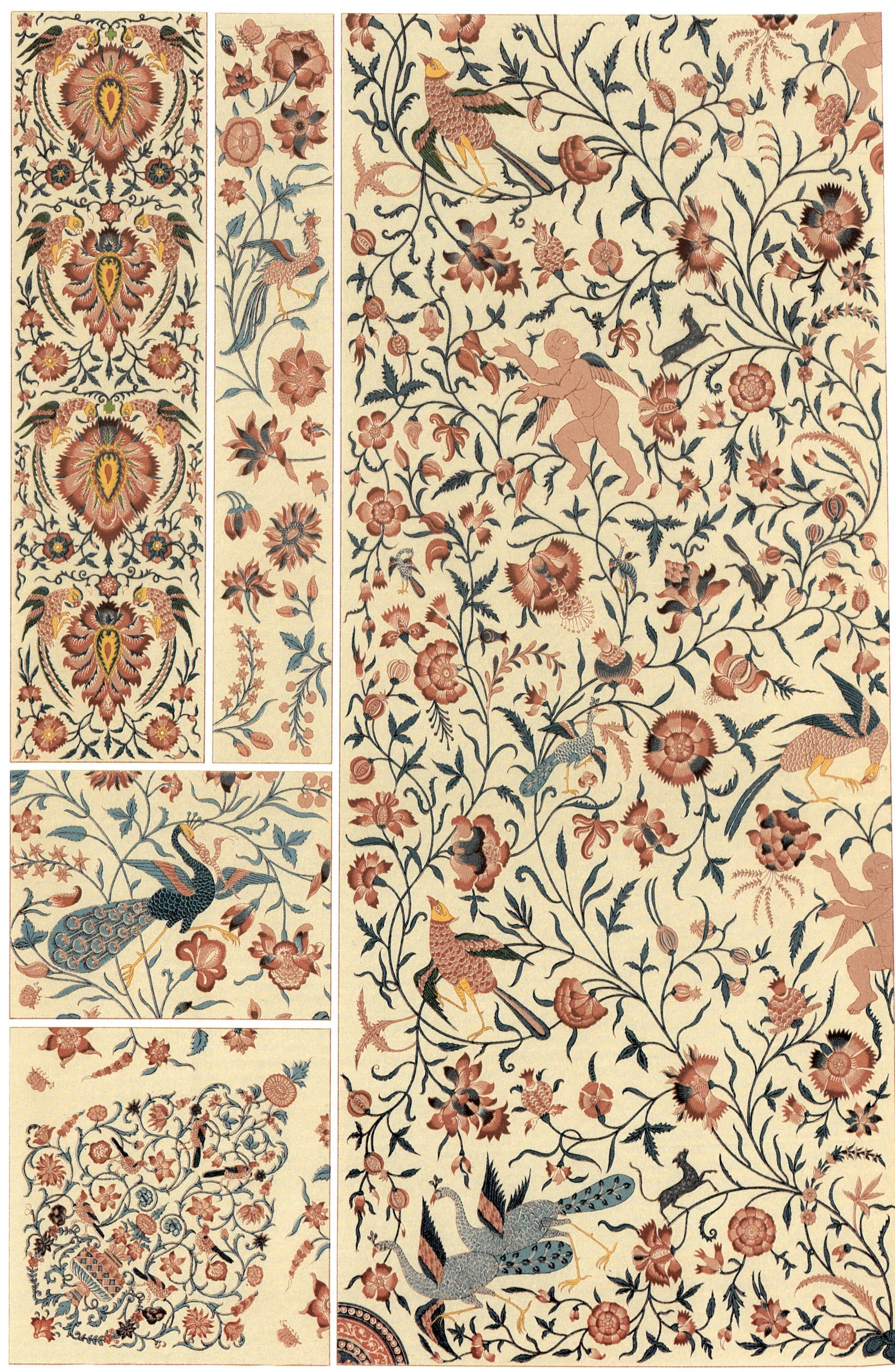

20. Persia: Designs from printed fabrics.

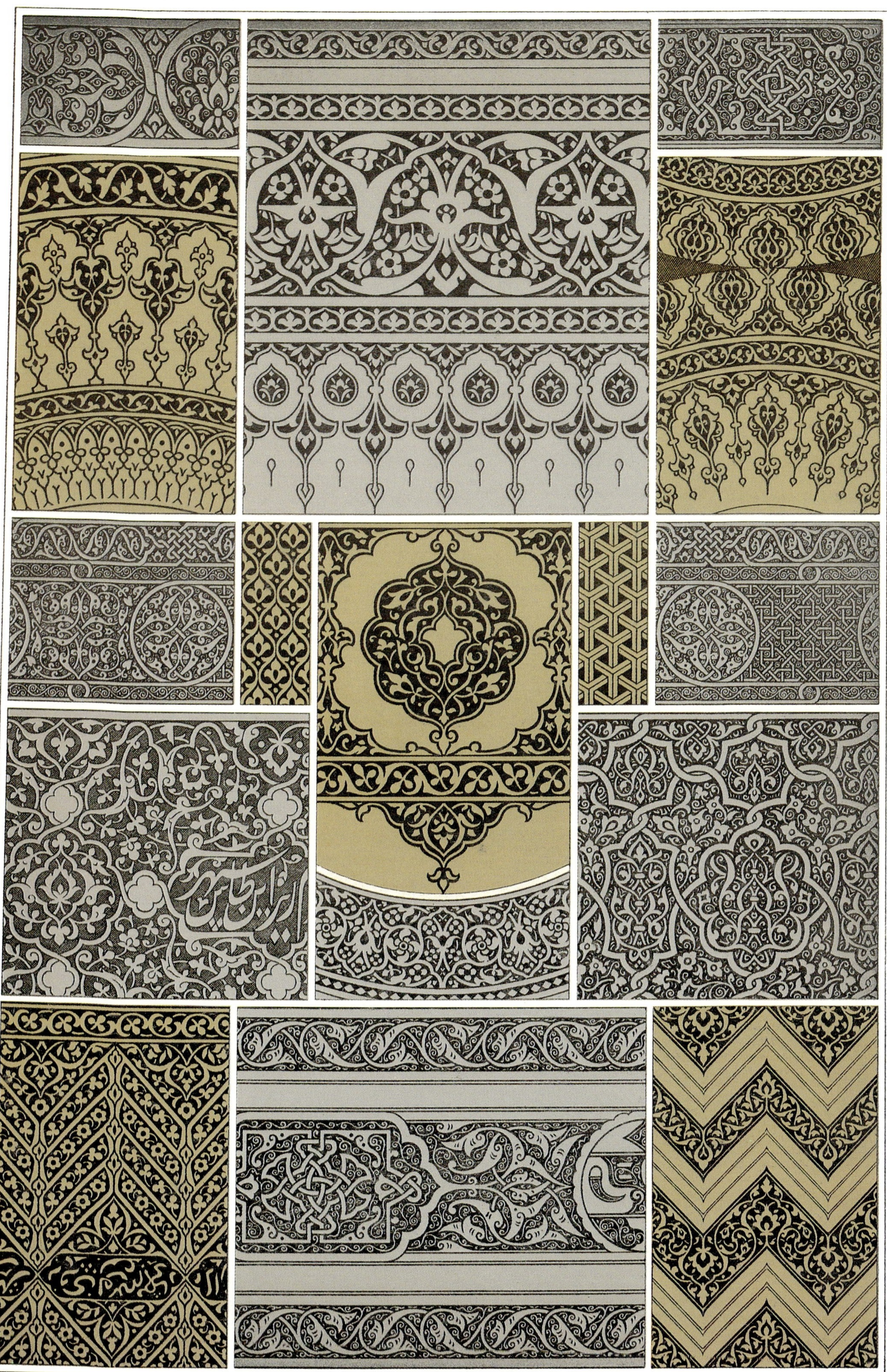

21. Persia: Designs from inlaid metal.

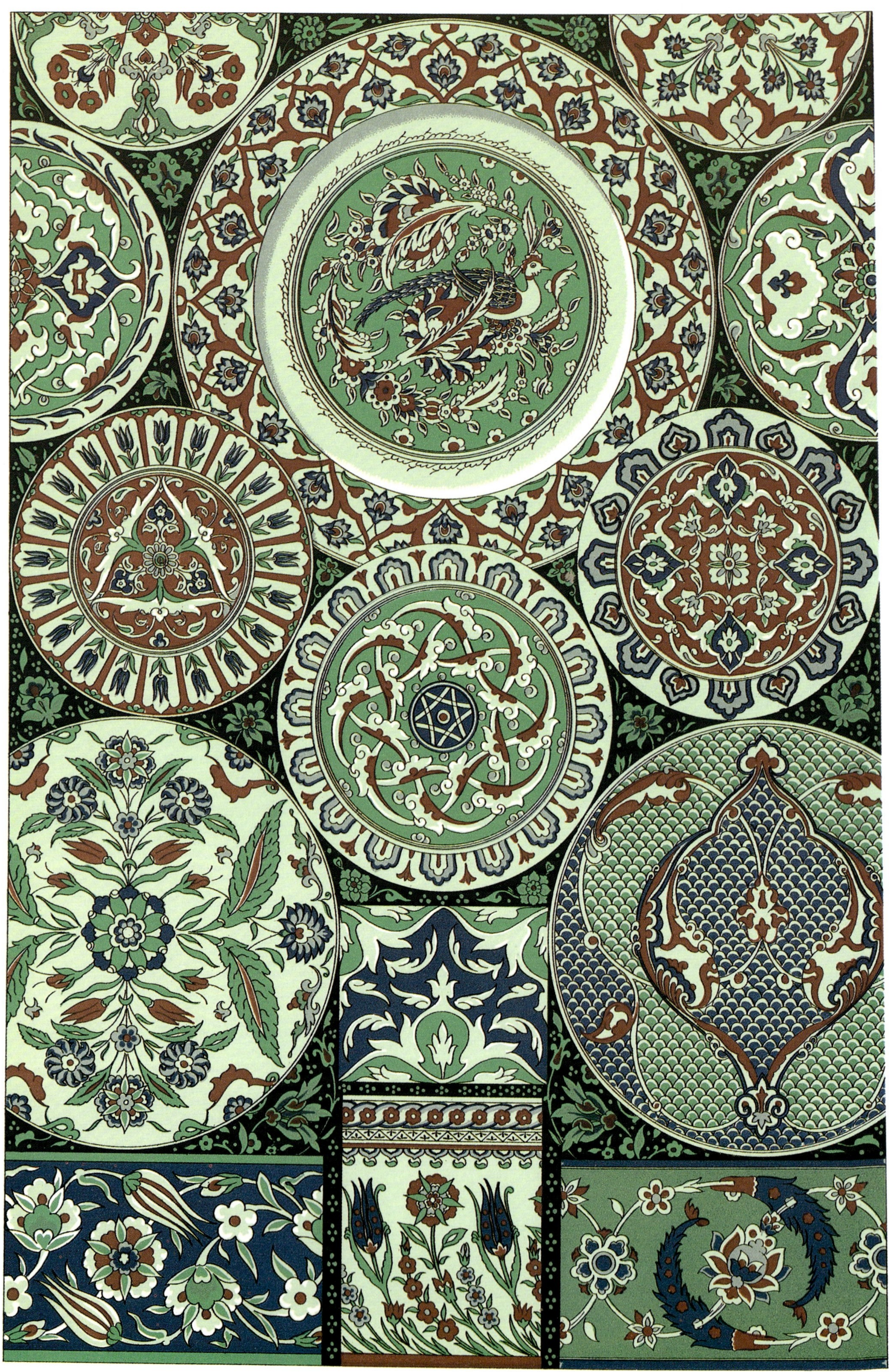

22. Persia: Designs from platters and architectural tiles.

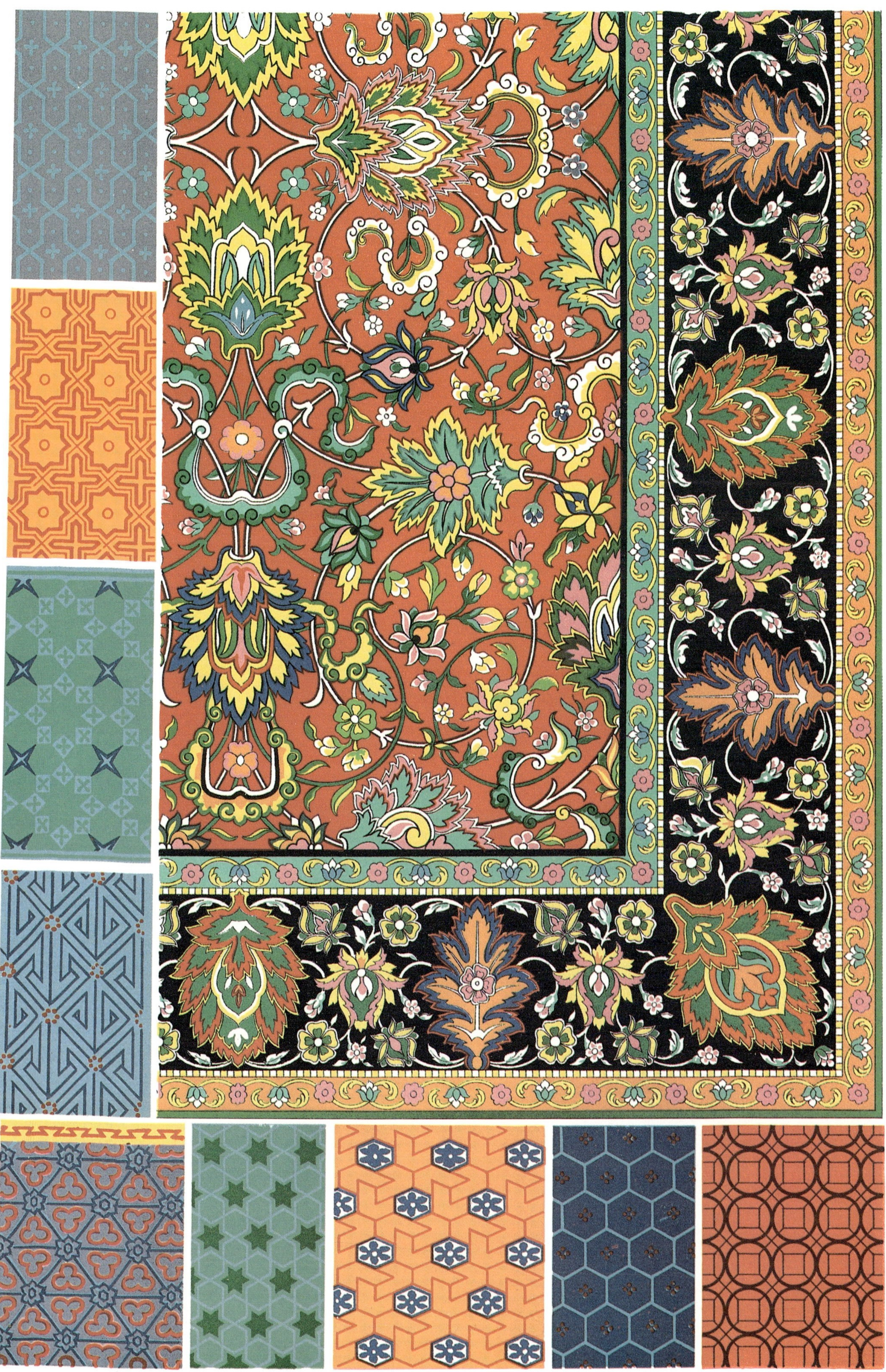

23. Persia: Carpet design and allover geometric designs from manuscripts.

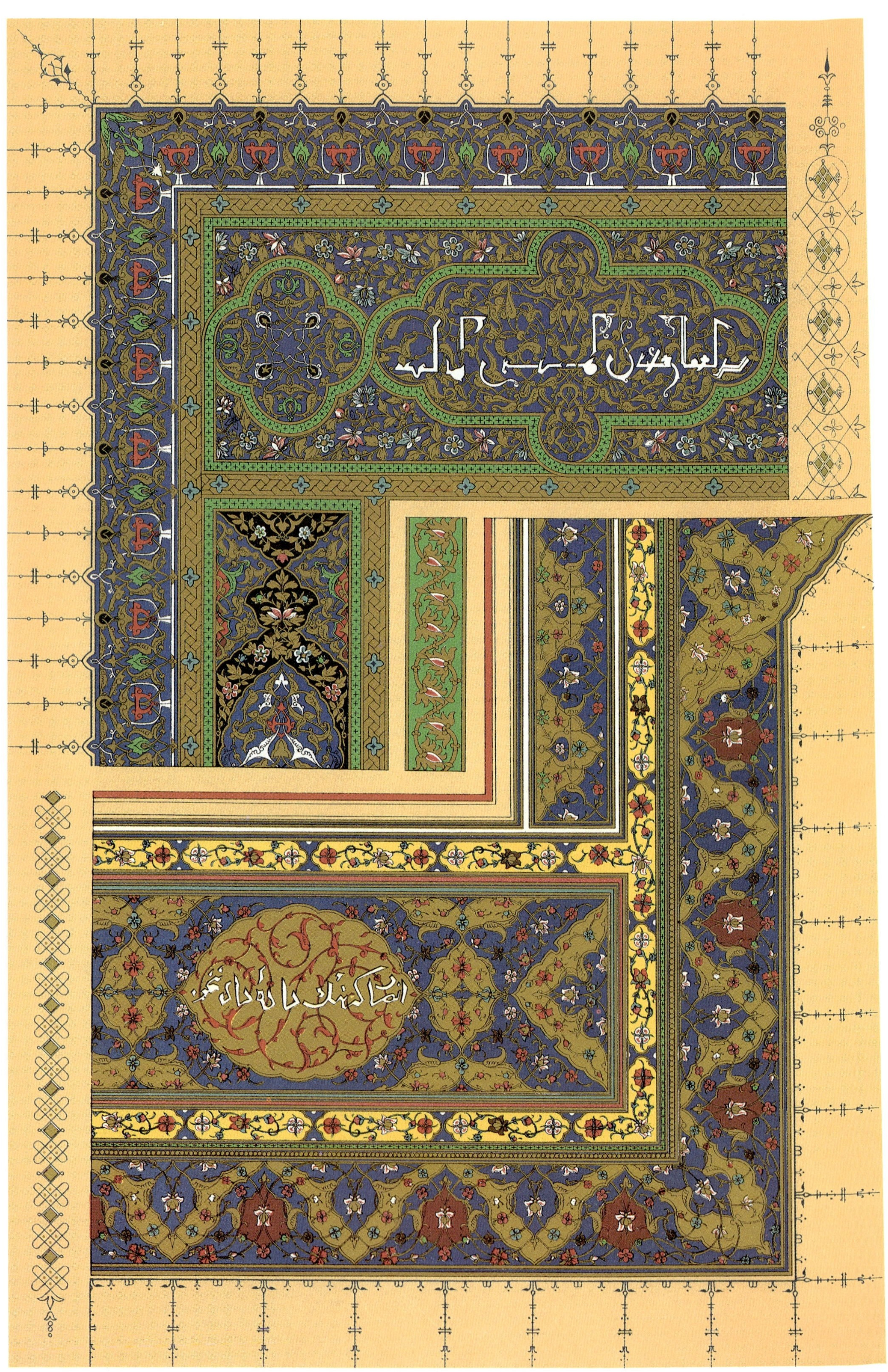

24. Persia: Designs from illuminated manuscripts.

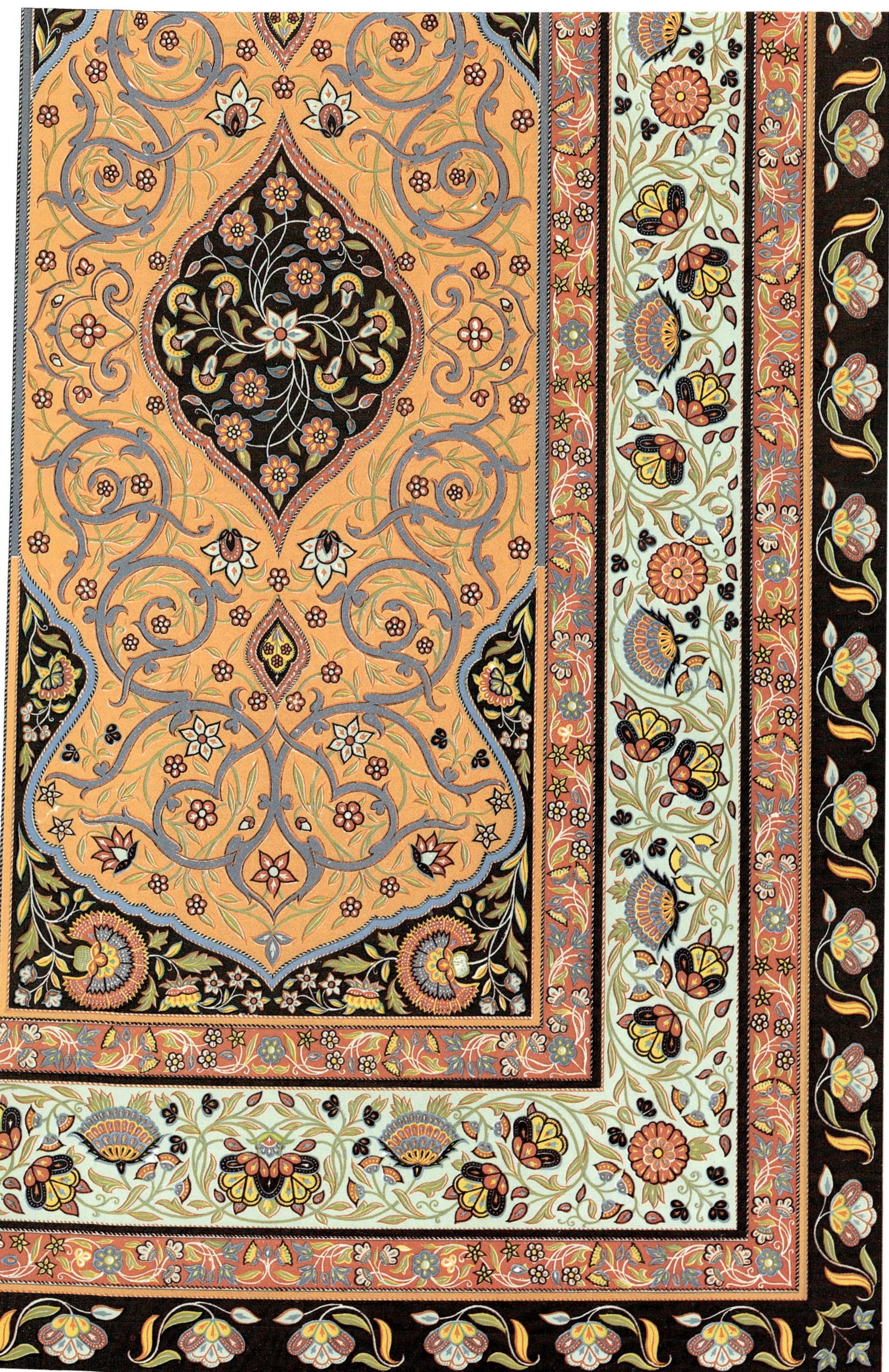

25. Persia: Design from a prayer rug.

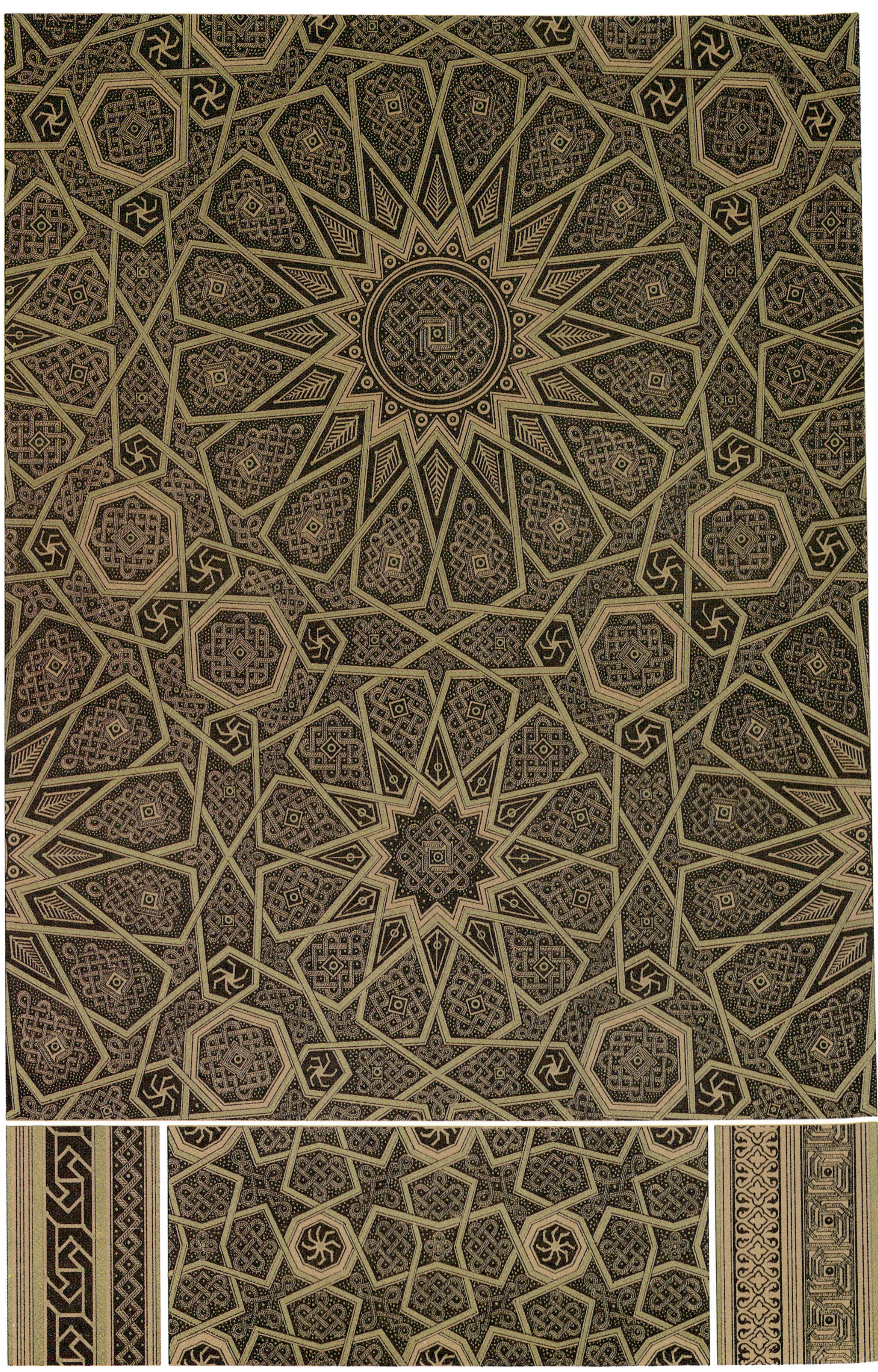

26. Islamic: Designs from a bookbinding.

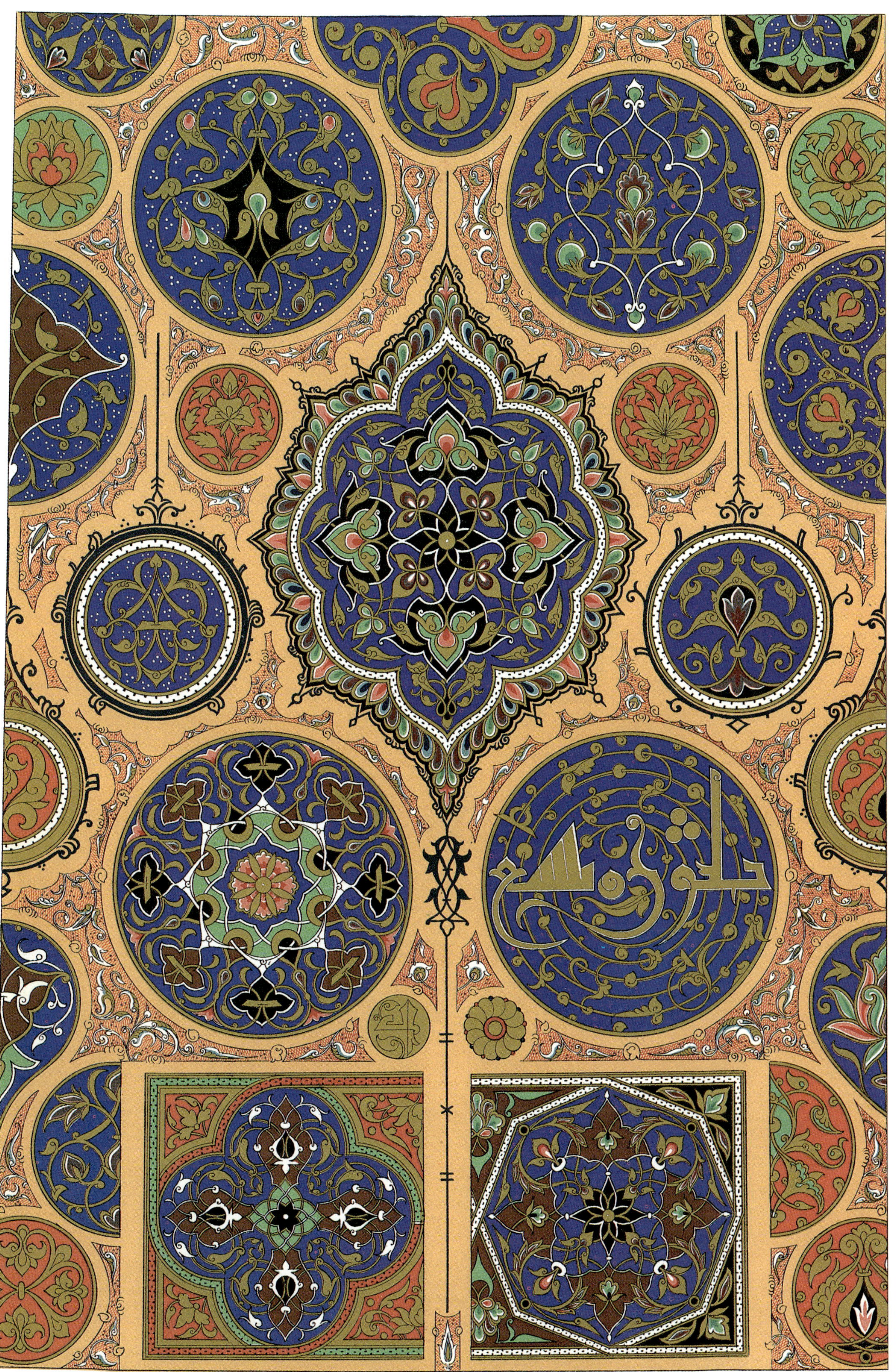

27. Islamic: Floral designs from an illuminated manuscript.

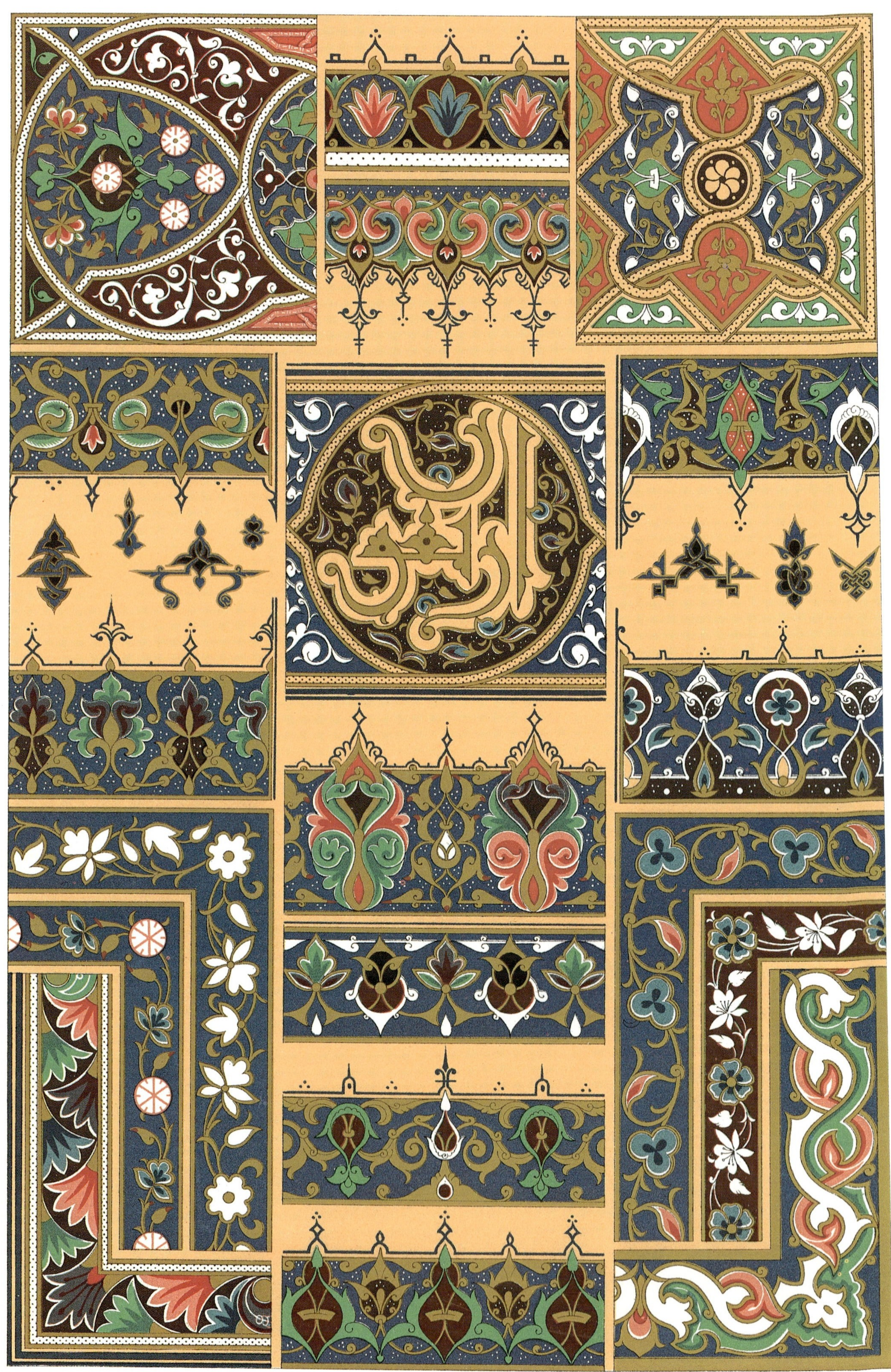

28. Islamic: Ornaments from an illuminated manuscript.

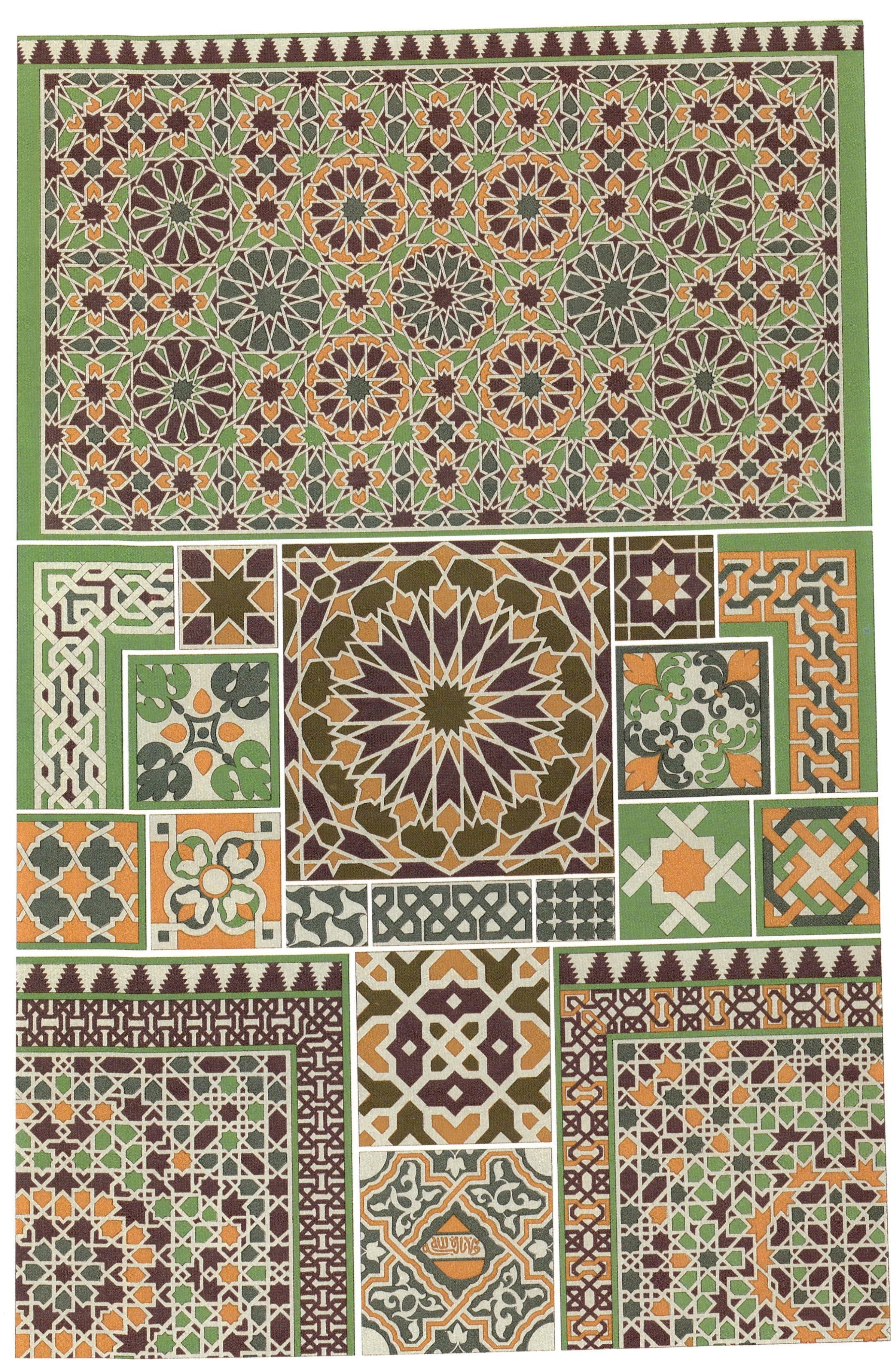

29. Moorish: Tile designs from the Alhambra and from the Seville Alcázar.

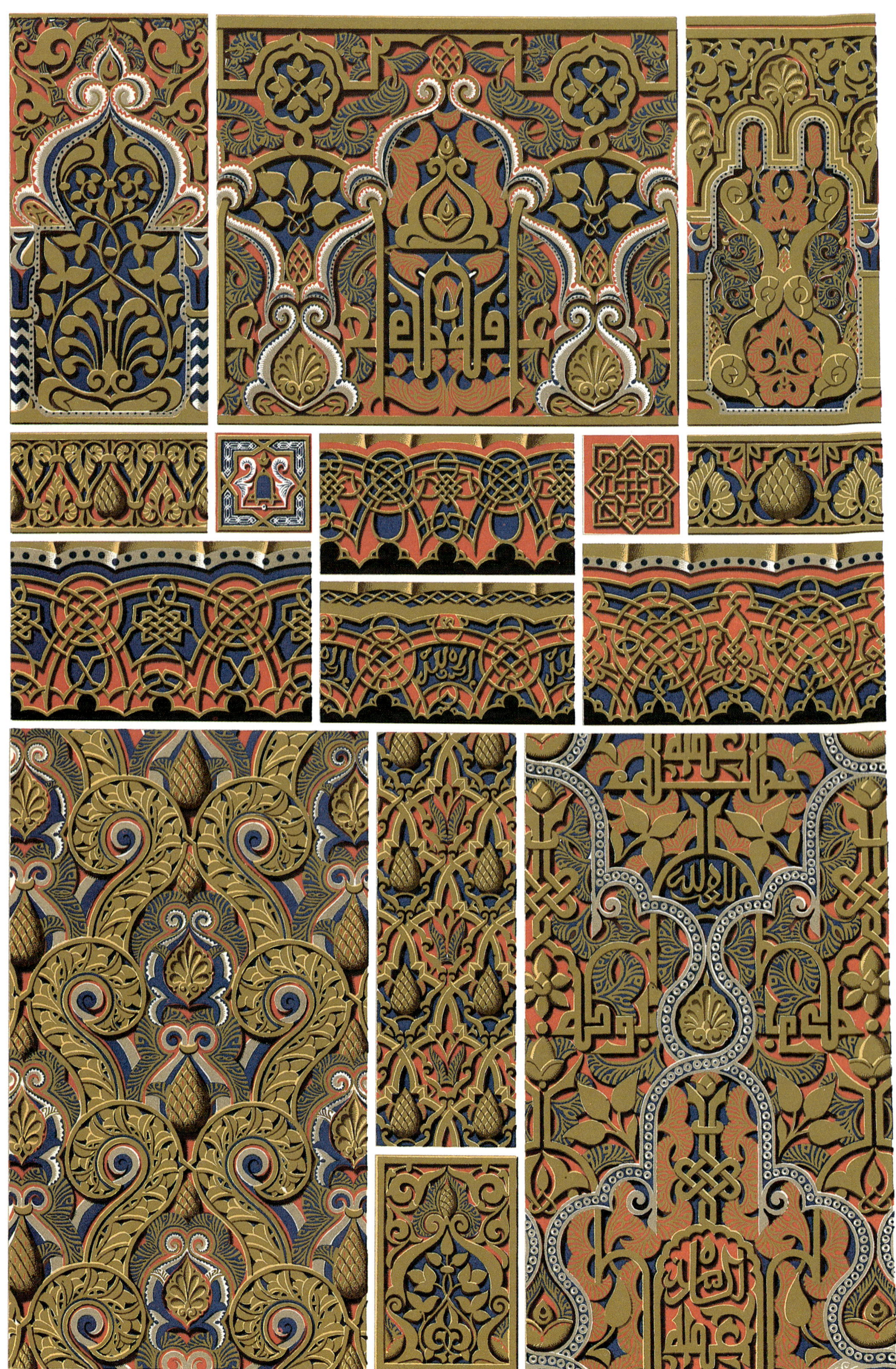

30. Moorish: Relief ornament from the Alhambra.

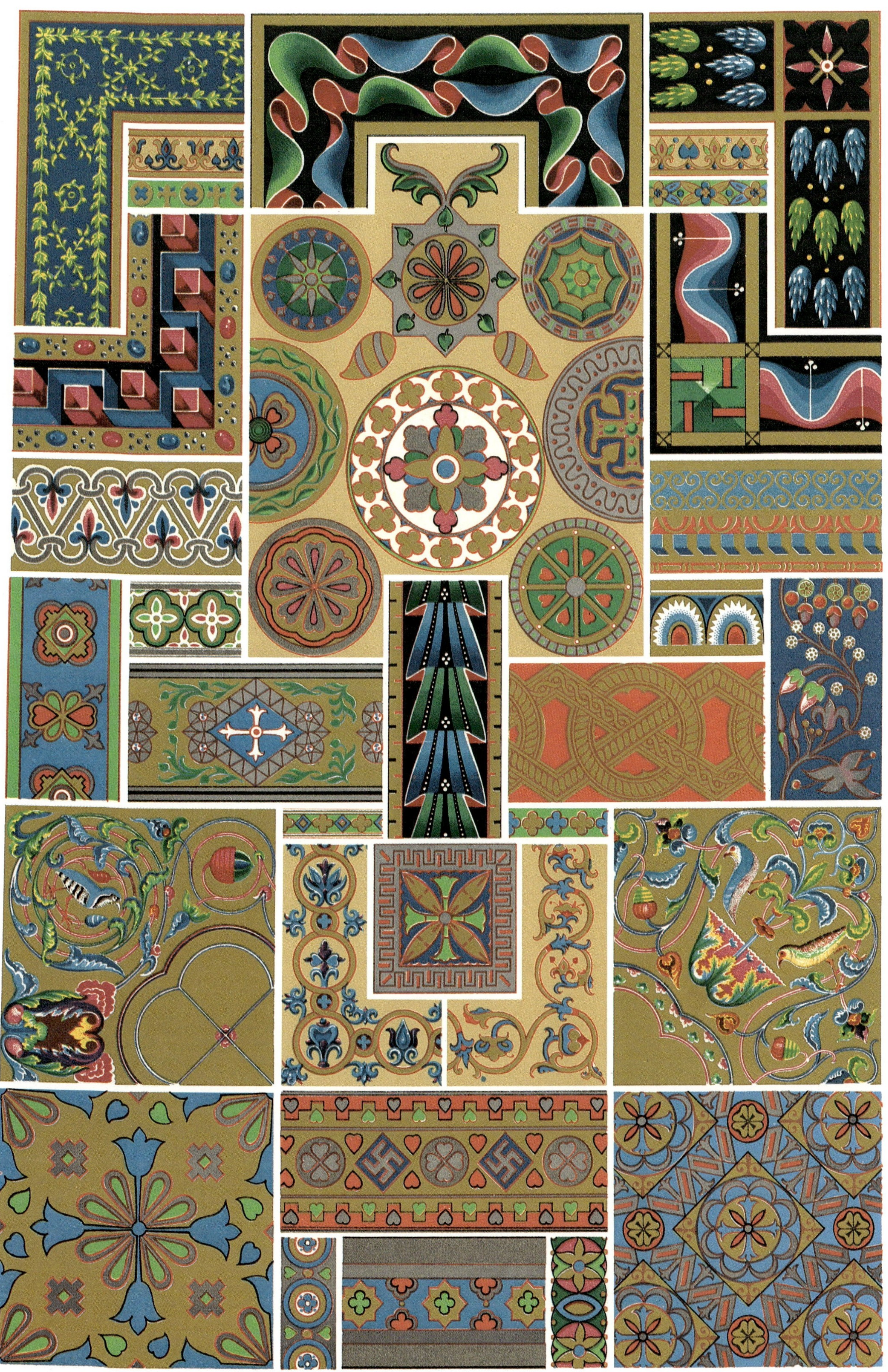

31. Byzantine: Designs from mural and manuscript paintings and from mosaics, Greece and Italy.

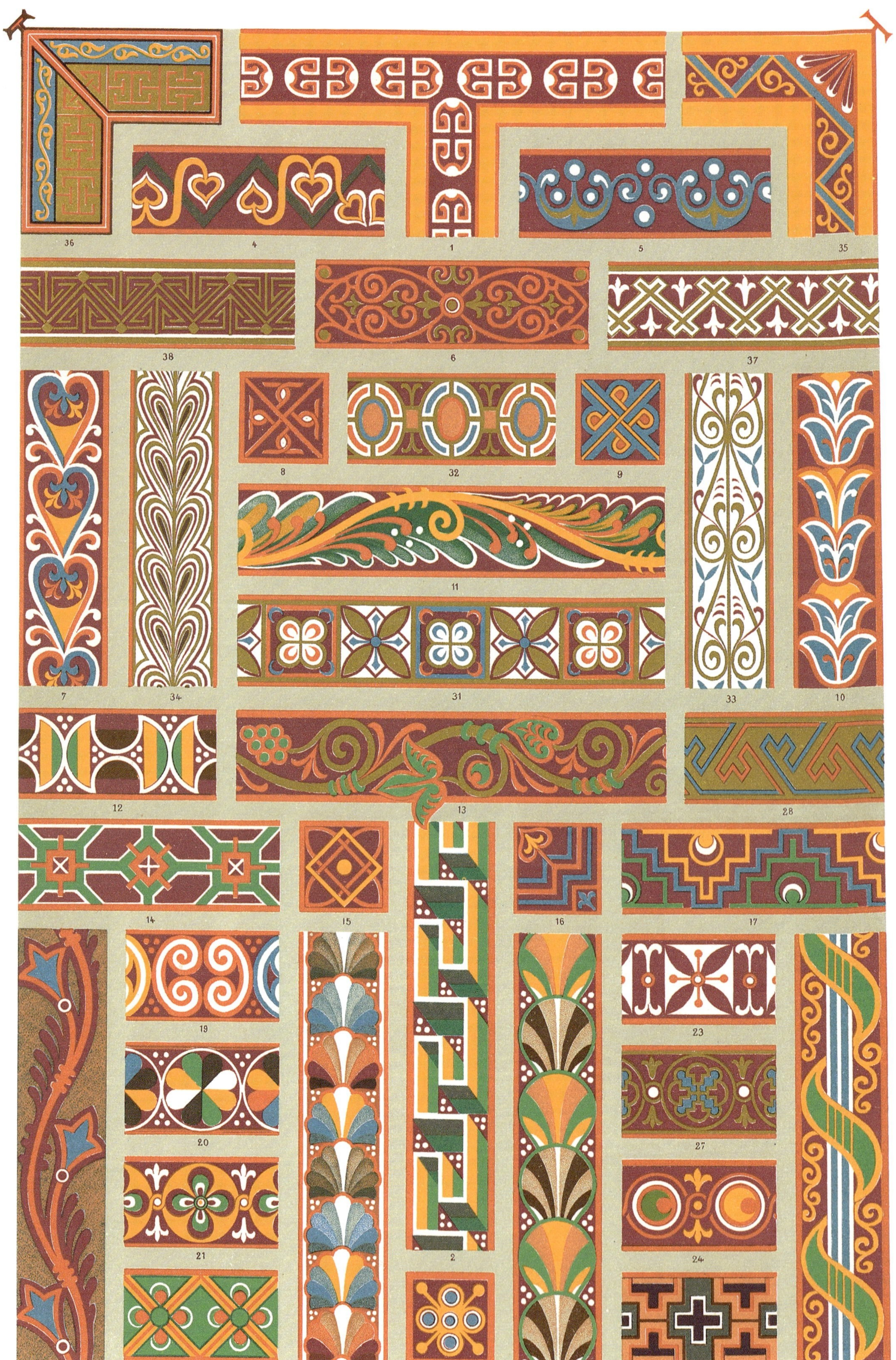

32. Early Medieval: Designs from illuminated manuscripts, France.

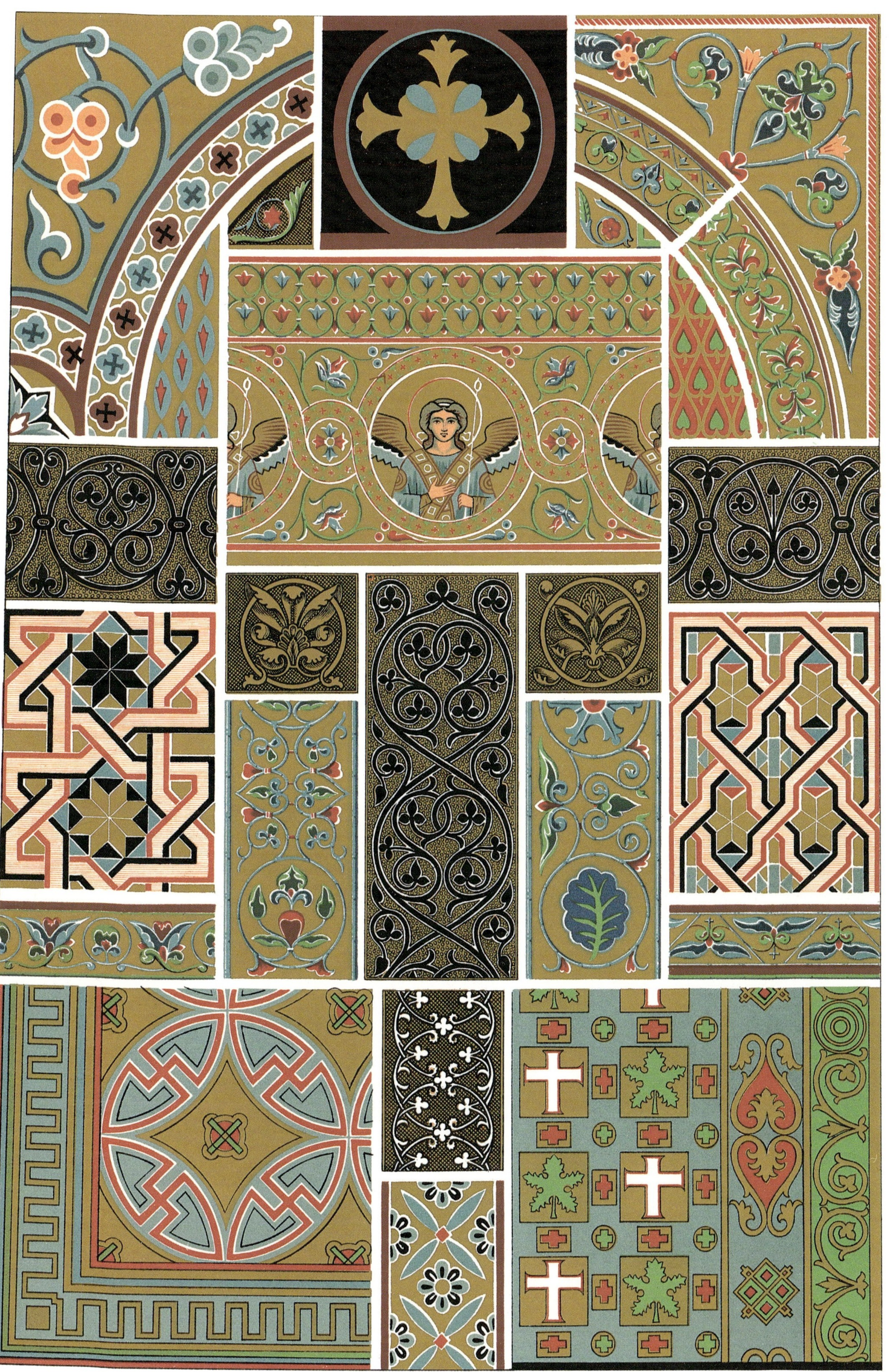

33. Byzantine: Designs from architecture and manuscripts, Greece and Italy.

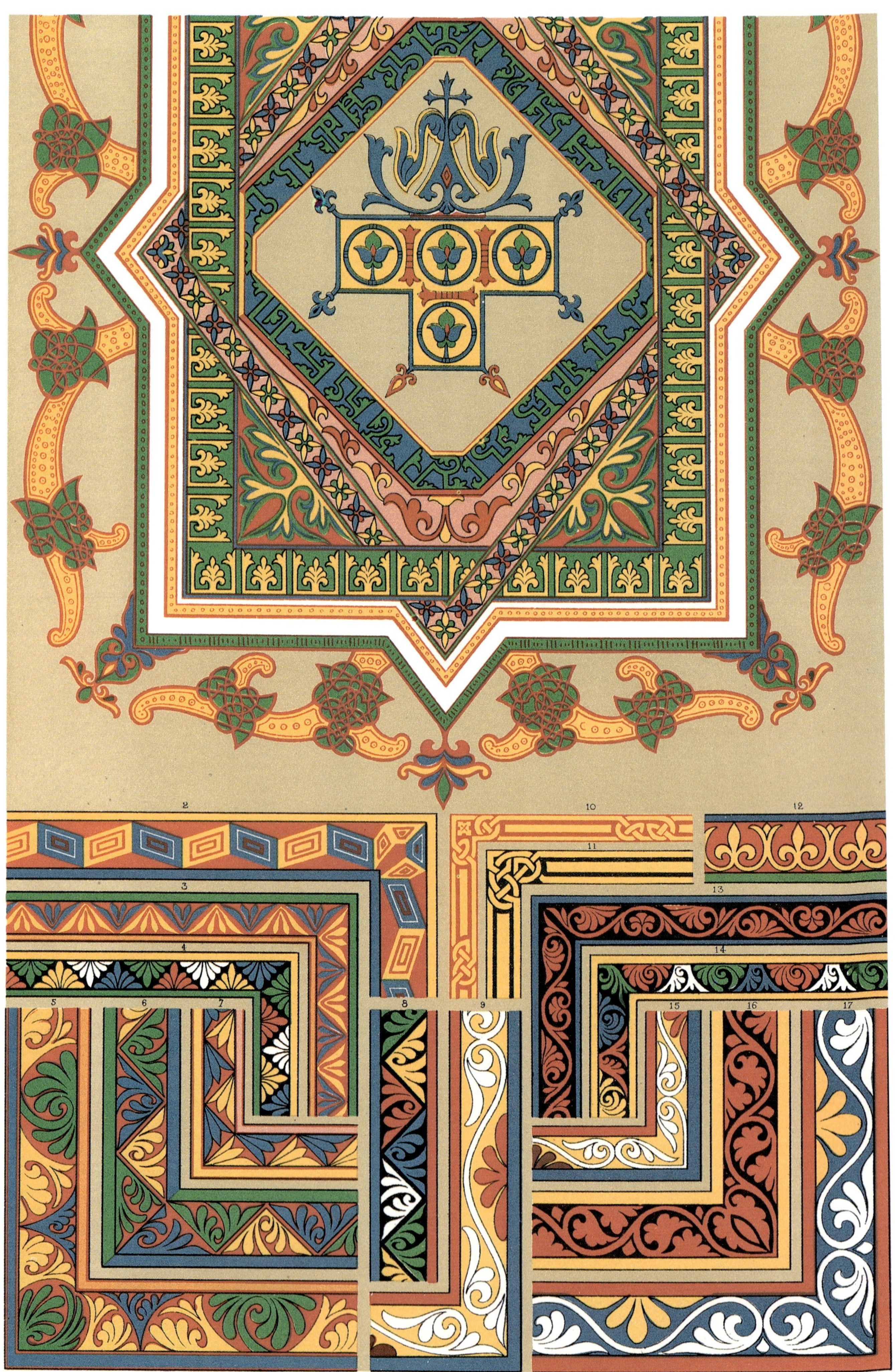

34. Byzantine: Designs from manuscripts.

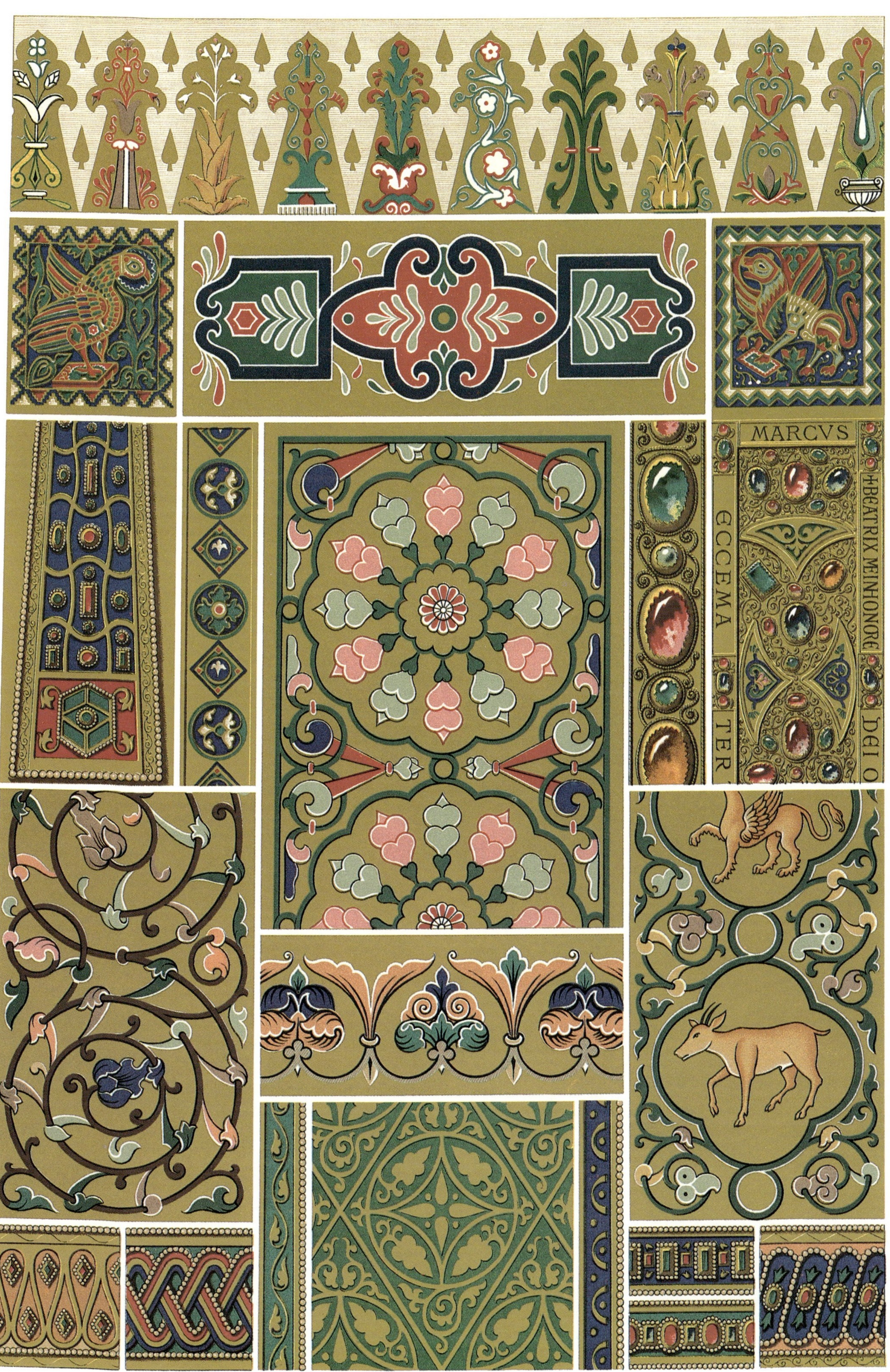

35. Byzantine: Designs from mosaics (Sicily), frescoes (Asia Minor) and enamels.

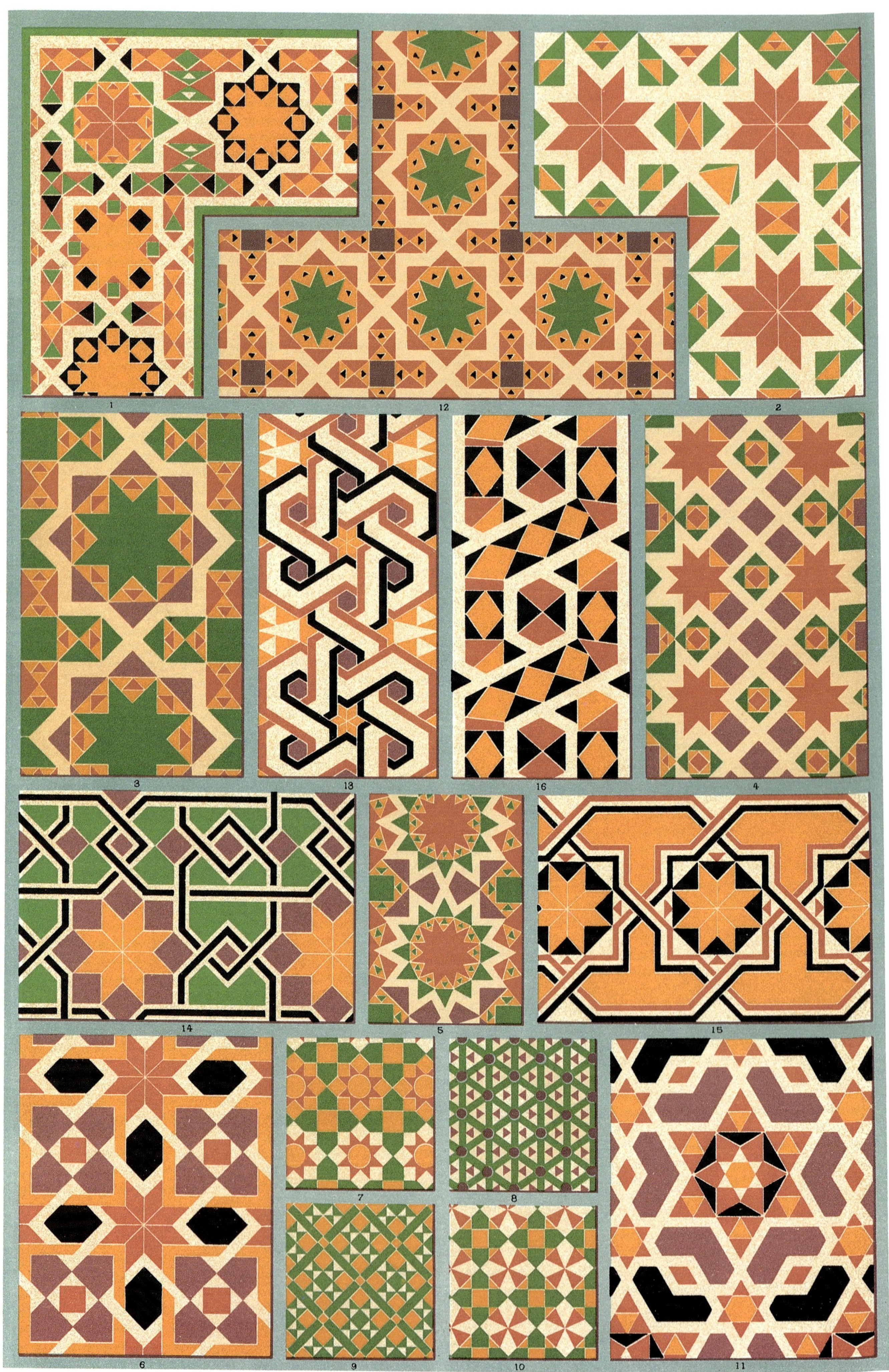

36. Byzantine/Early Medieval: Mosaics from Palermo and Salerno.

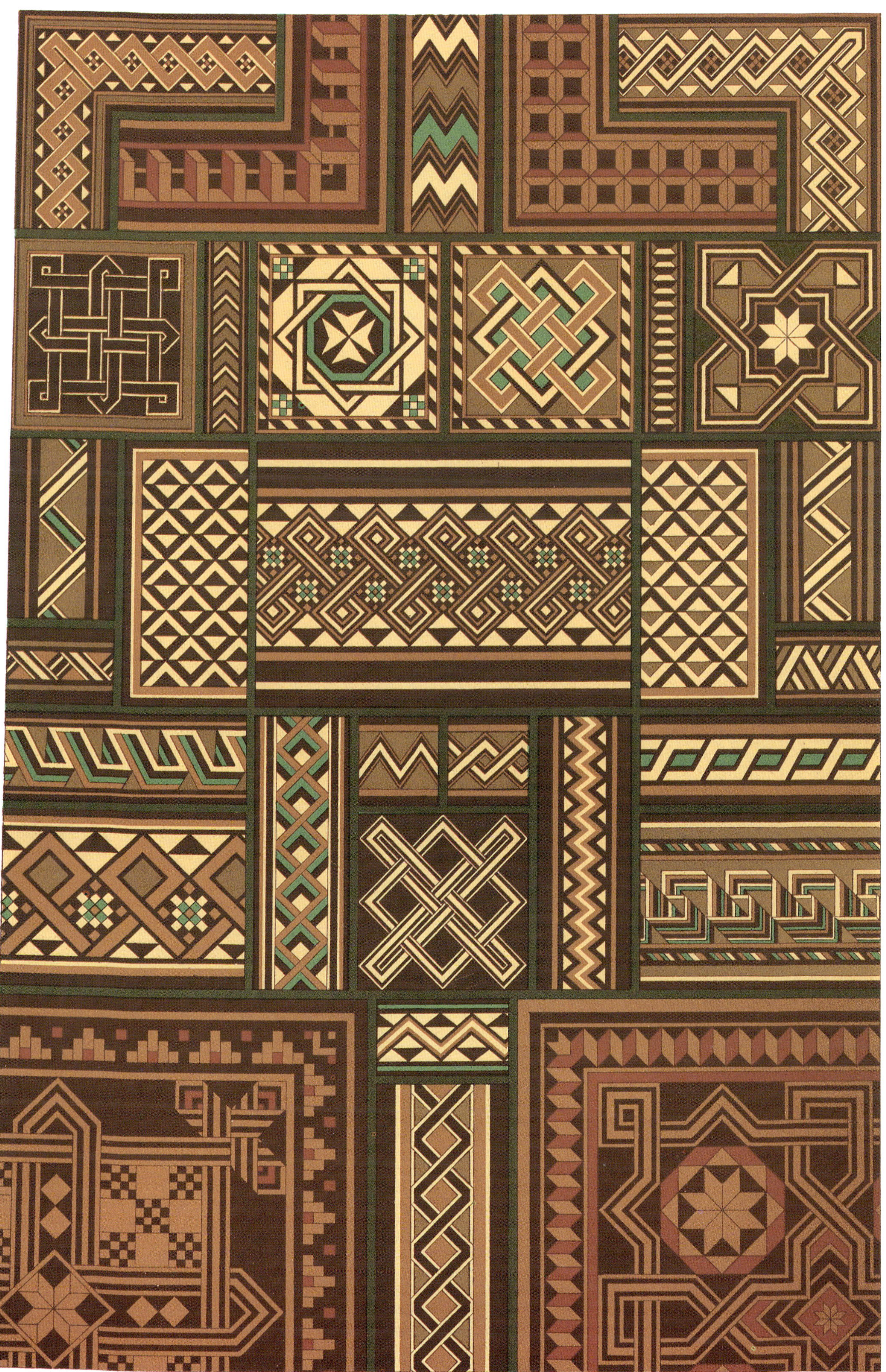

37. Medieval: Designs from ivory and wood inlays, France and Italy, 14th and 15th centuries.

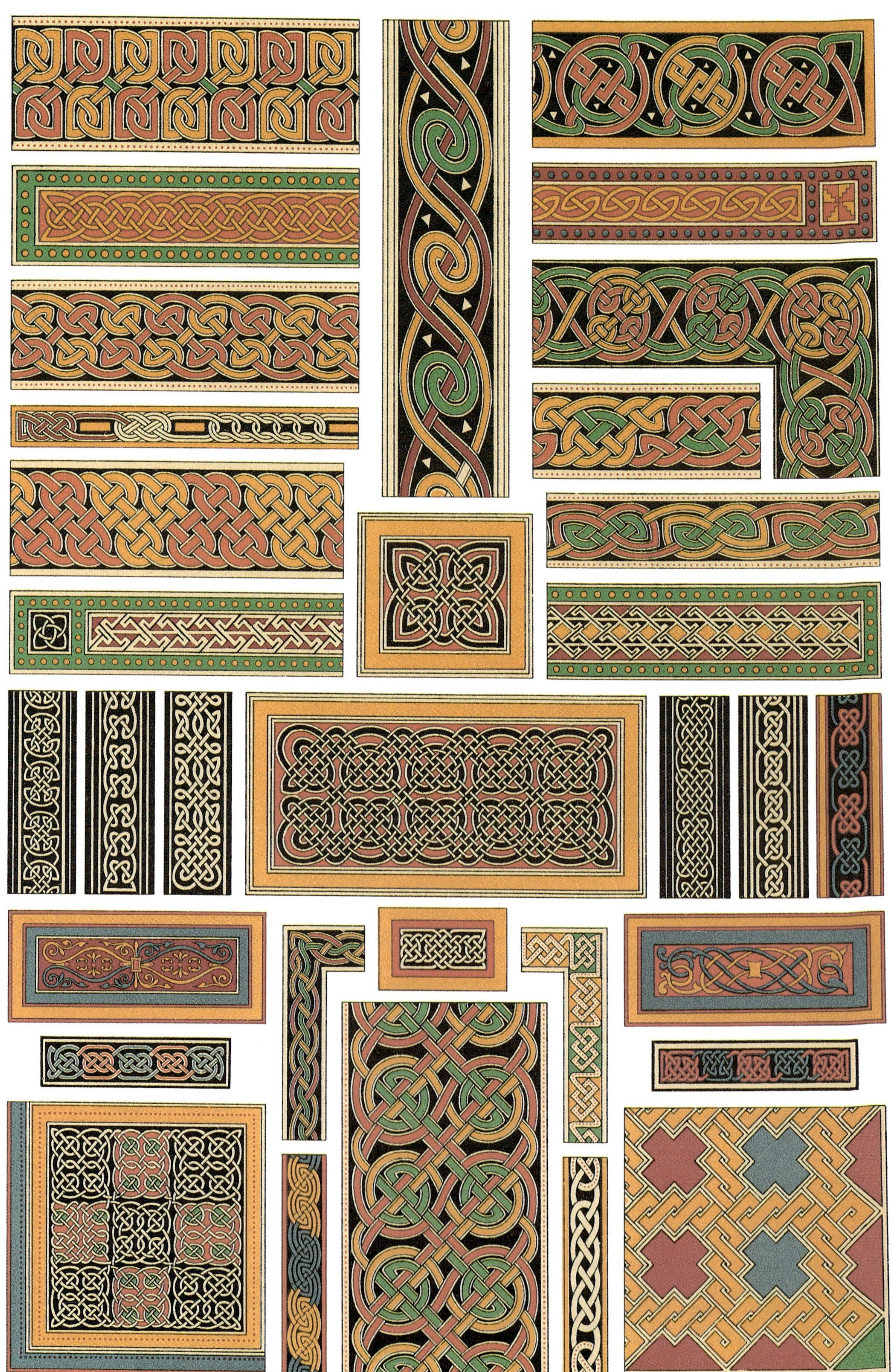

38. Medieval: "Celtic" ornament from manuscripts, British Isles, 7th–9th centuries.

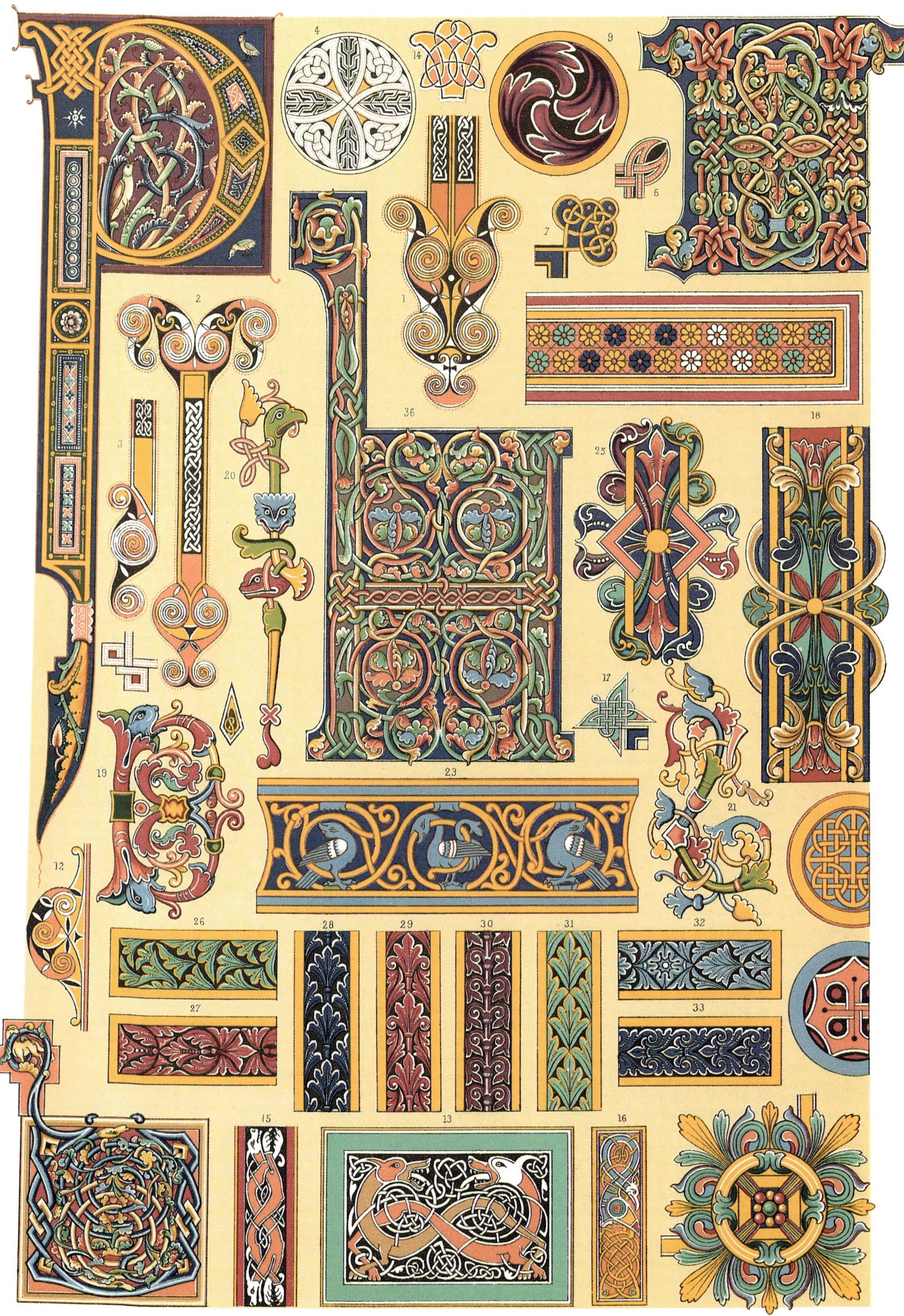

39. Medieval: "Celtic" ornament from British and continental manuscripts, 7th–11th centuries.

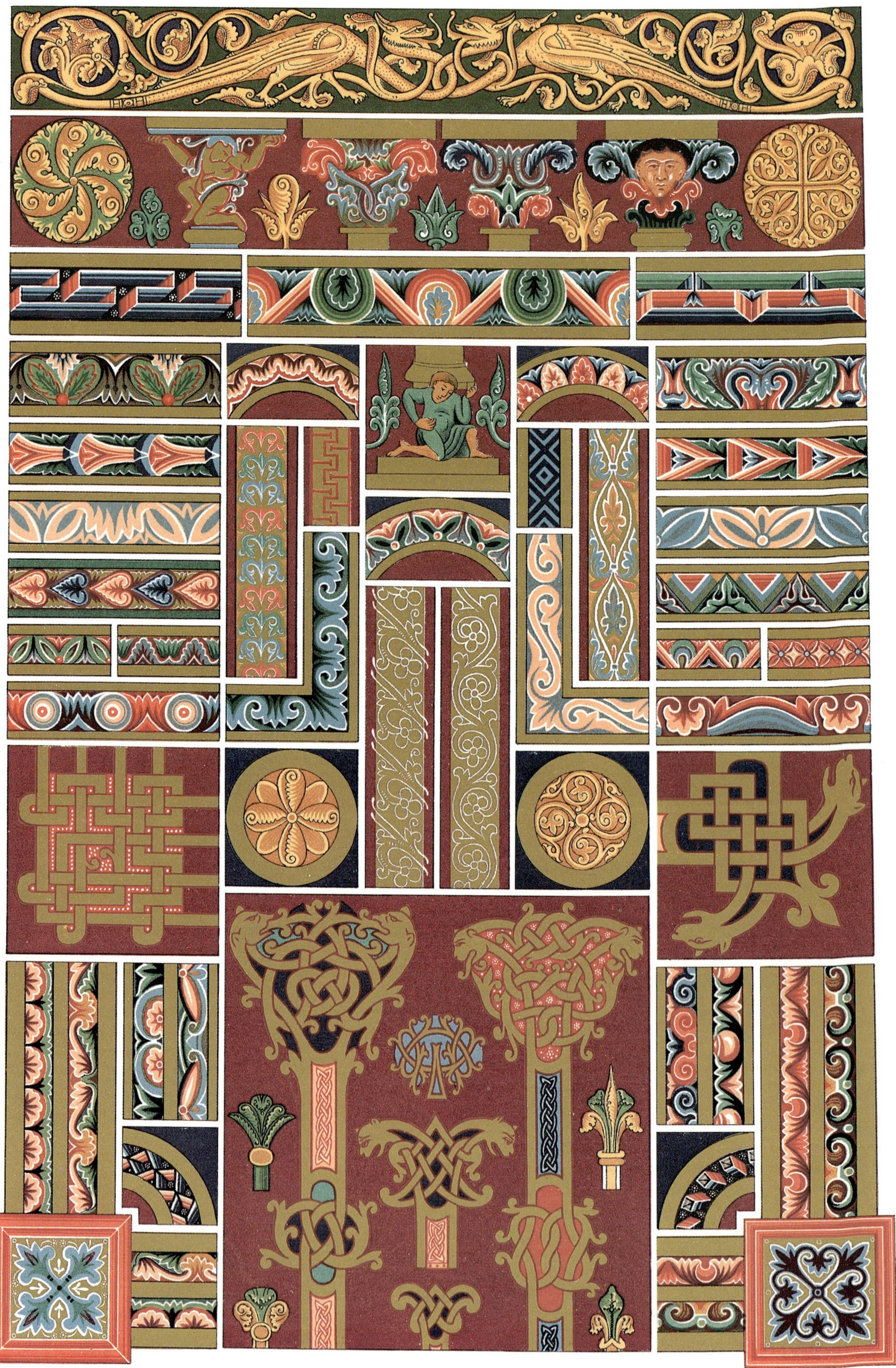

40. Medieval: Romanesque manuscript ornaments, 11th and 12th centuries.

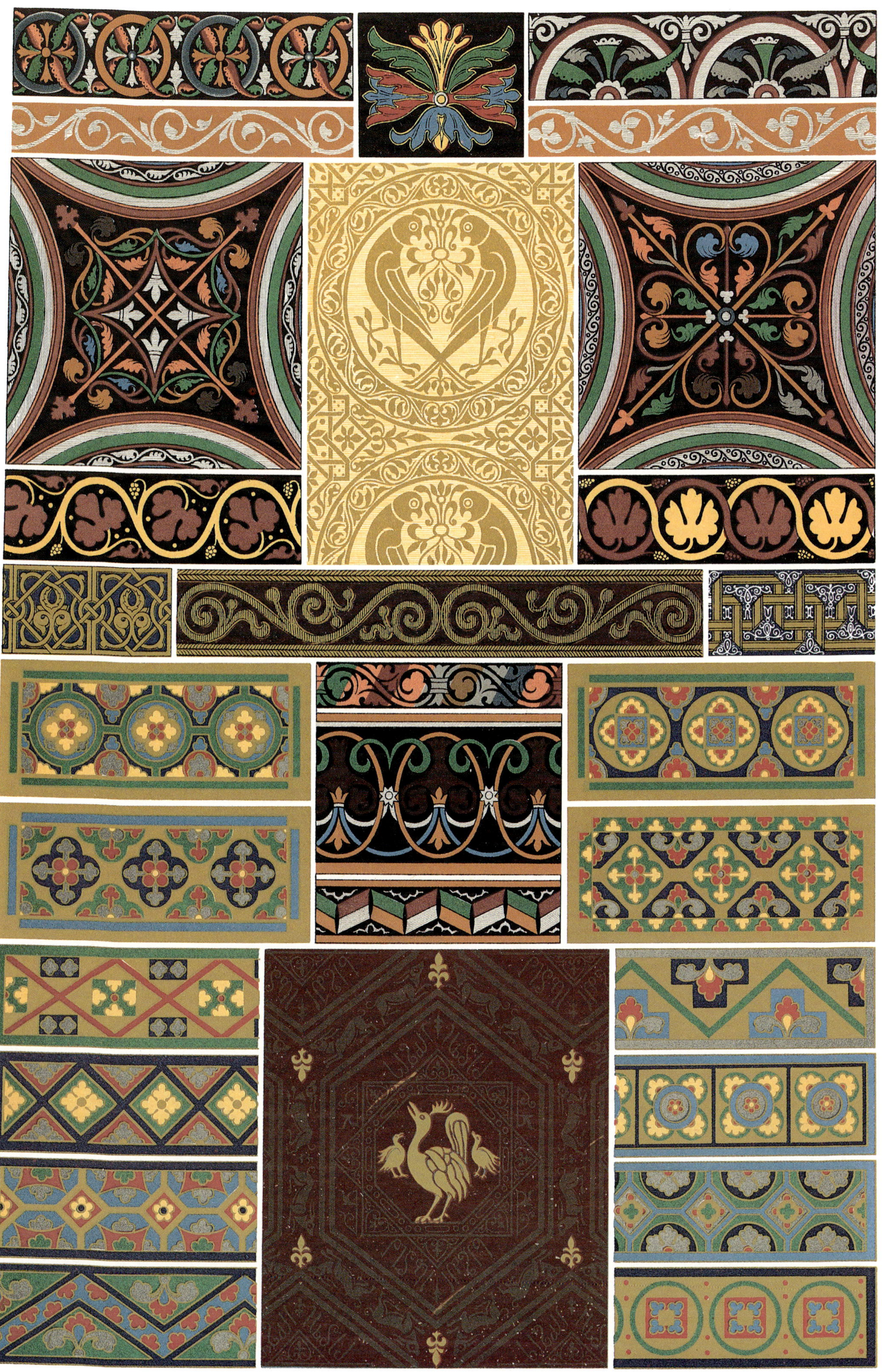

41. Medieval: Designs from embroideries, murals, manuscript illuminations and enamels.

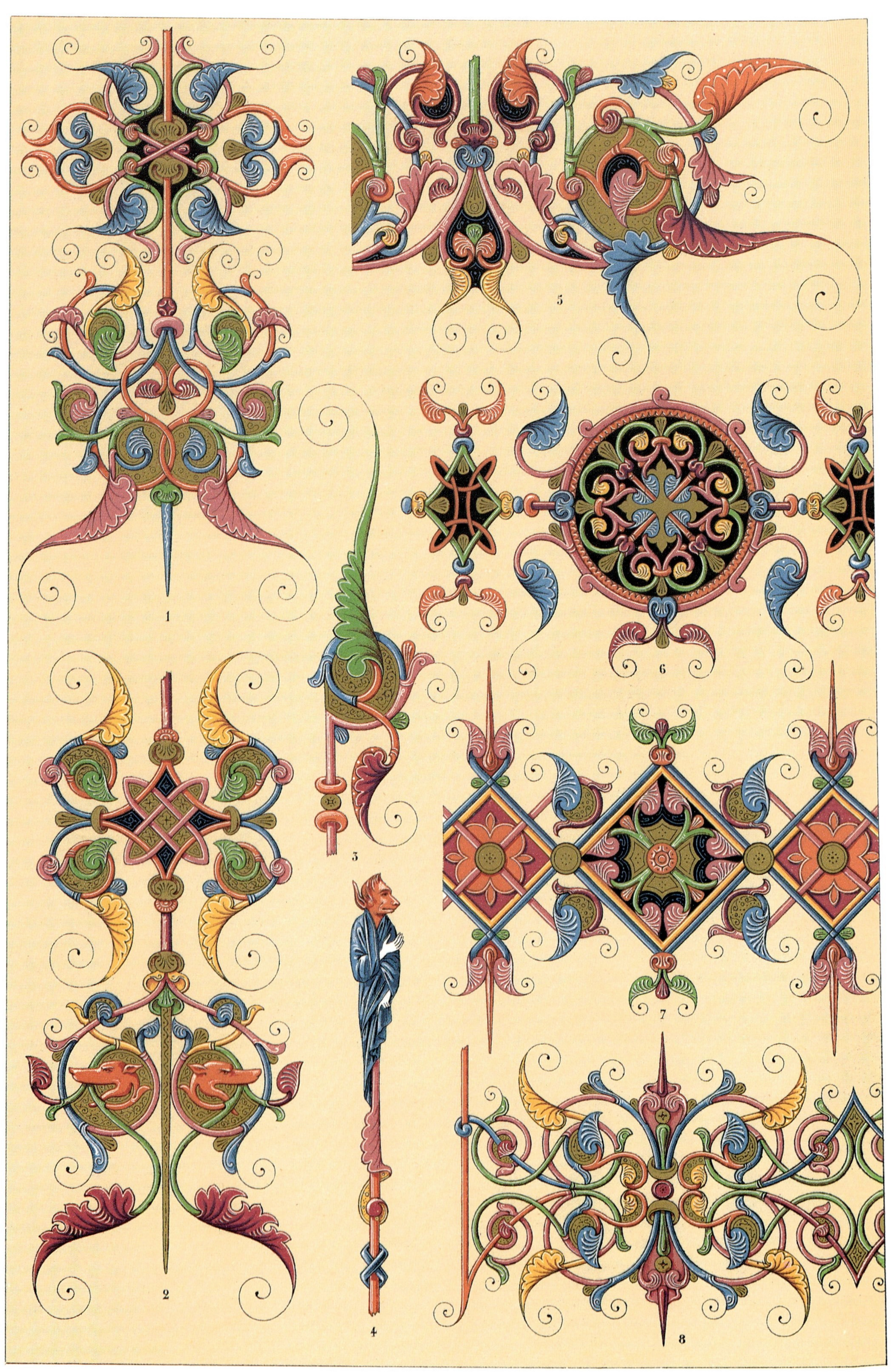

42. Medieval: Ornaments from a 14th-century Italian manuscript.

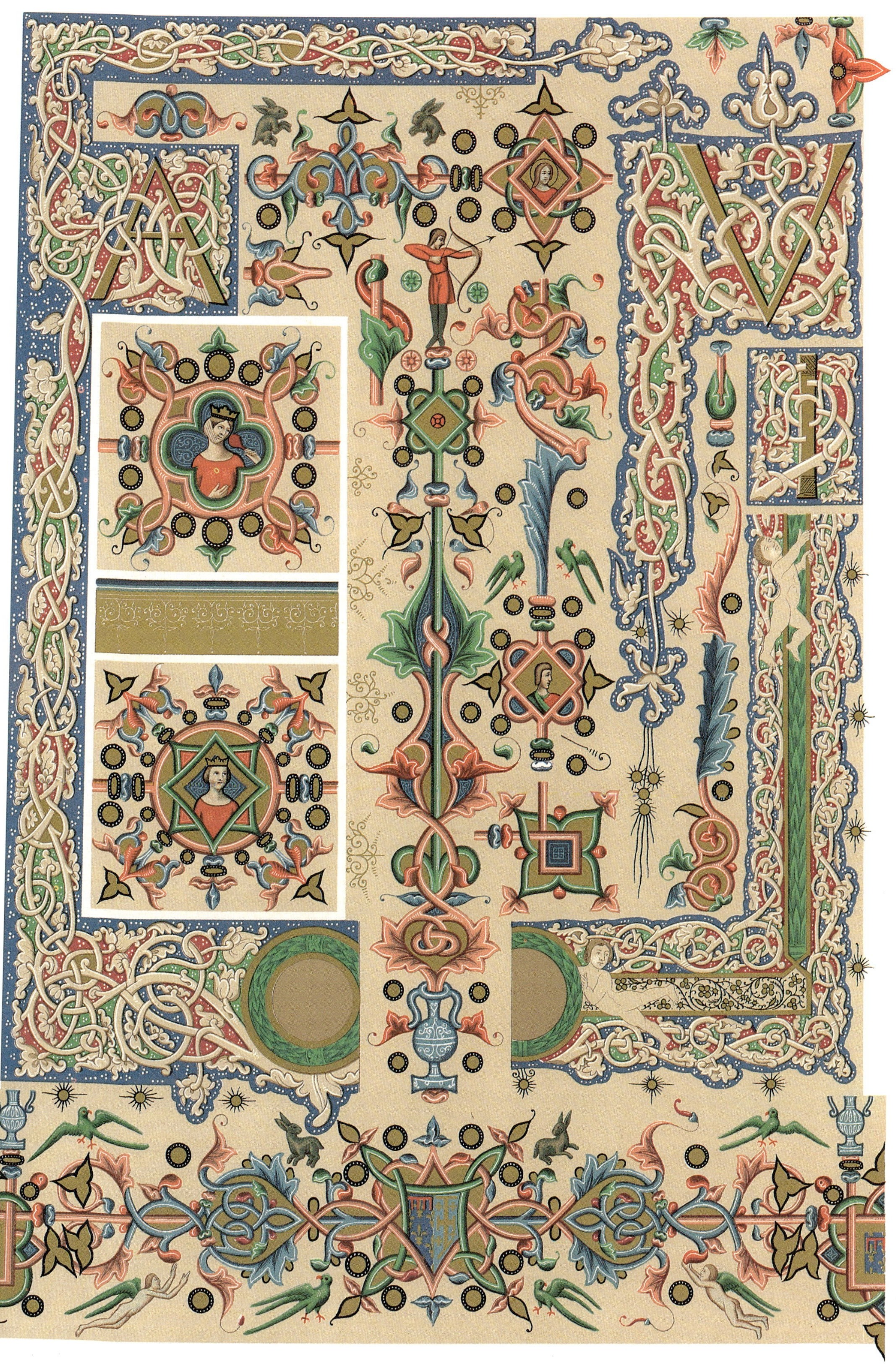

43. Medieval: Ornaments from 14th- and 15th-century Italian manuscripts.

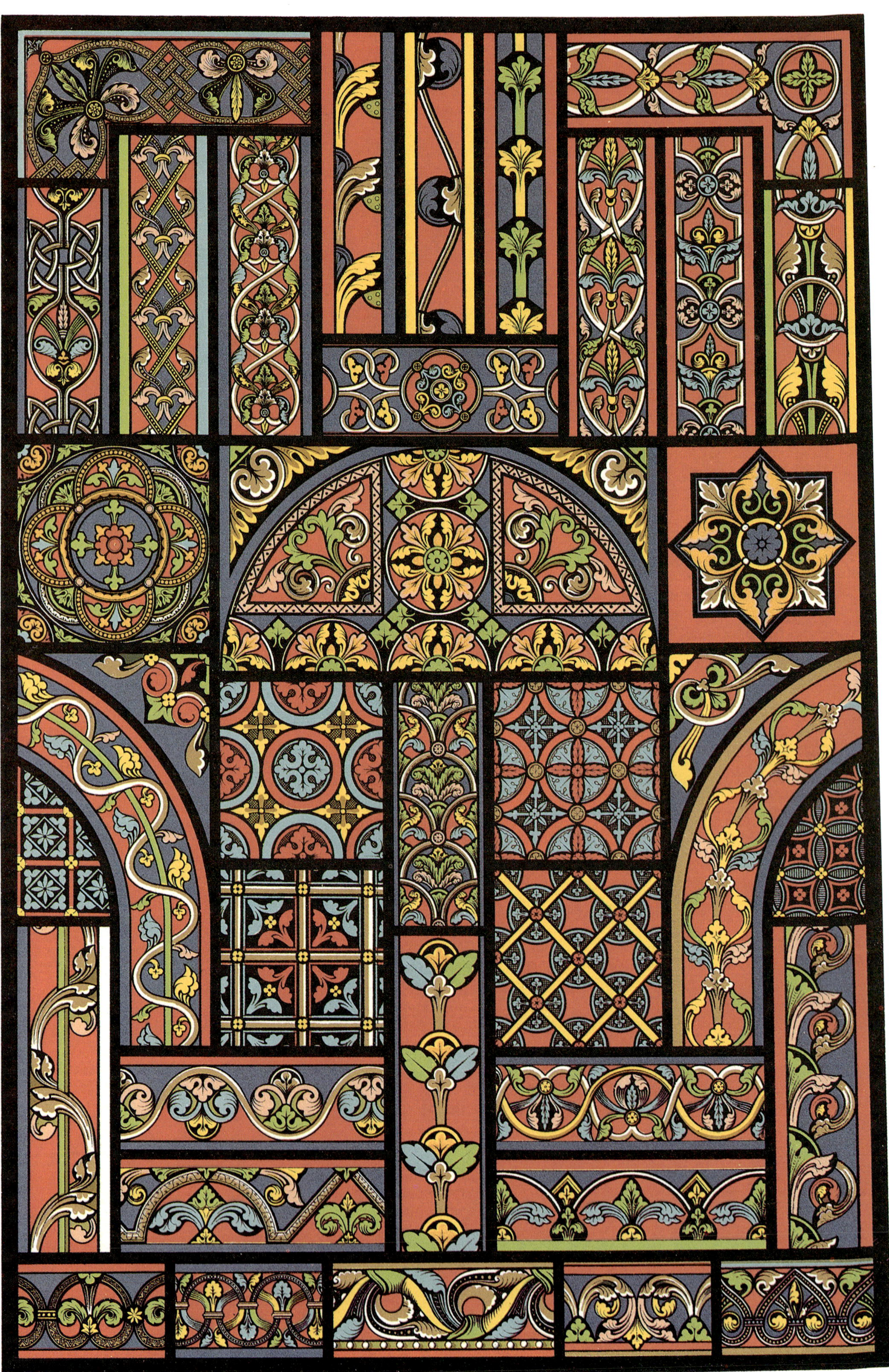

44. Medieval: Stained glass, 12th–14th centuries (various French and German cathedrals).

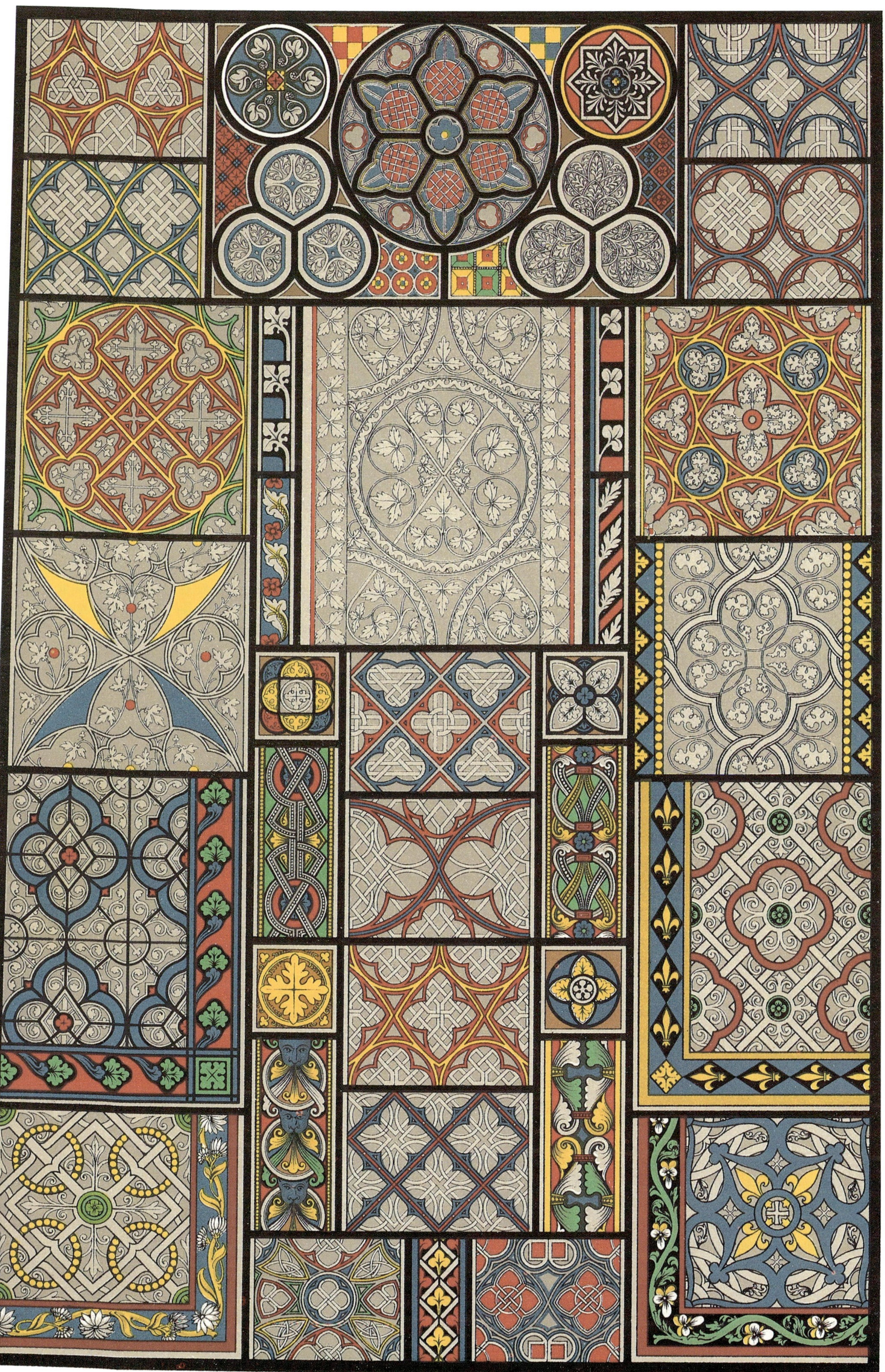

45. Medieval: Stained glass, 13th–15th centuries (Cologne, Bourges, Chartres, Strasbourg, Tournai).

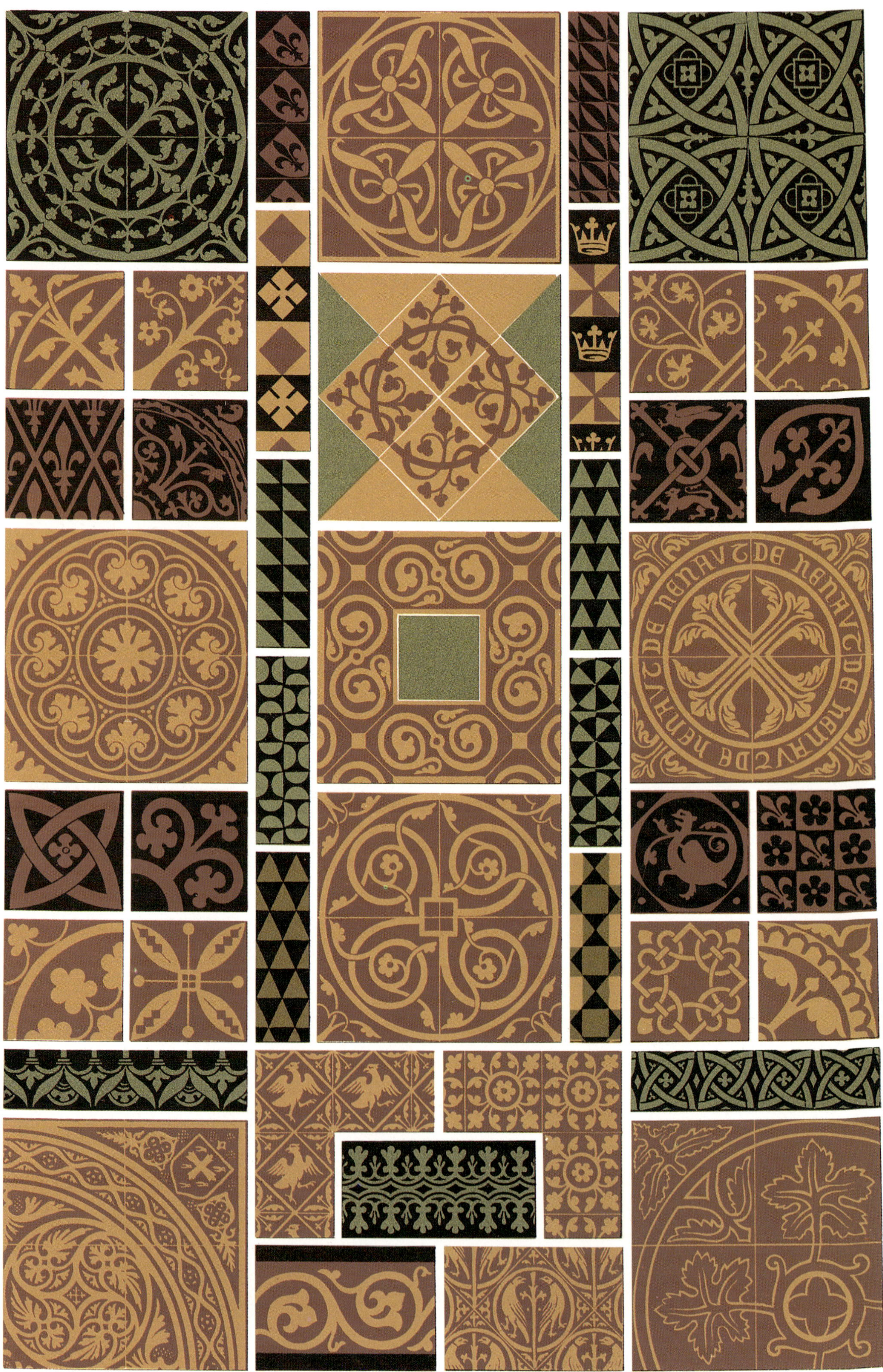

46. Medieval: Designs from wall and floor tiles, 13th and 14th centuries.

47. Medieval: Designs from textiles depicted in 16th-century manuscript illuminations.

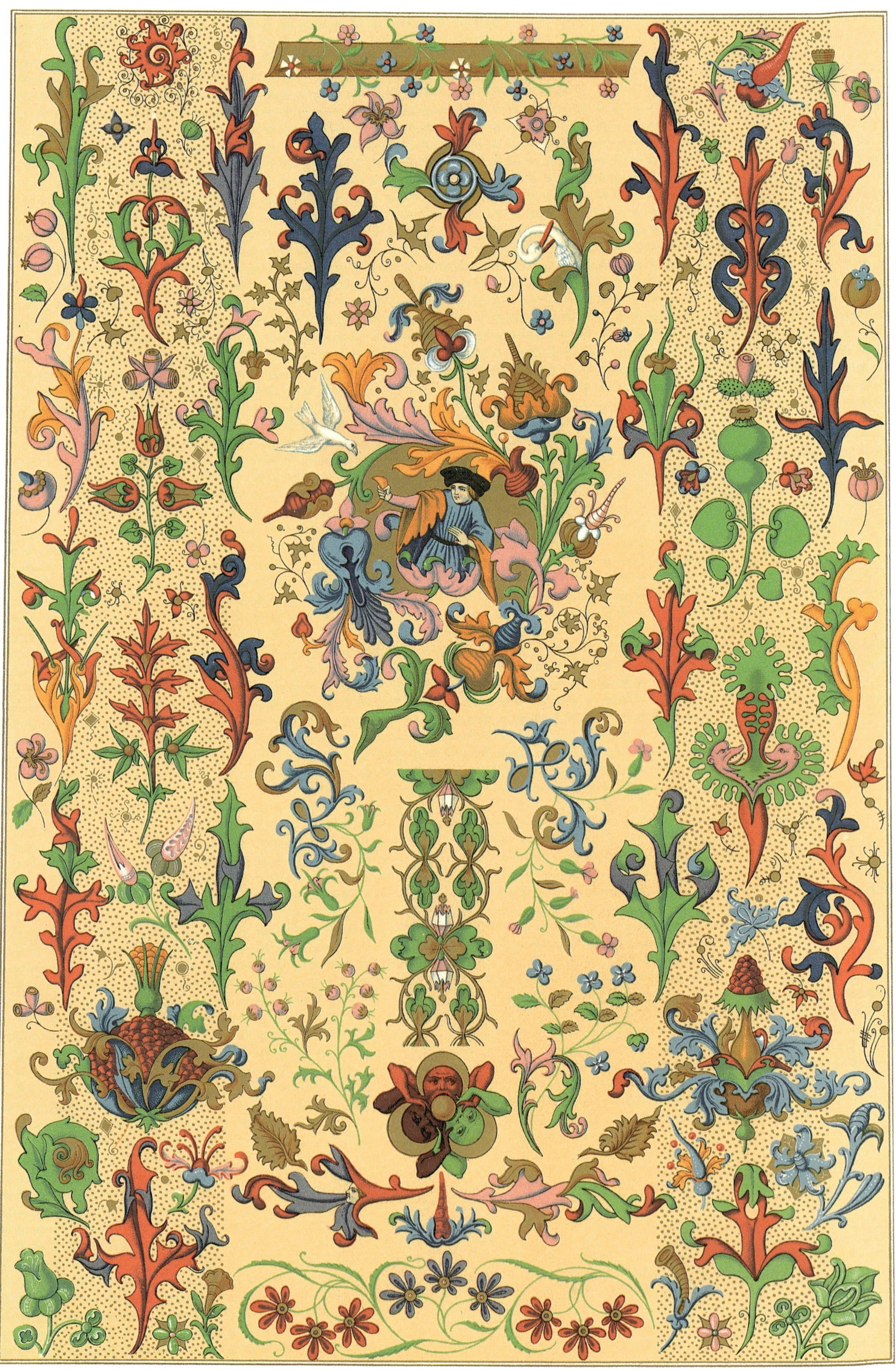

48. Medieval: Floral ornament from 15th-century manuscripts.

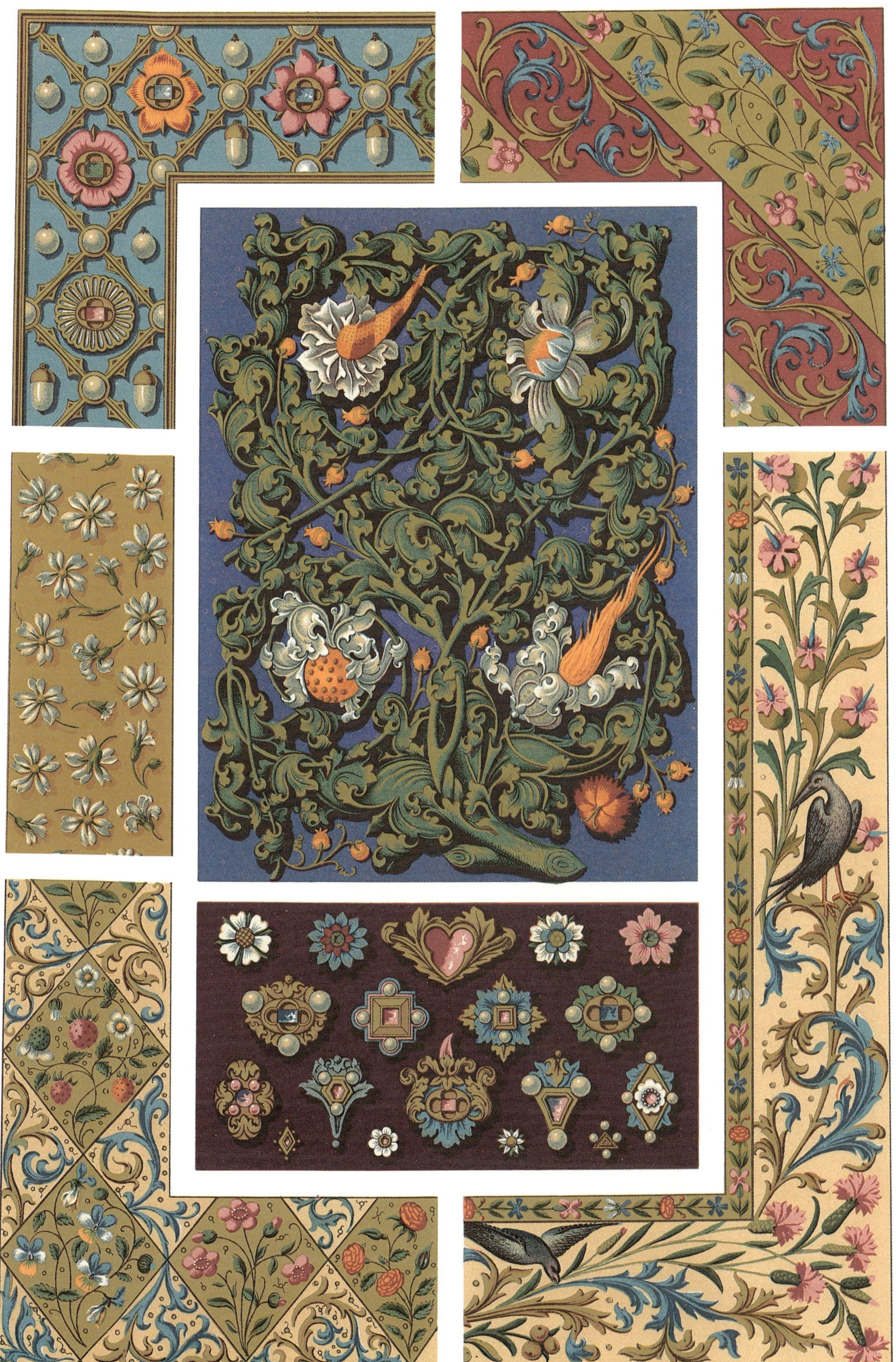

49. Medieval: Flowers and jewels from 15th-century manuscripts.

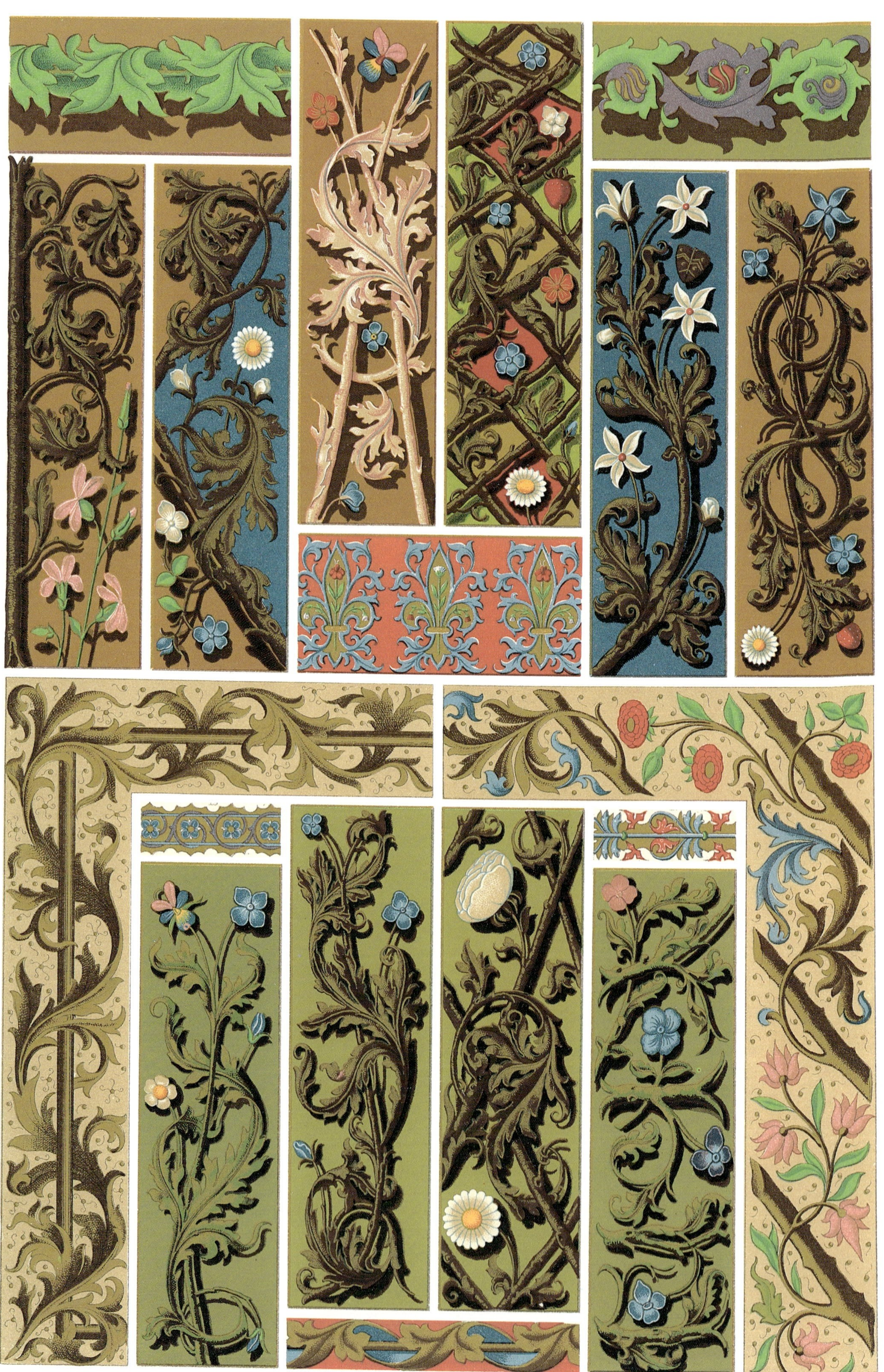

50. Medieval: Ornaments from 15th-century French and Flemish manuscripts.

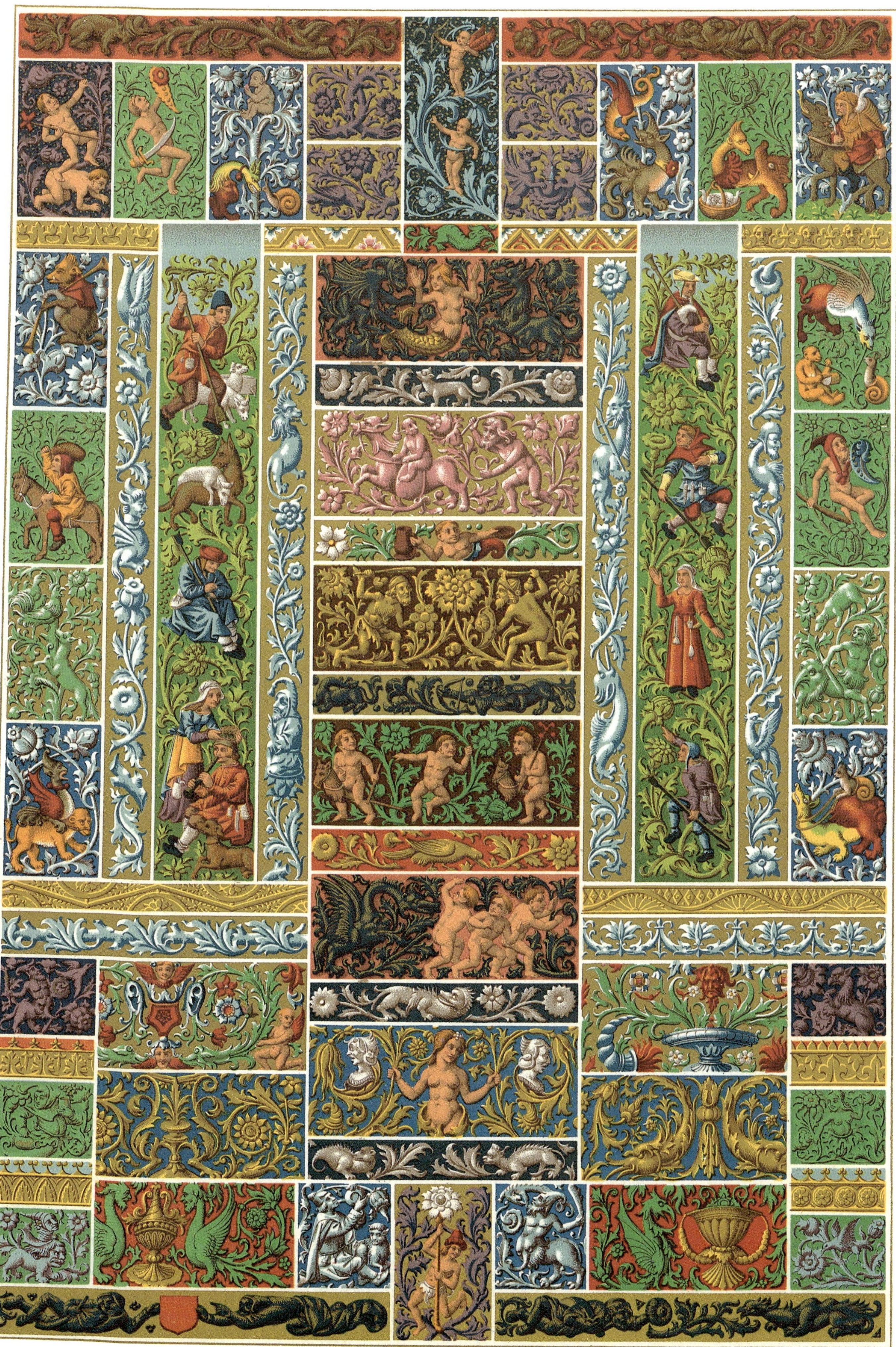

51. Renaissance: Ornaments from a printed (but hand-colored) French book of hours, 1508.

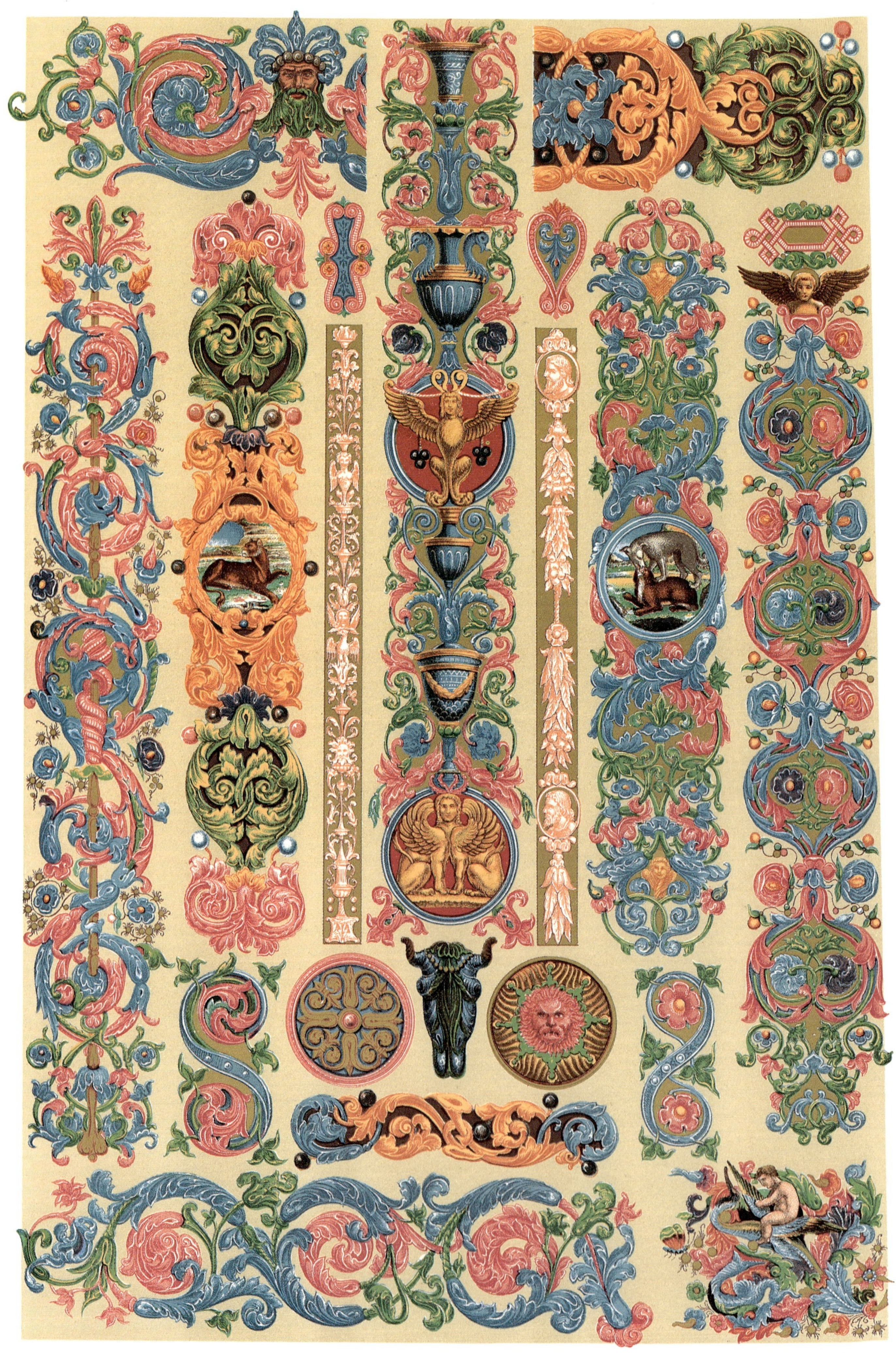

52. Renaissance: Ornaments from a late 15th-century Italian manuscript.

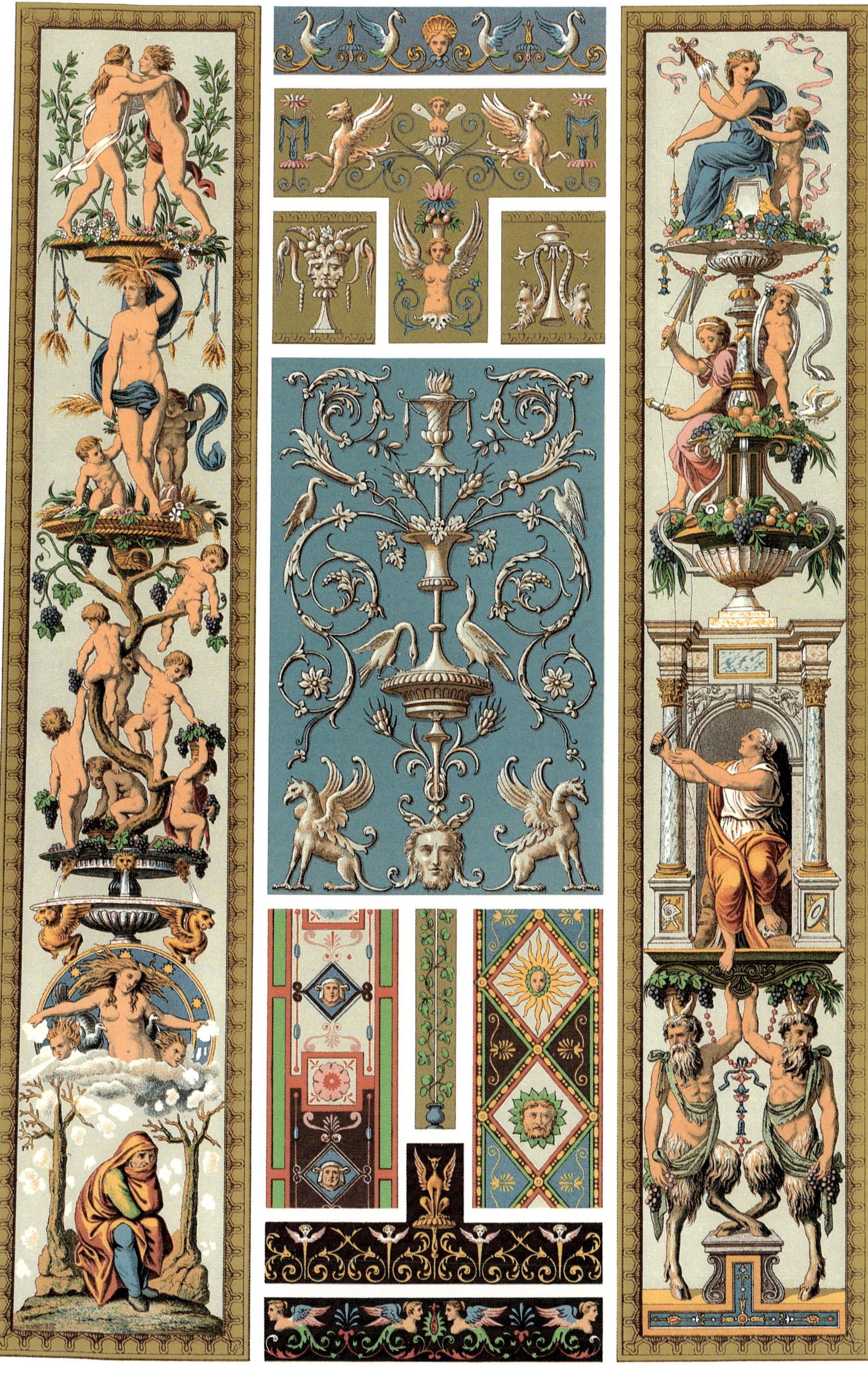

53. Renaissance: From Raphael's frescoes in the Vatican, early 16th century.

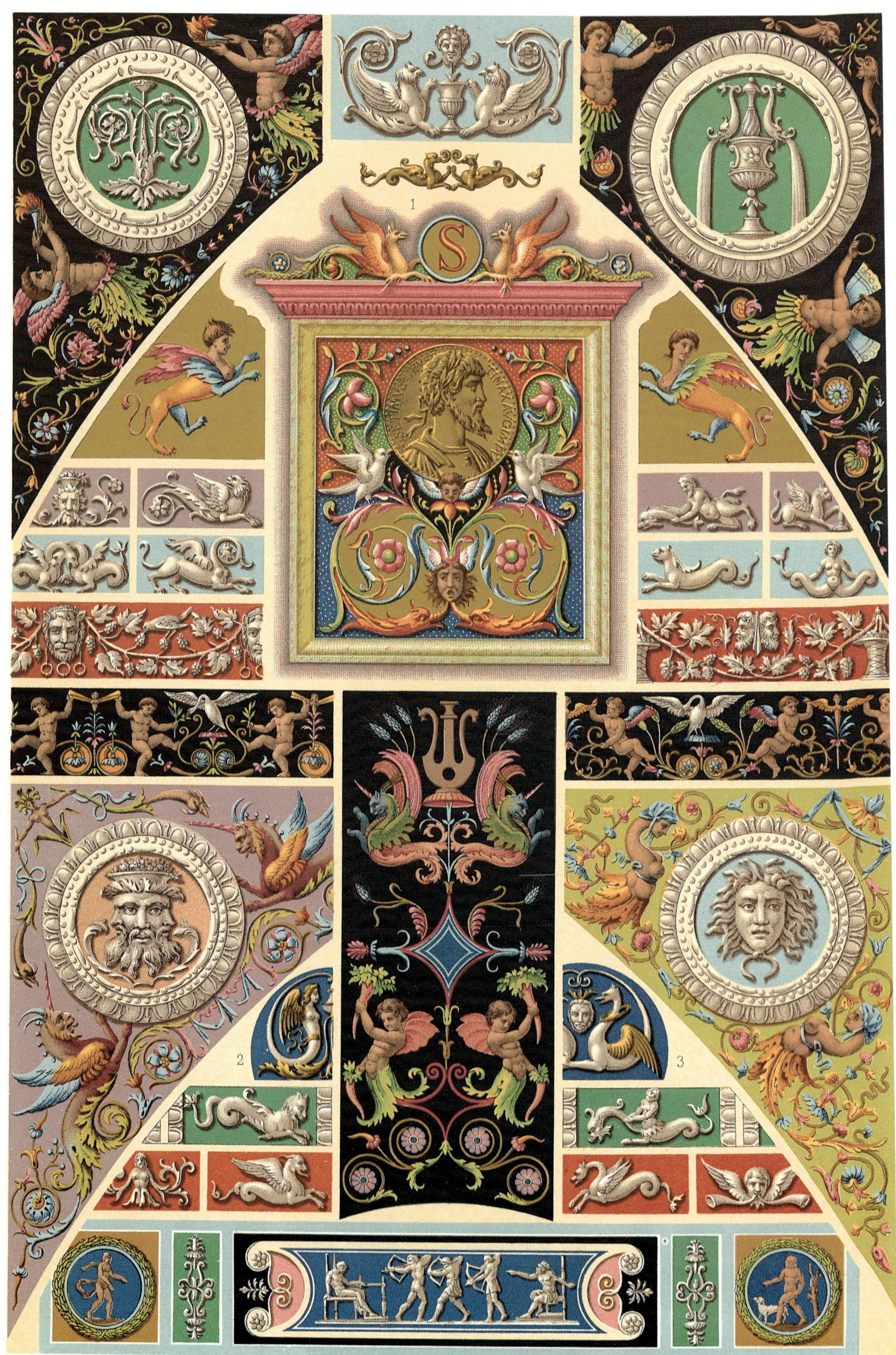

54. Renaissance: From 16th-century frescoes in Milan and in the Vatican (by Raphael and others).

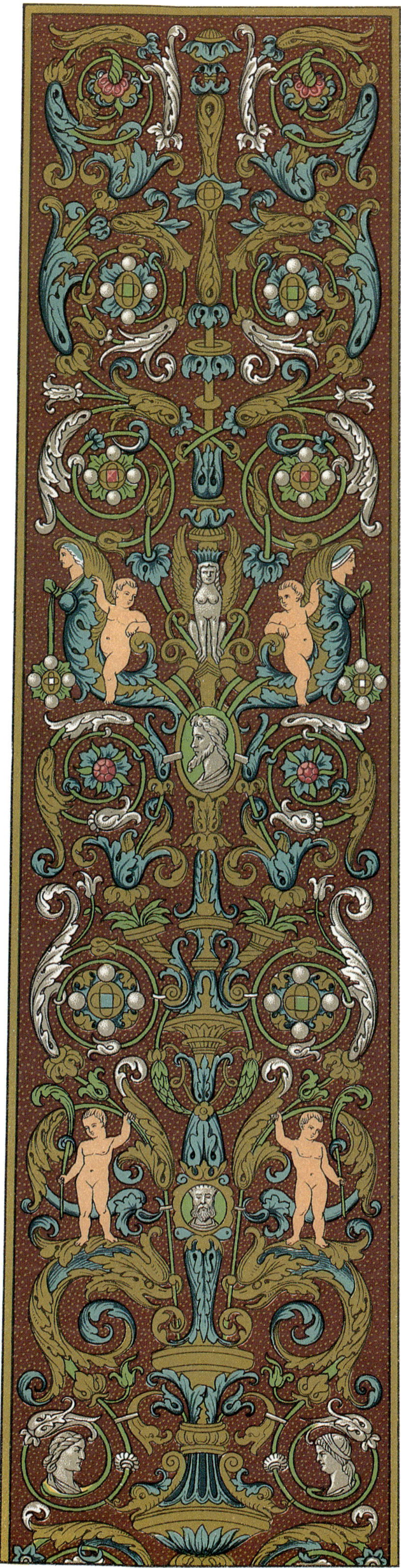
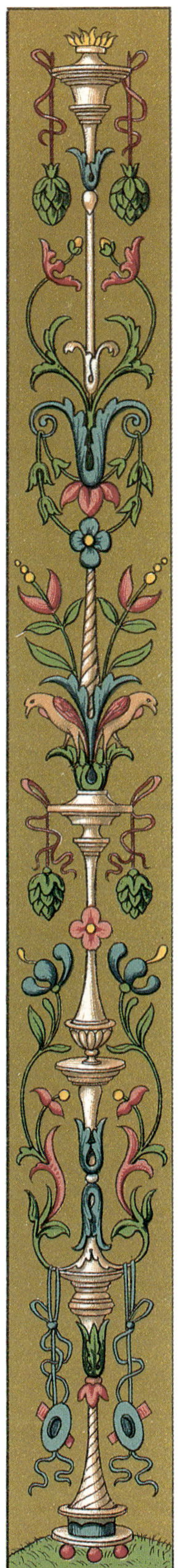
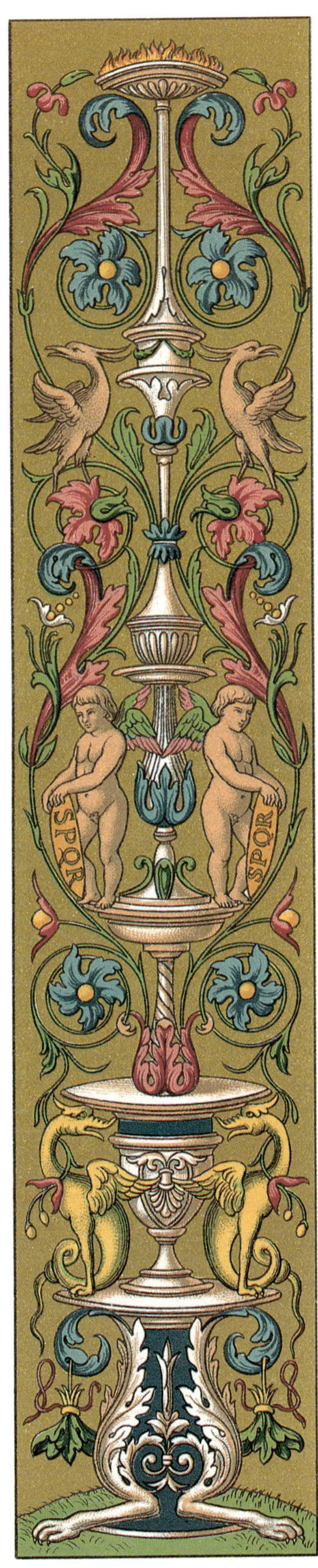

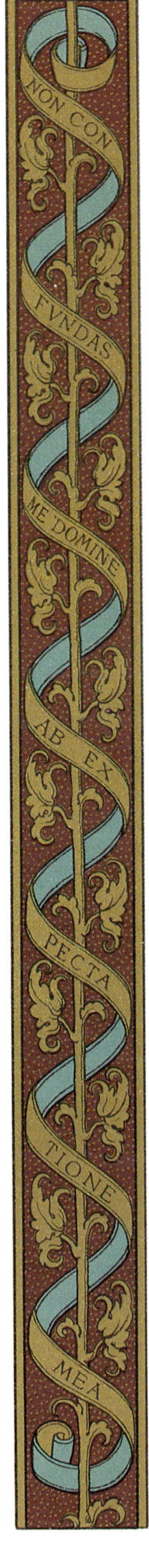

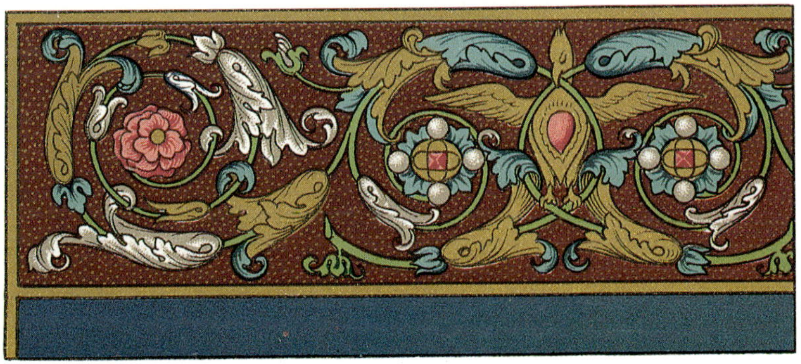

55. Renaissance: Miniatures from Italianate manuscripts of the early 16th century.

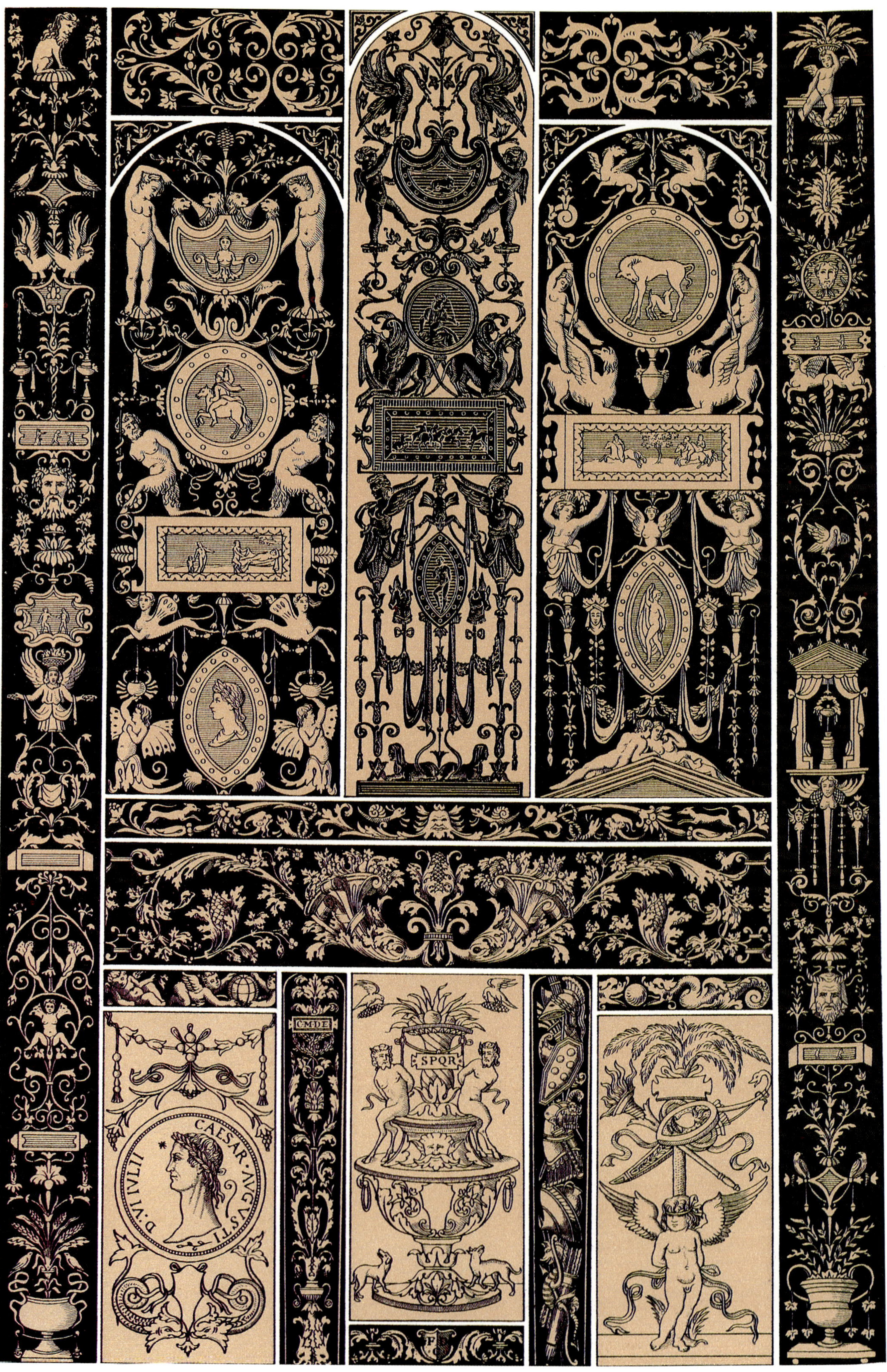

56. Renaissance: Designs from engraved ivories, including furniture inlays.

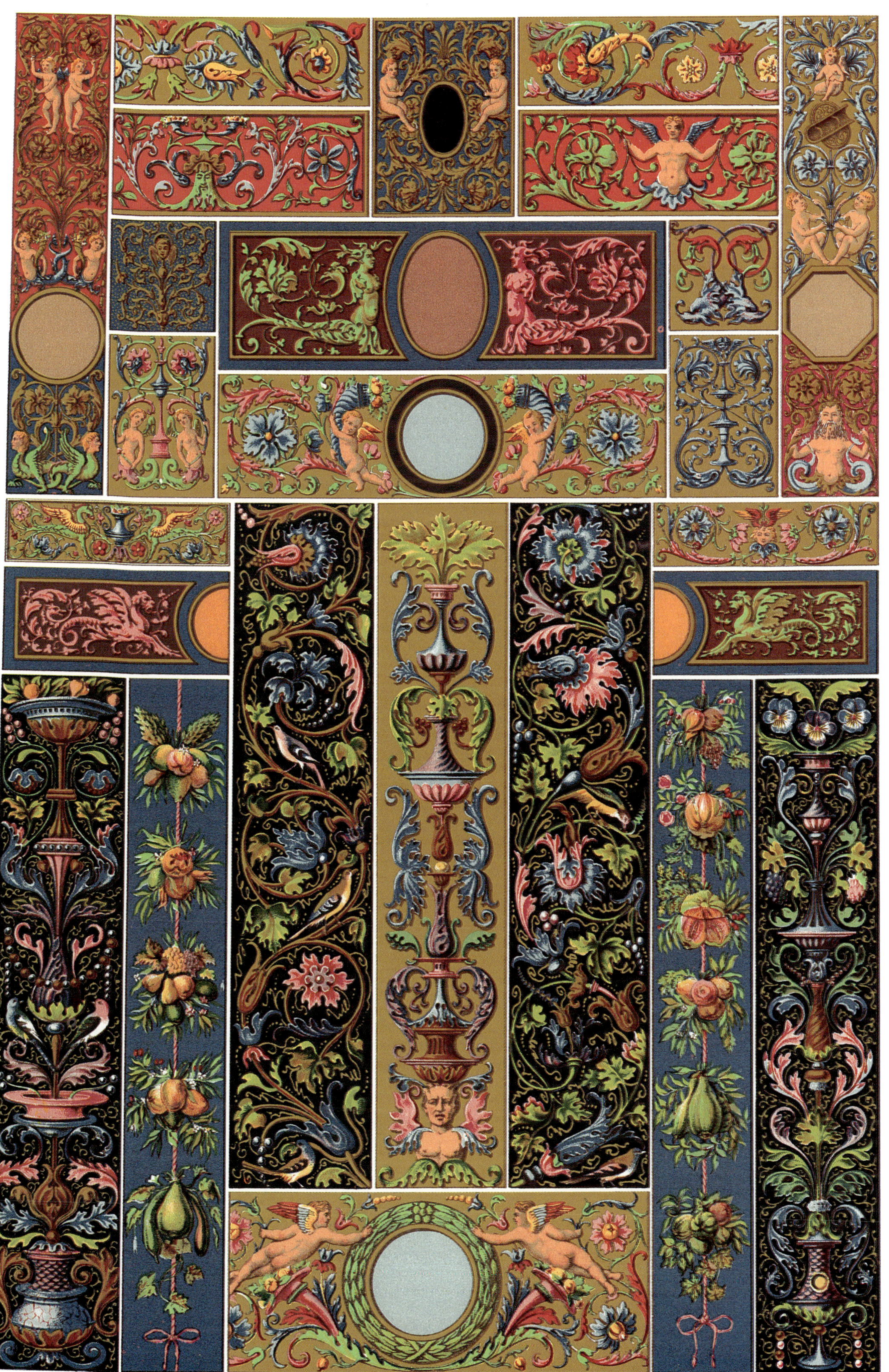

57. Renaissance: From Italian frescoes and manuscripts, 15th and 16th centuries.

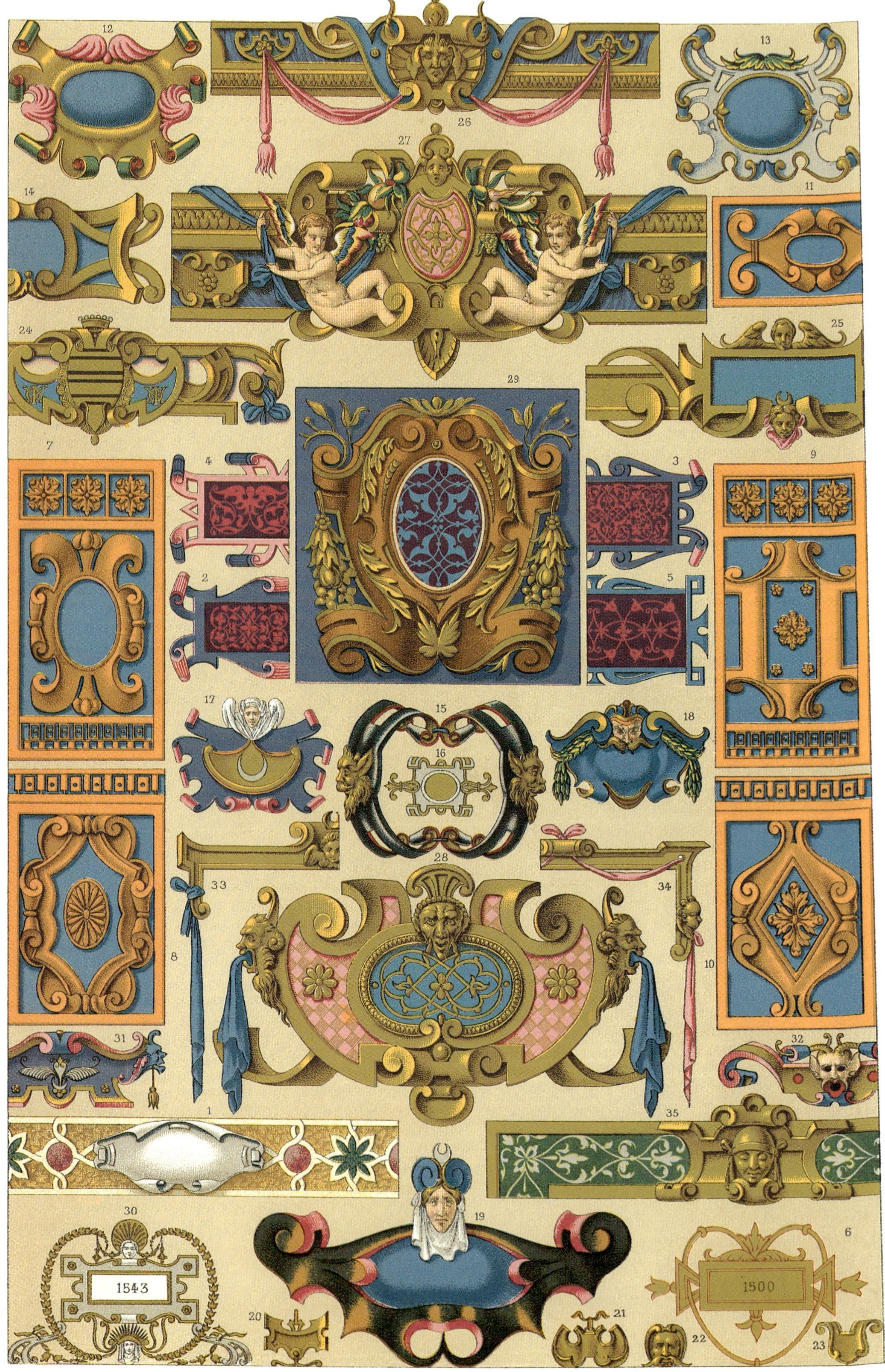

58. Renaissance: Cartouches, Italianate, 15th and early 16th centuries.

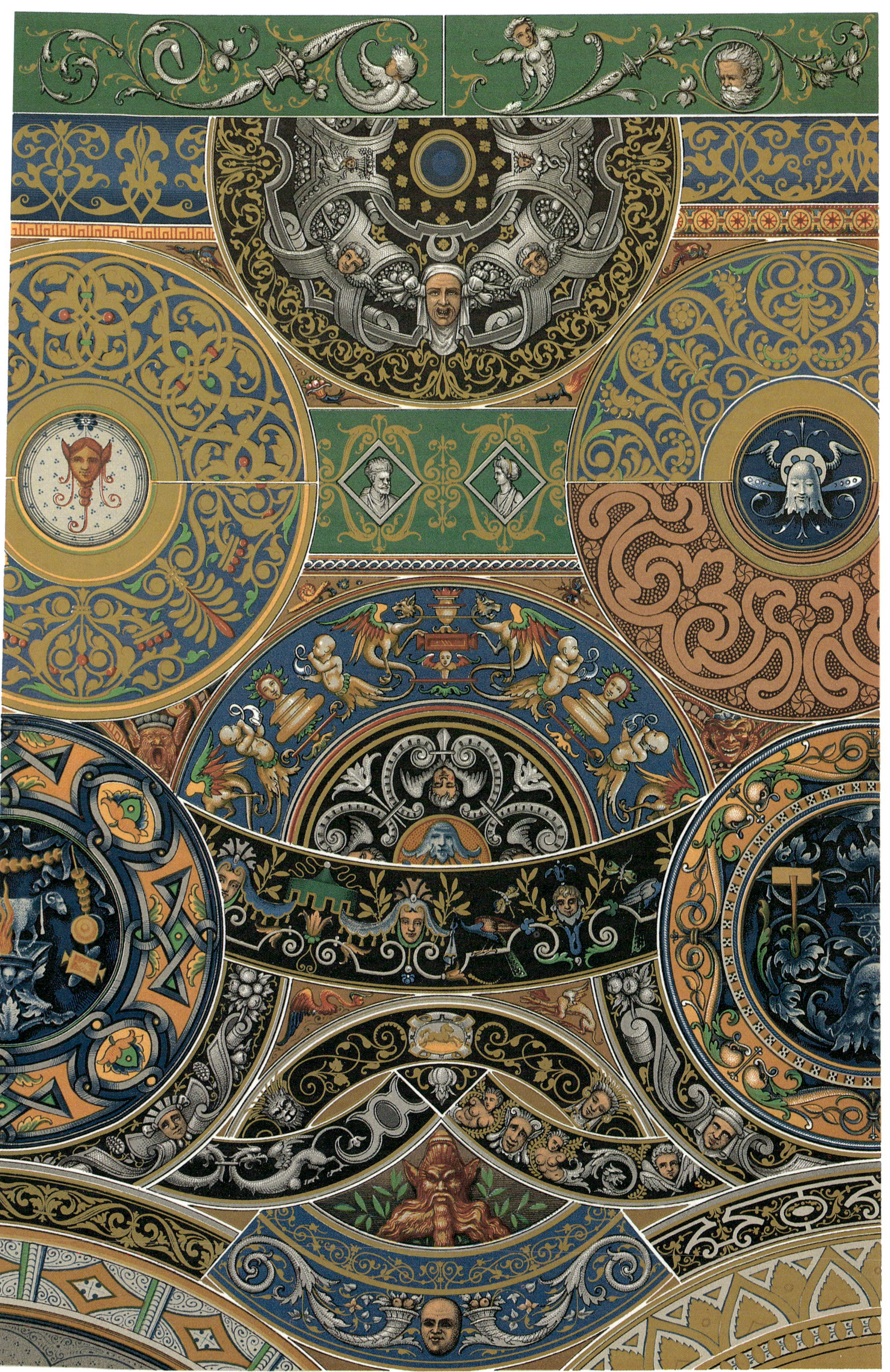

59. Renaissance: From Limoges enamels and Italian faience, 16th century.

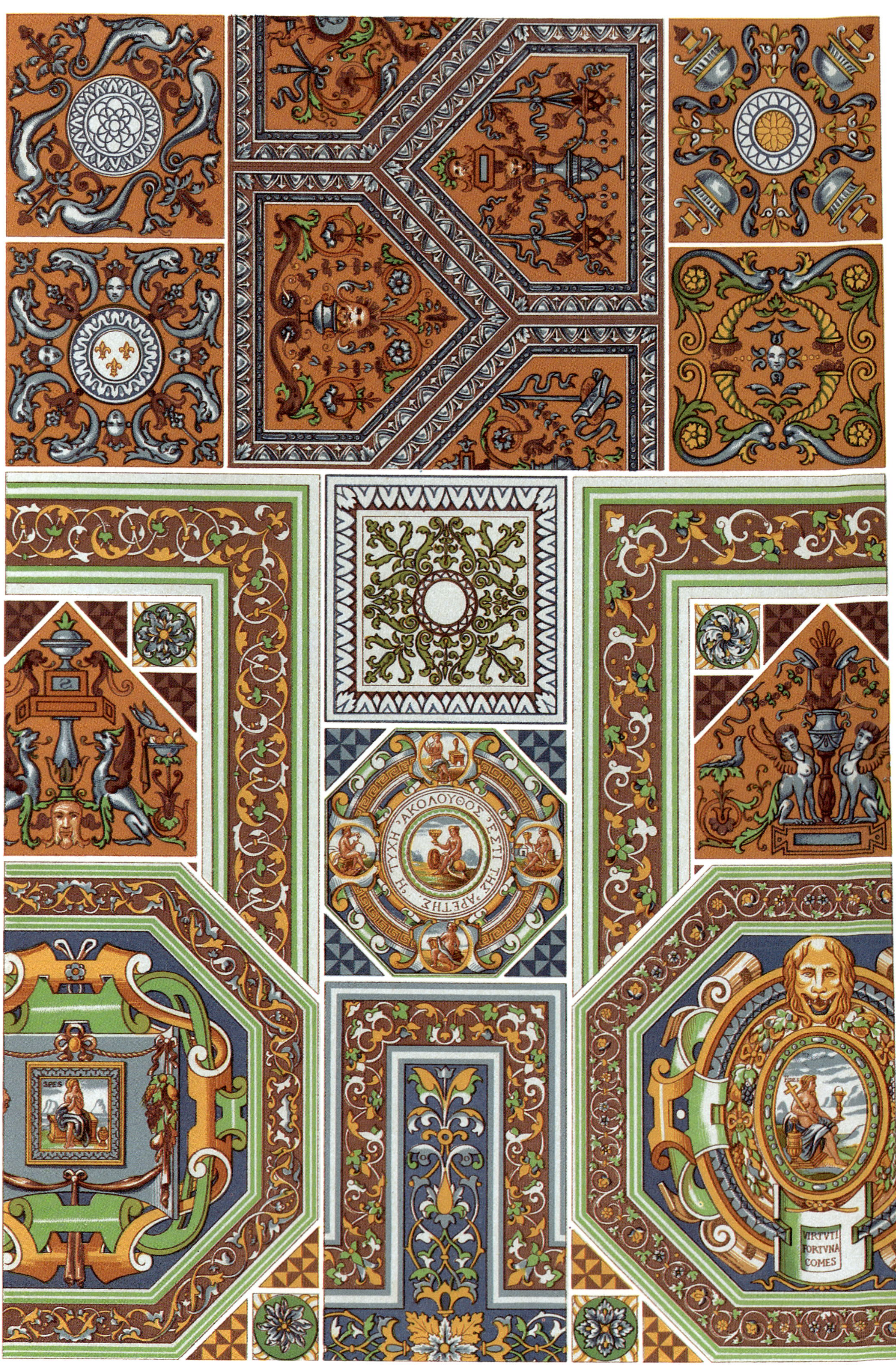

60. Renaissance: Glazed tiles.

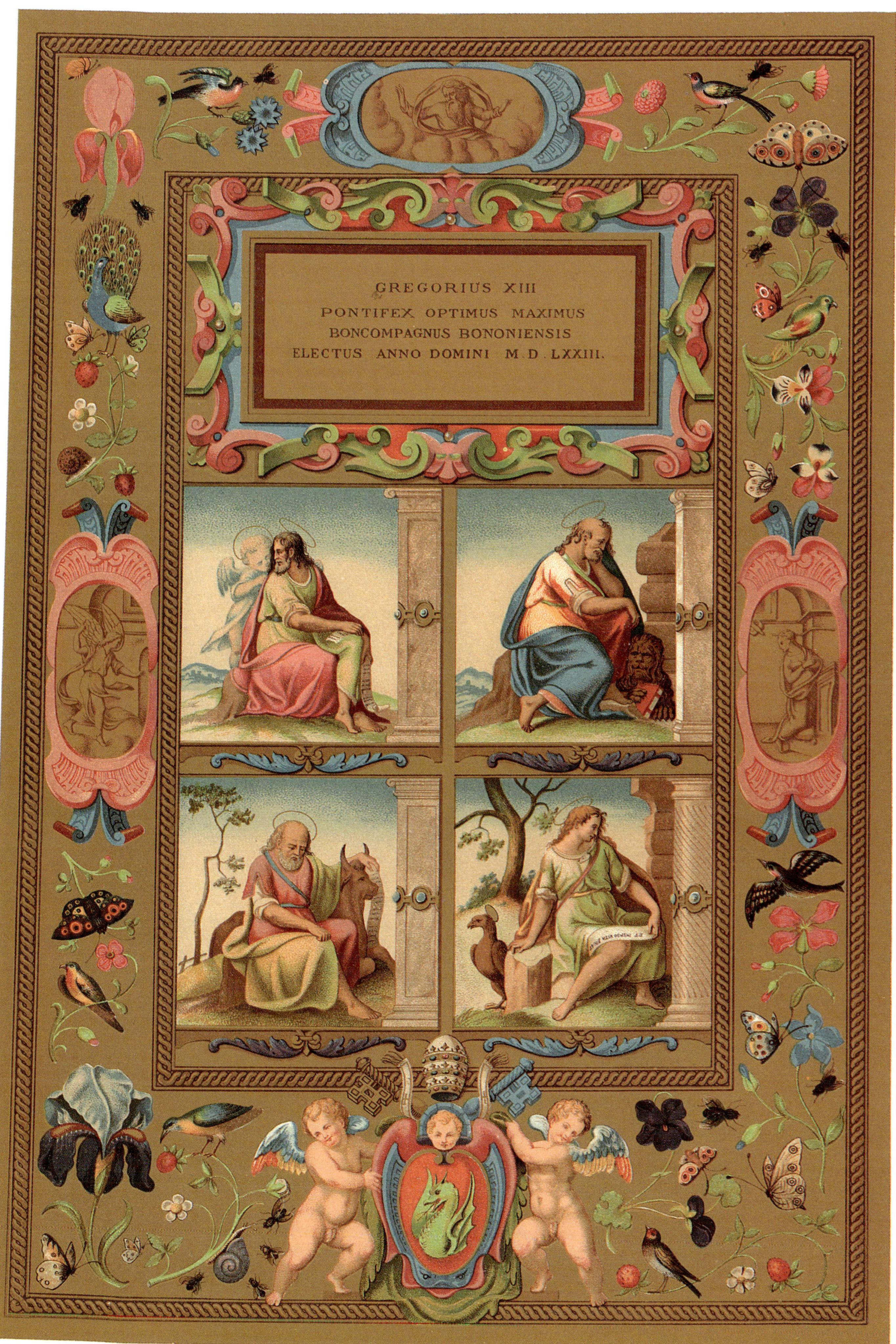

61. Renaissance: Painting on vellum, on the election of Pope Gregory XIII, 1573.

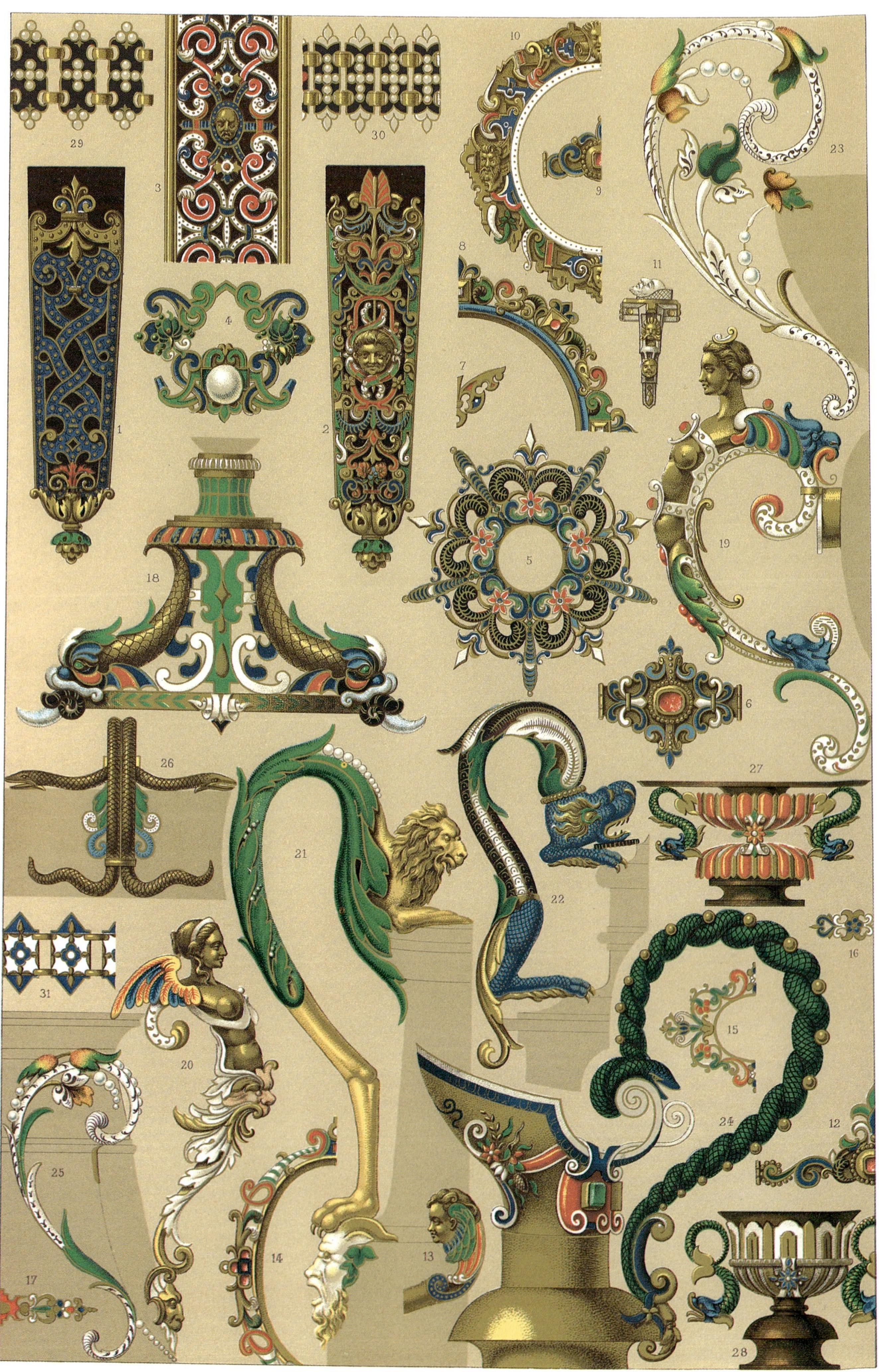

62. 16th & 17th Centuries: Enameled metalwork and jewelry.

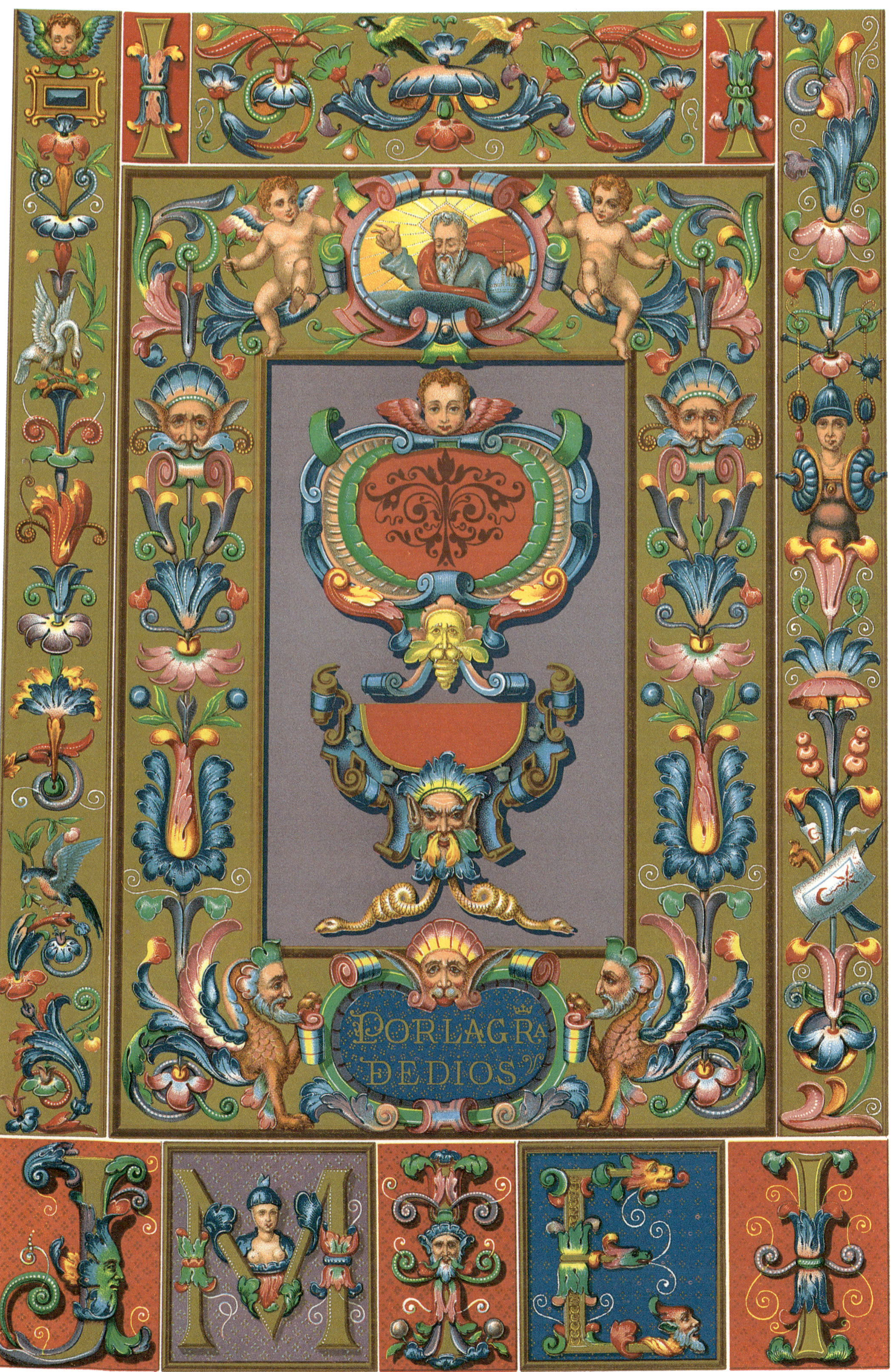

63. Renaissance: From Spanish illuminated manuscripts, late 16th century.

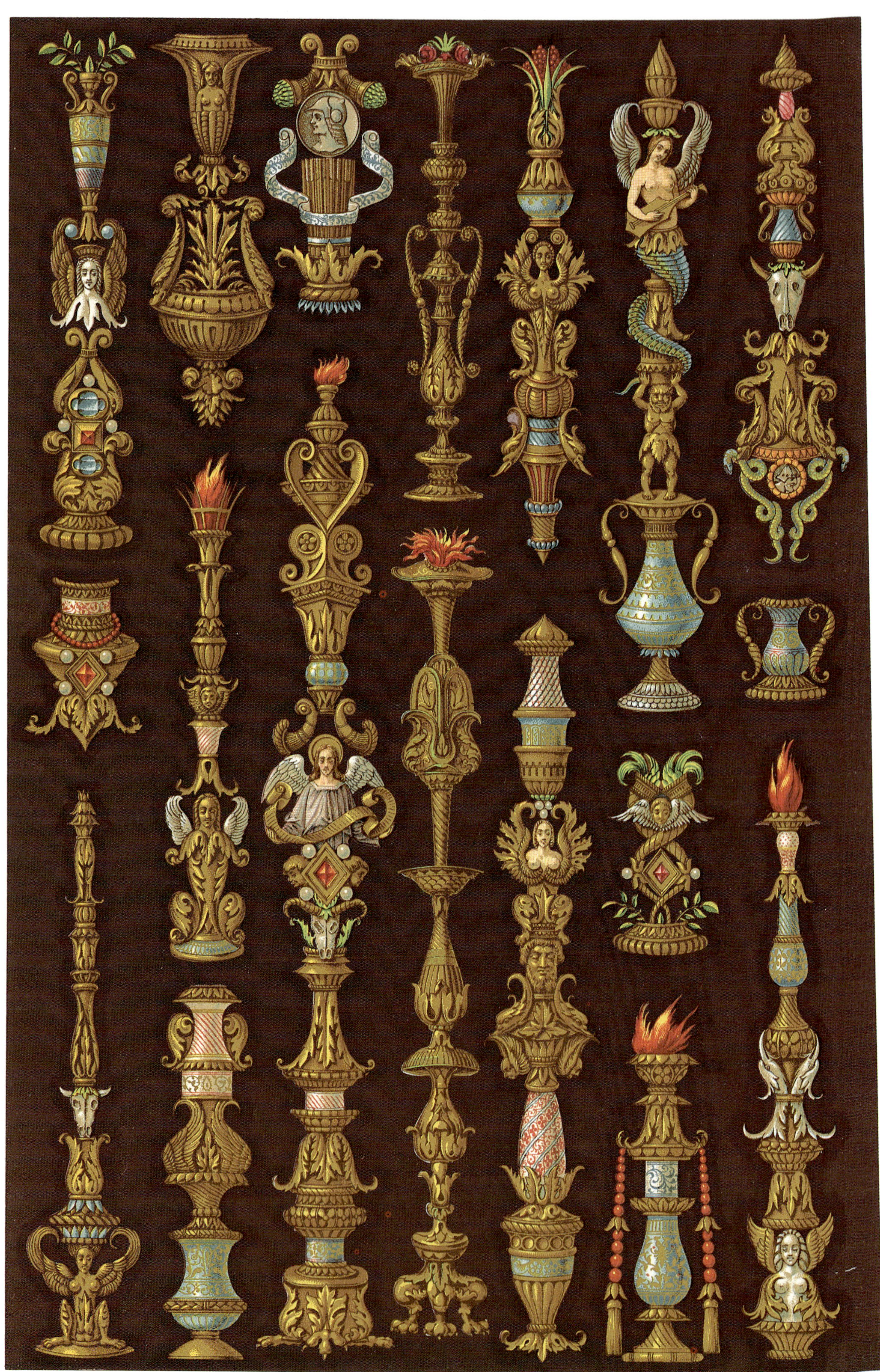

64. Renaissance: From French and Italian illuminated manuscripts.

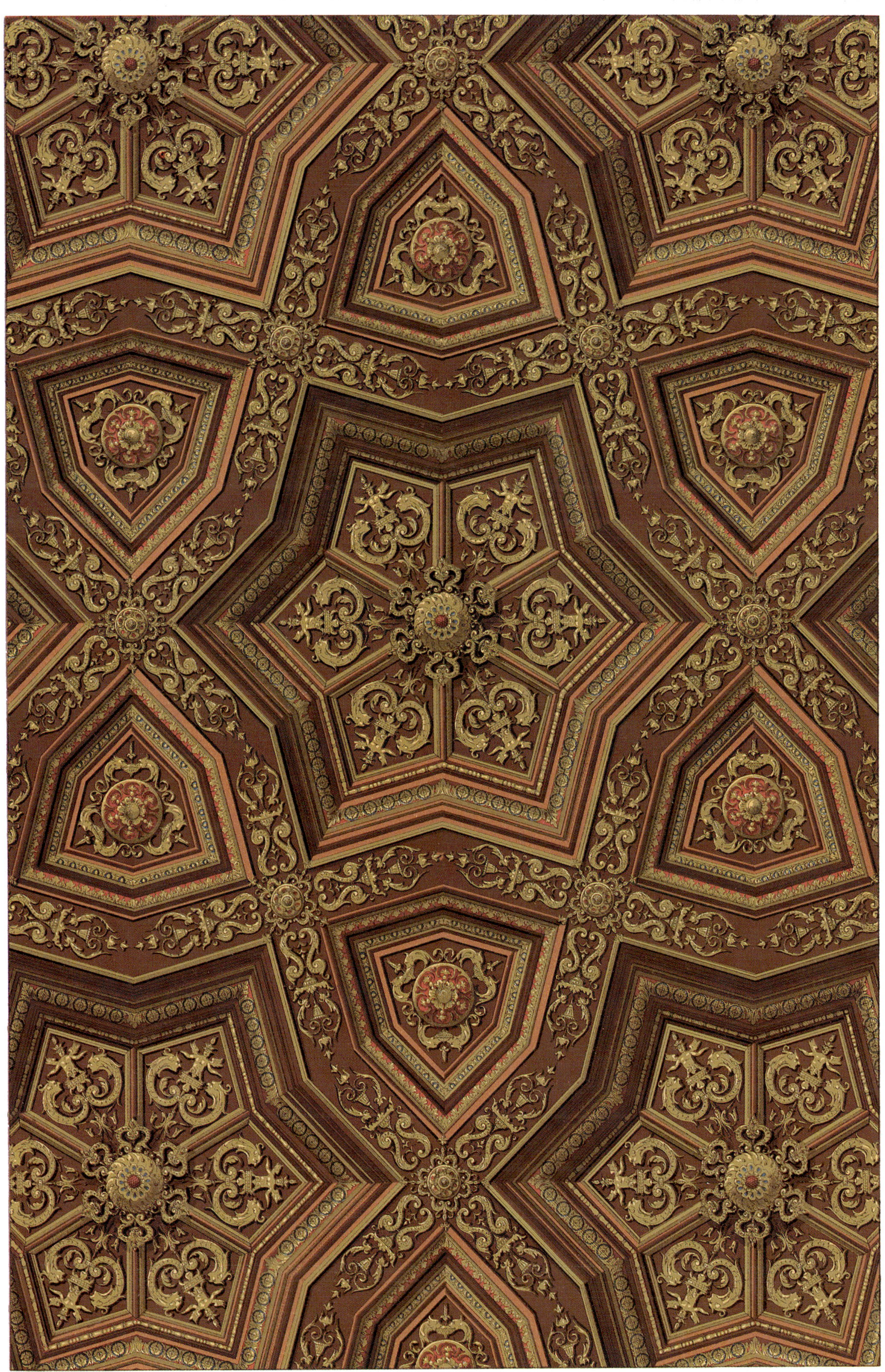

65. Renaissance: Ceiling from the Palais de Justice, Rouen, ca. 1500.

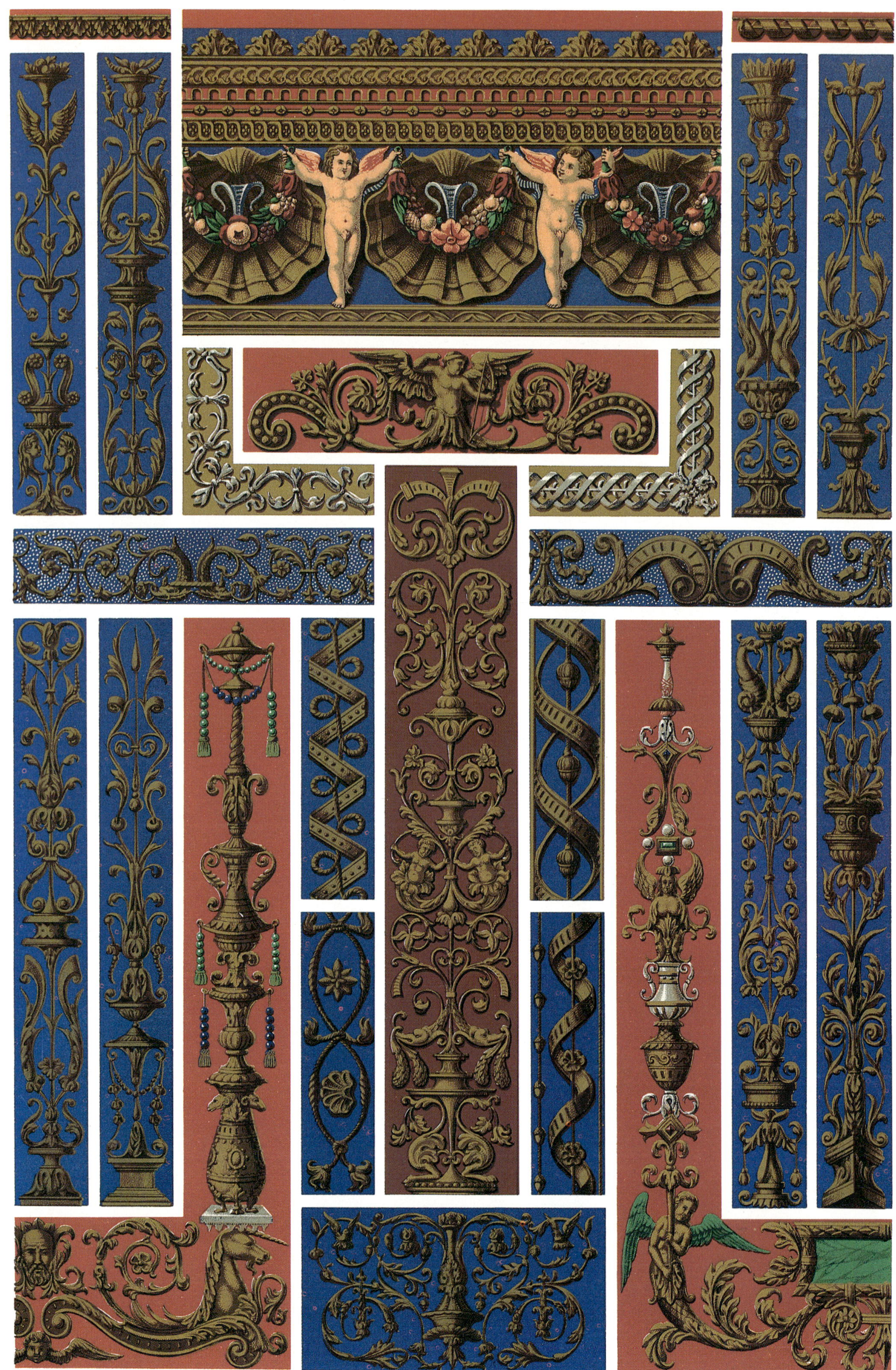

66. Renaissance: Stone and wood carvings, and manuscript illuminations, France, 16th century.

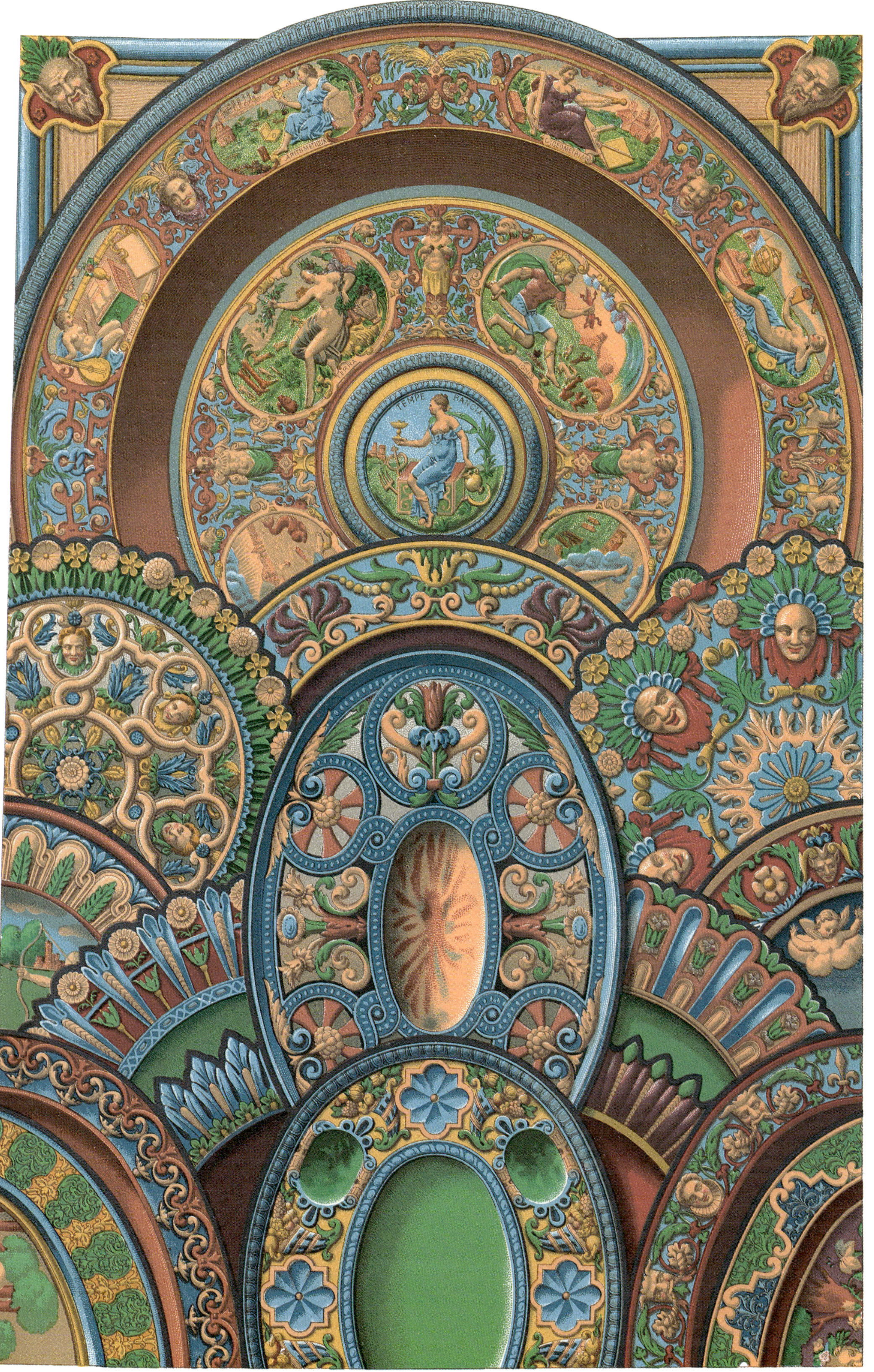

67. Renaissance: Glazed earthenware by Bernard Palissy, France, 16th century.

68. Renaissance: From Venetian book covers and marquetry.

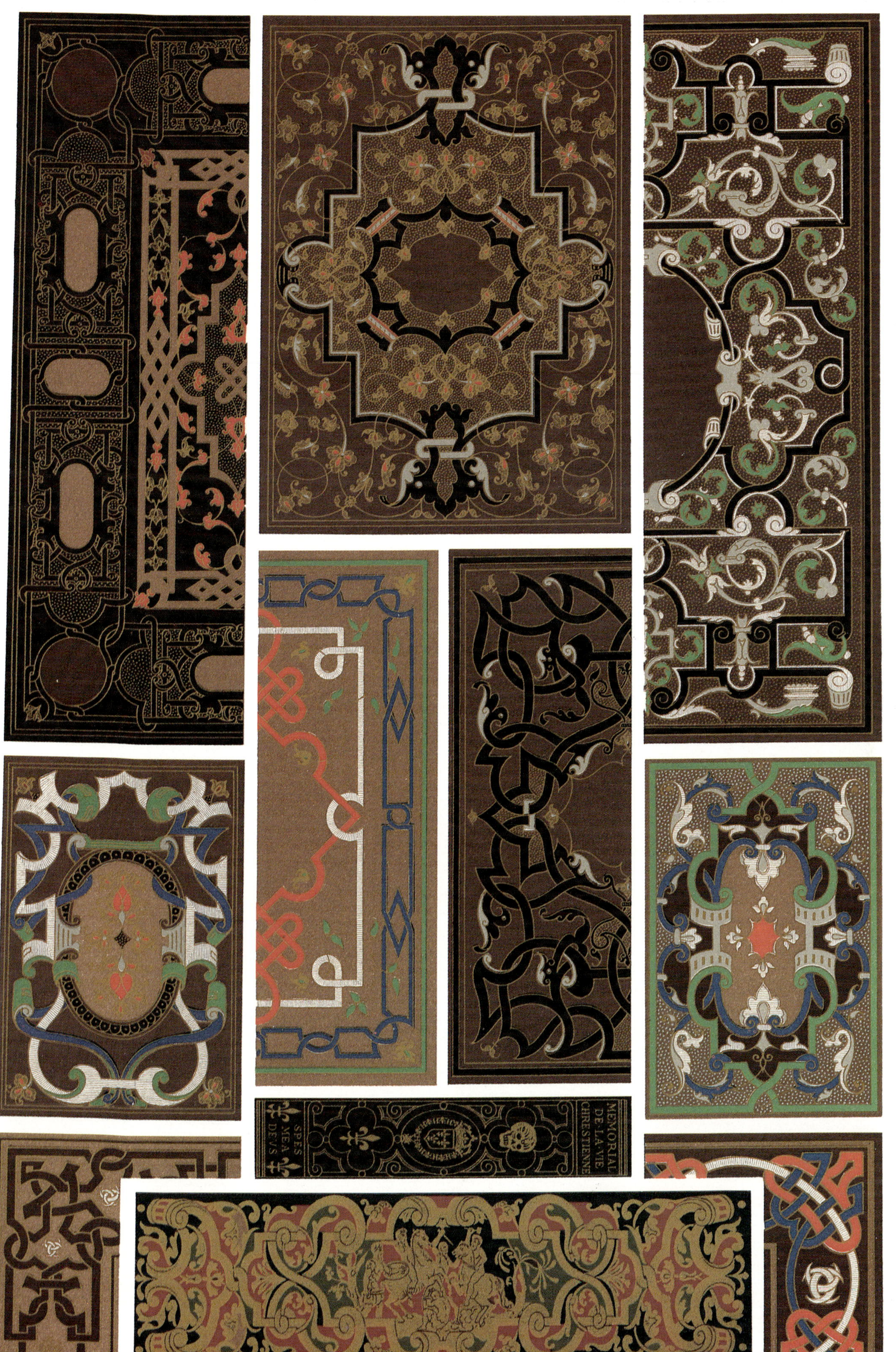

69. 16th & 17th Centuries: From French and Italian book covers.

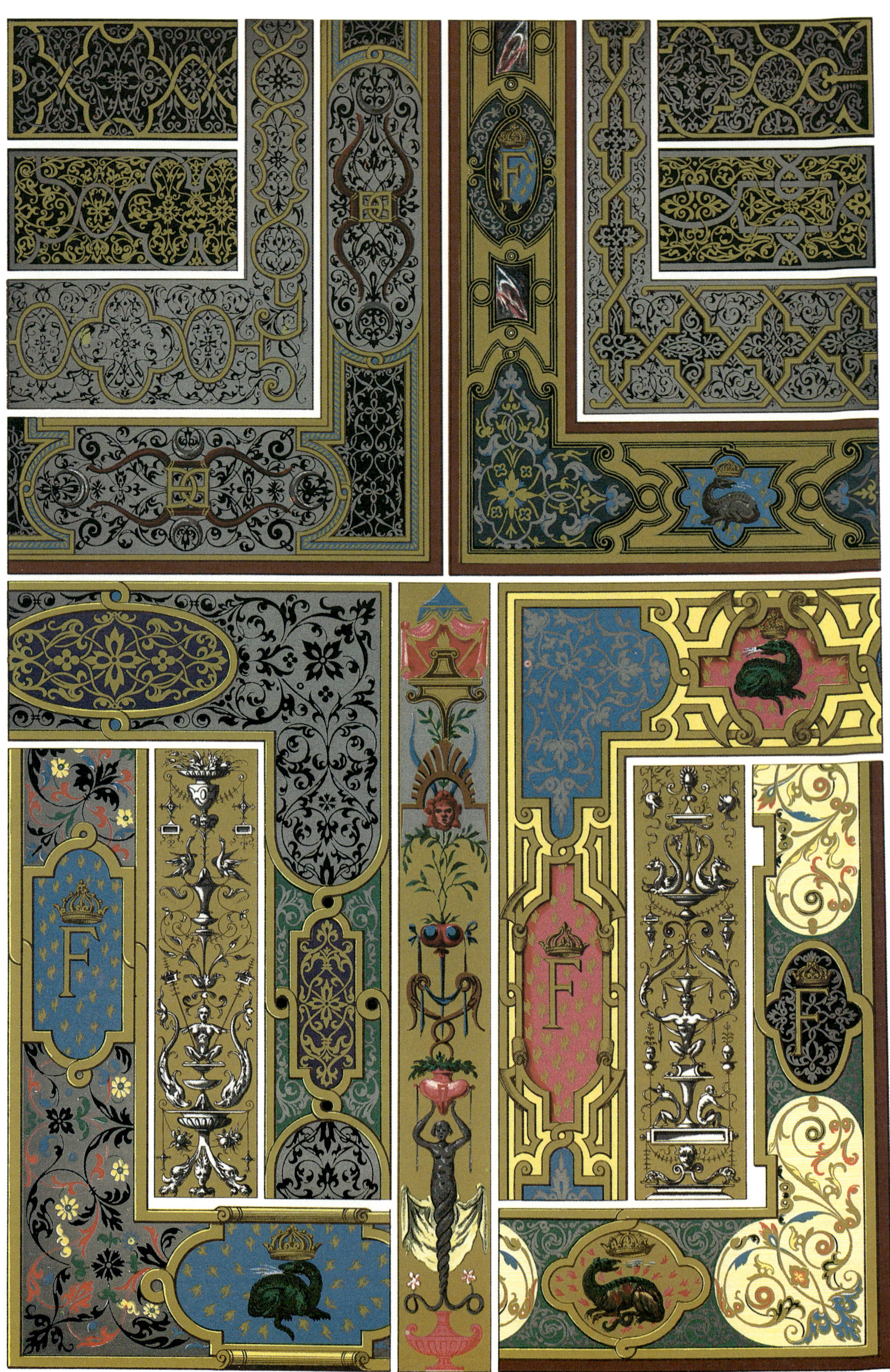

70. Renaissance: Painted and typographic book ornament, France, 16th century.

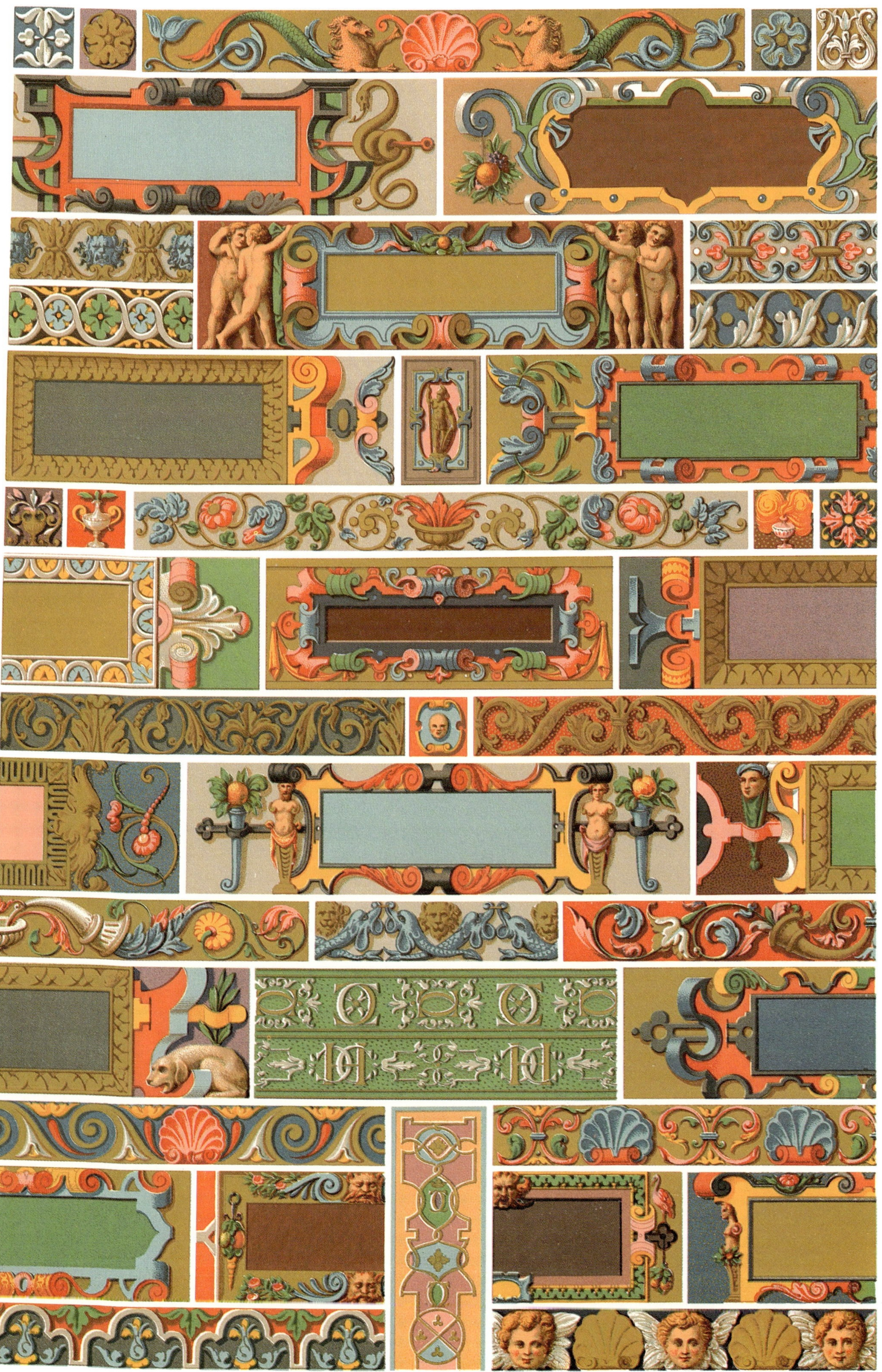

71. Renaissance: Ornament from books and architectural painting, France, 16th century.

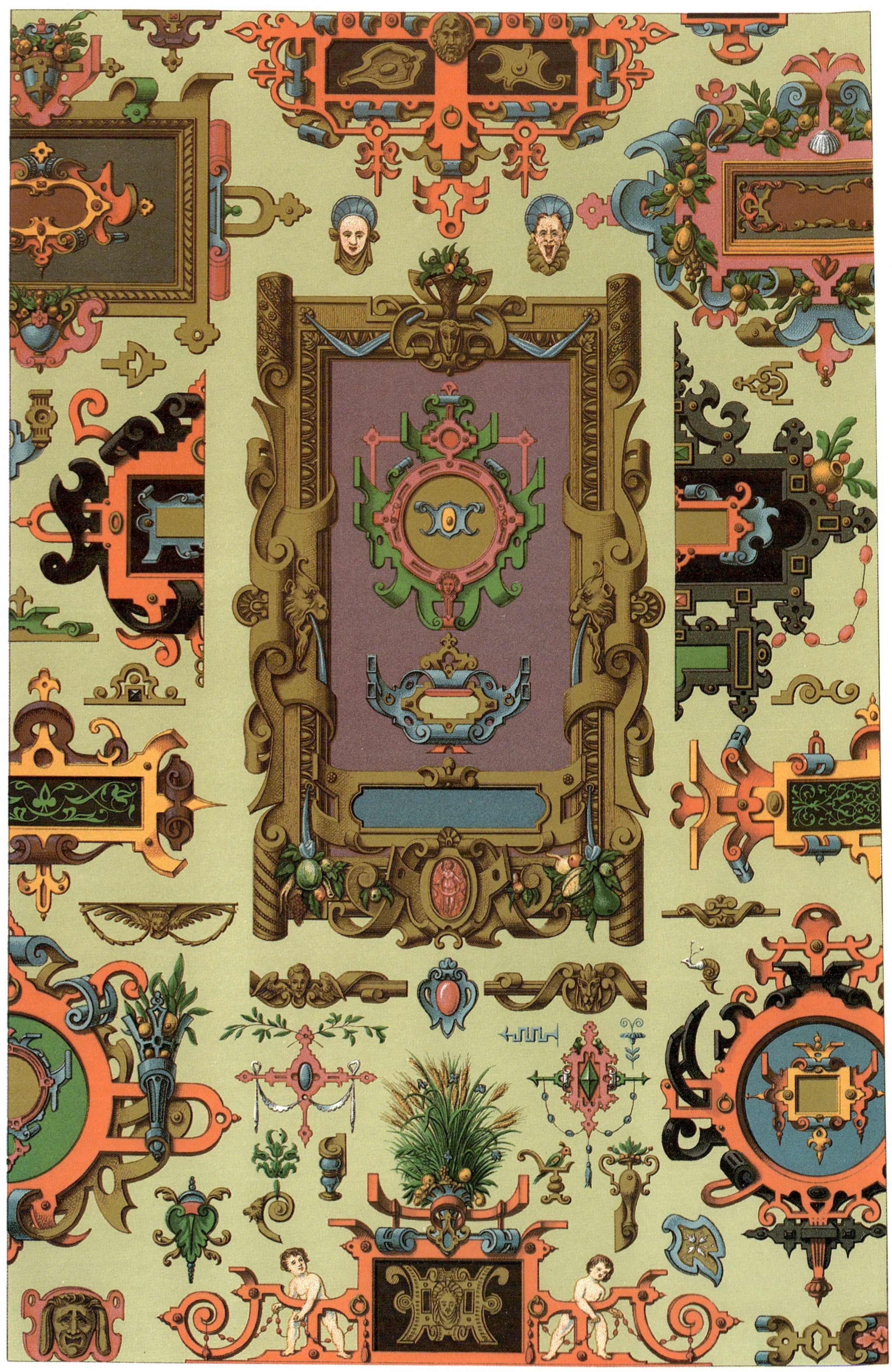

72. 16th & 17th Centuries: Cartouches from French and Flemish manuscripts and maps.

73. 16th & 17th Centuries: From embroidered wall hangings.

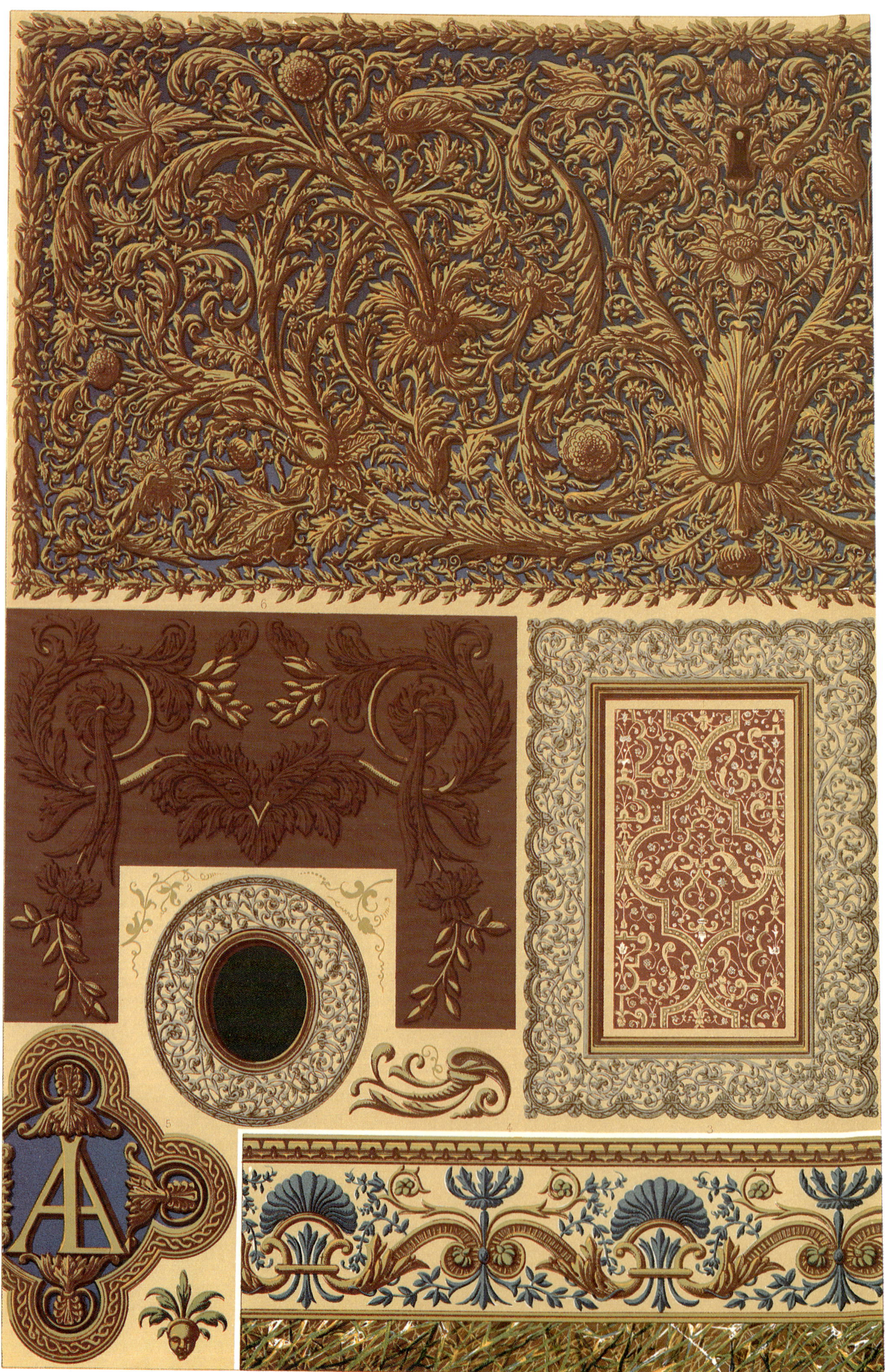

74. 17th Century: Louis XIII ornament from furniture and architecture.

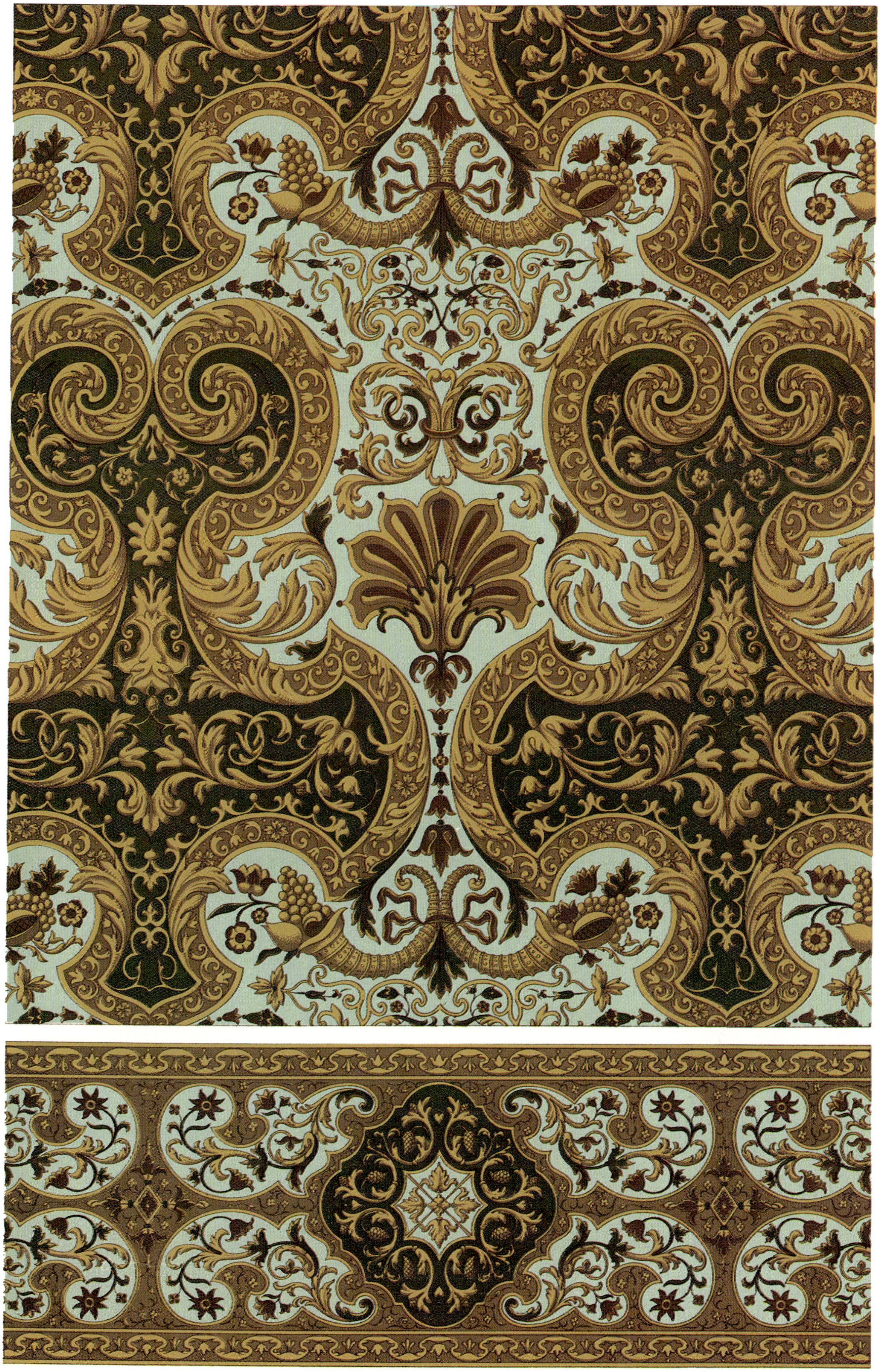

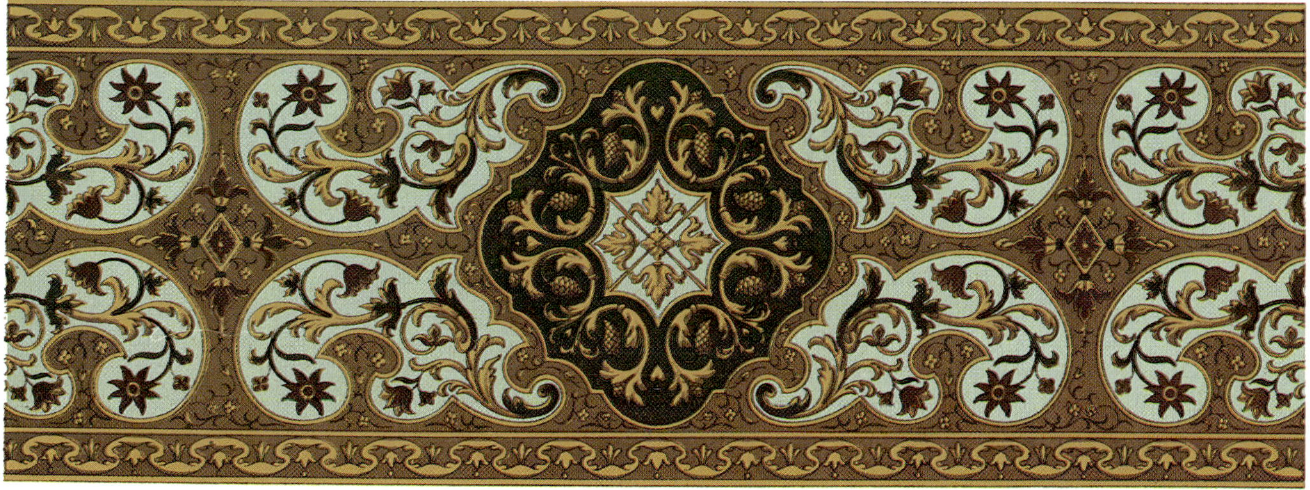

75. 17th Century: Louis XIII ornament from a gilt leather hanging.

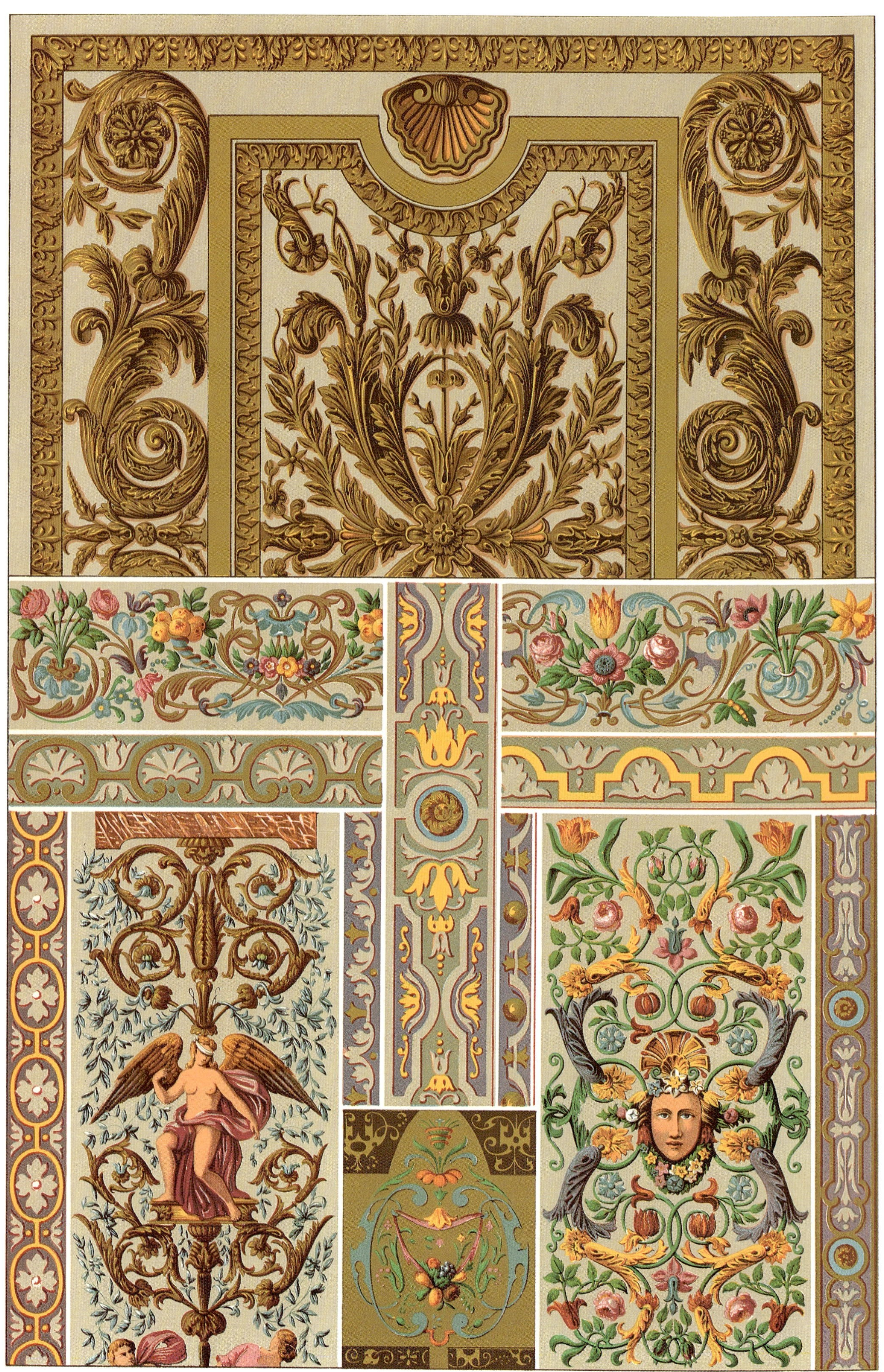

76. Early 17th Century: From murals, manuscripts and metalwork.

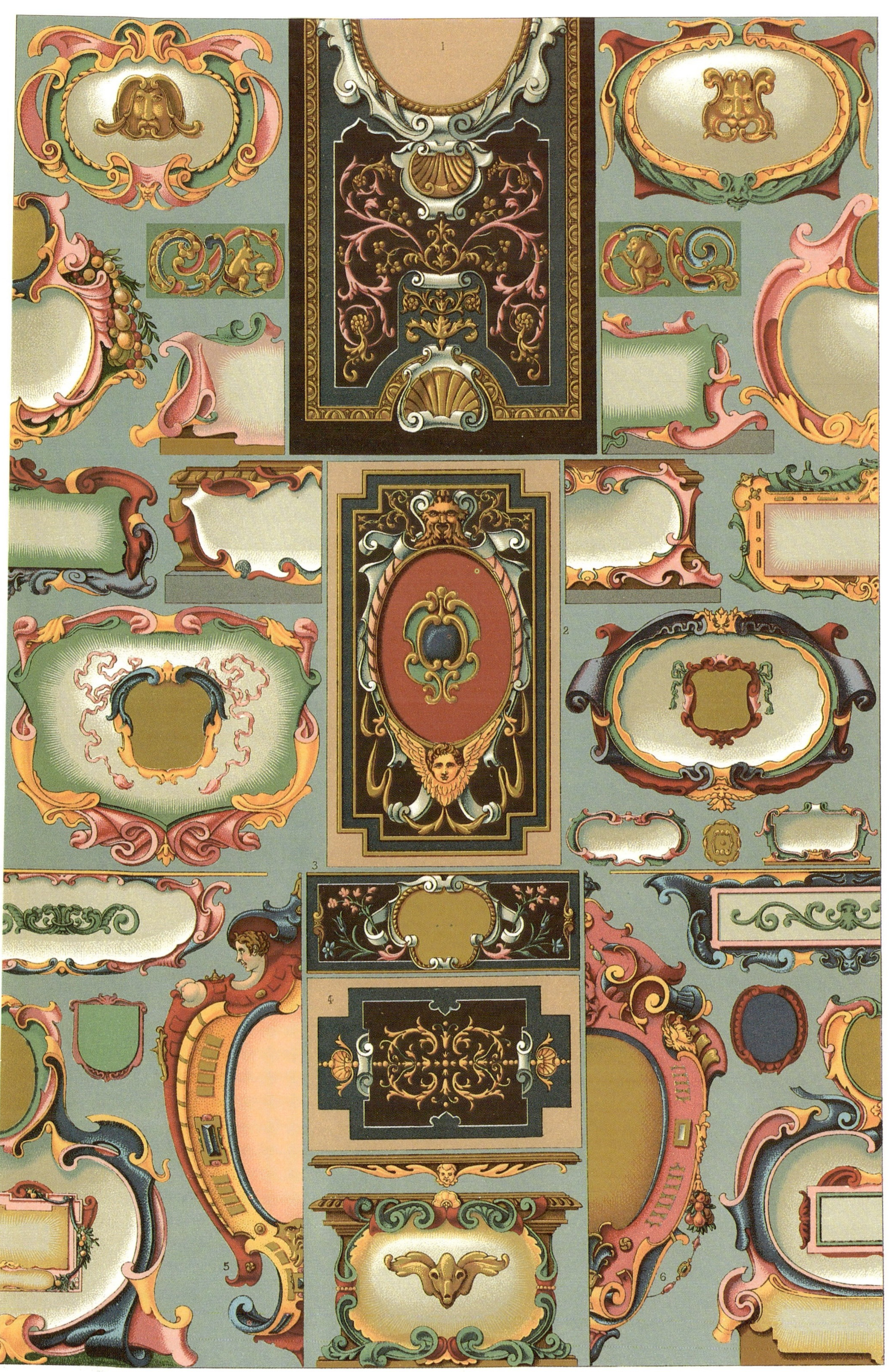

77. Early 17th Century: Cartouches from French and Flemish architectural maps.

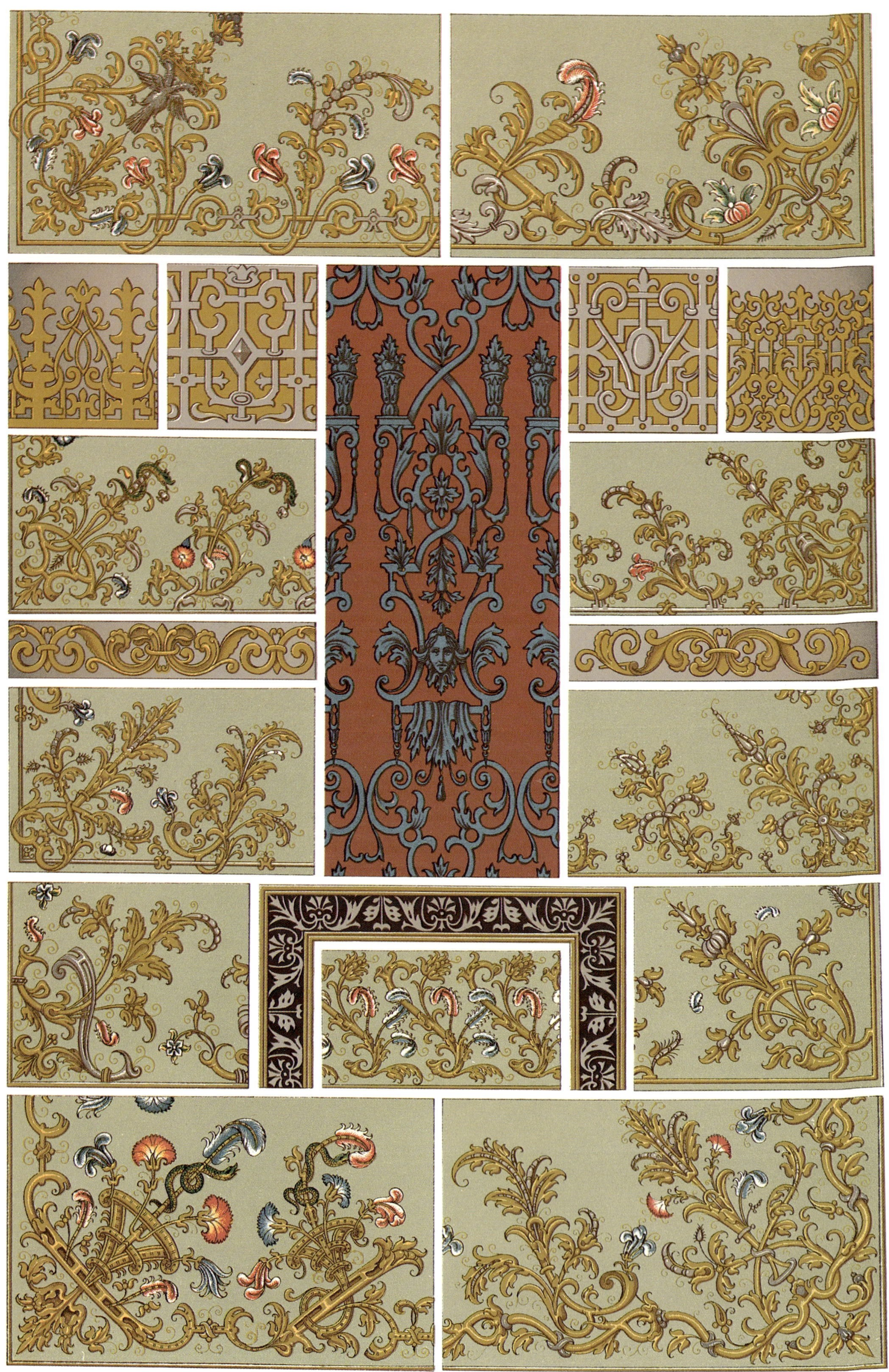

78. Early 17th Century: From embroideries, leatherwork, woodwork and book décor.

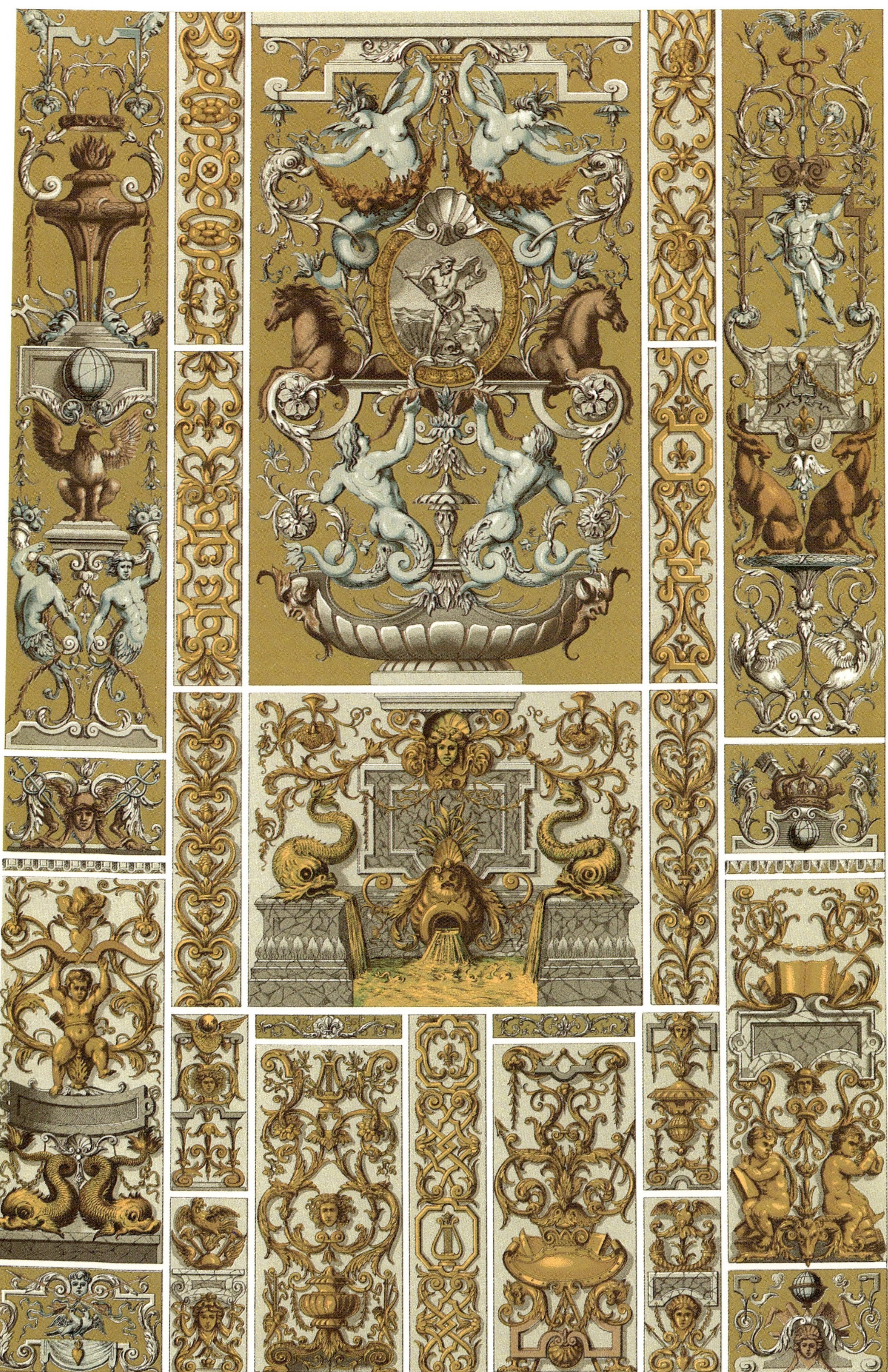

79. 17th Century: From murals in the Louvre designed by Jean Bérain.

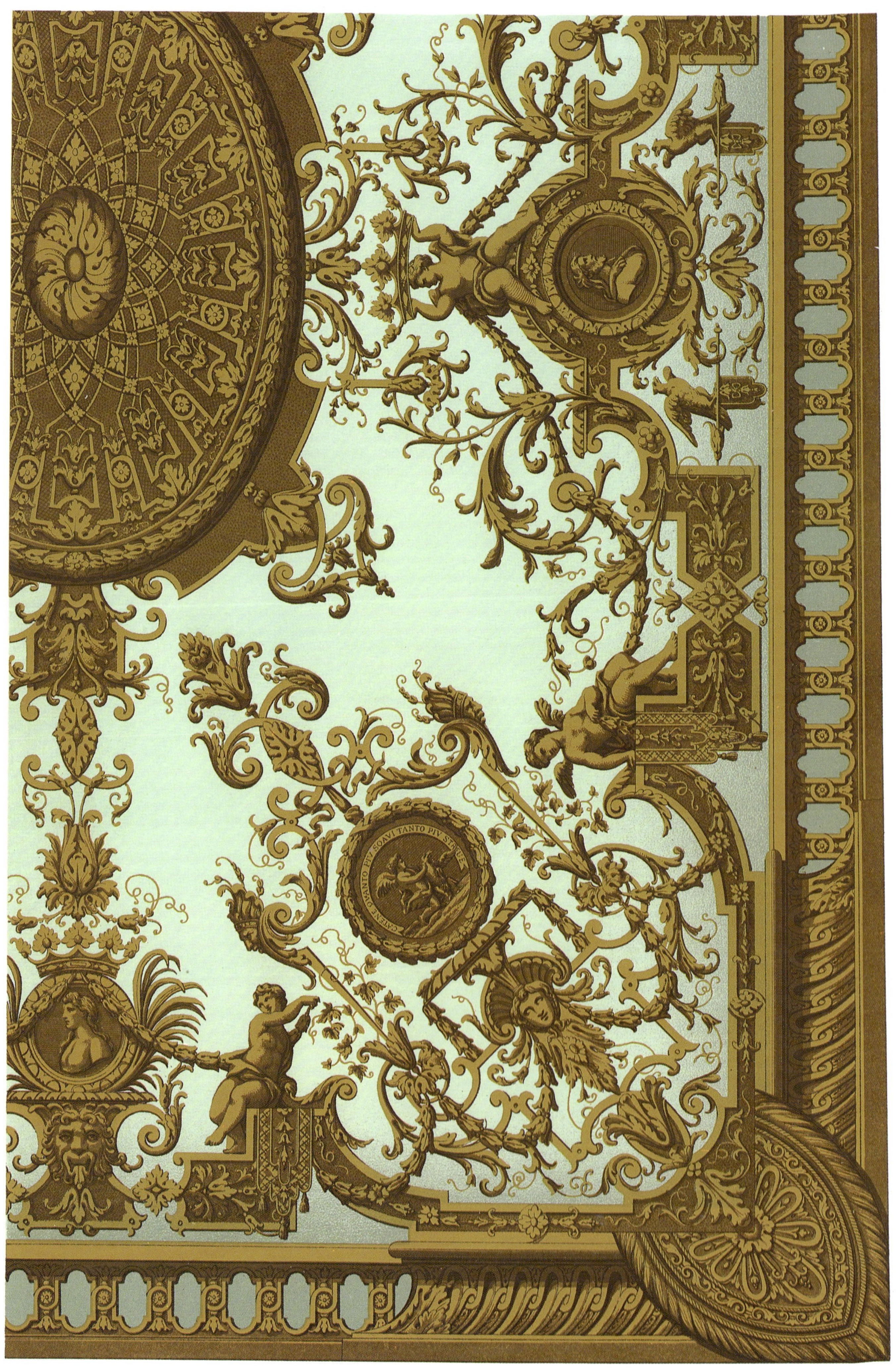

80. Later 17th Century: From a ceiling in a Parisian mansion.

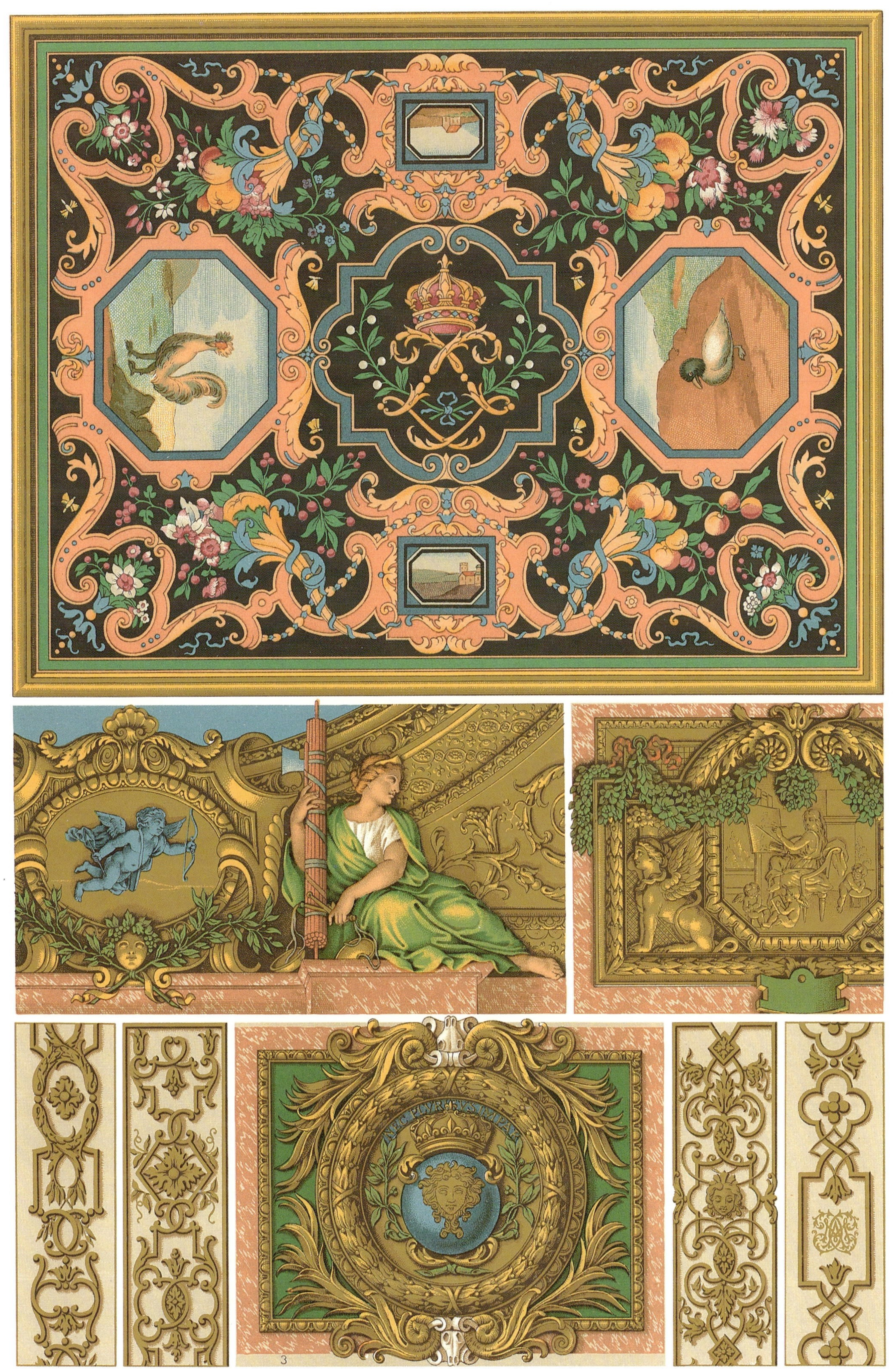

81. 17th Century: From architectural paintings at Versailles and a furniture marble inlay.

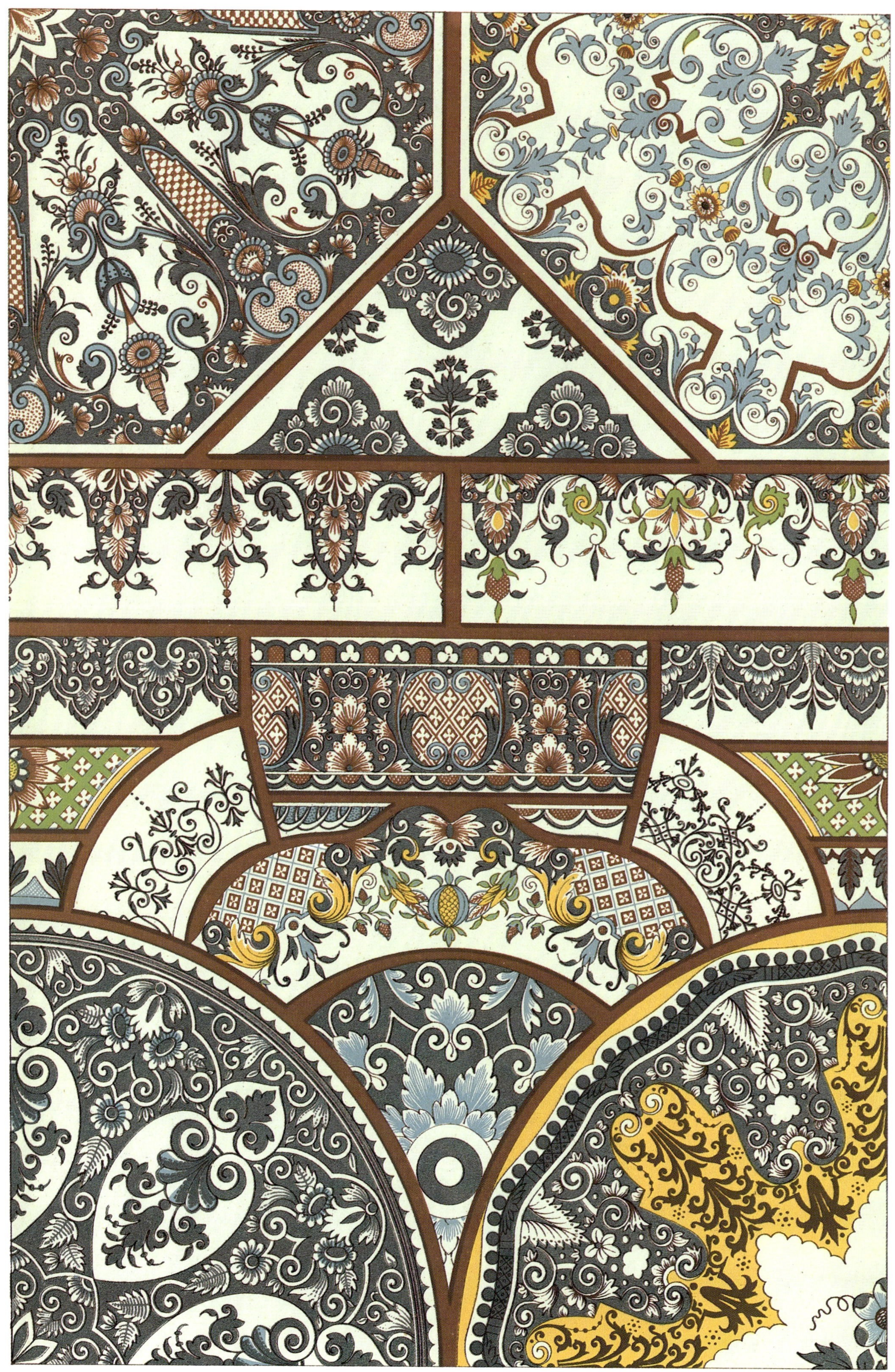

82. 17th & 18th Centuries: From Rouen, Lille and Moustiers faience.

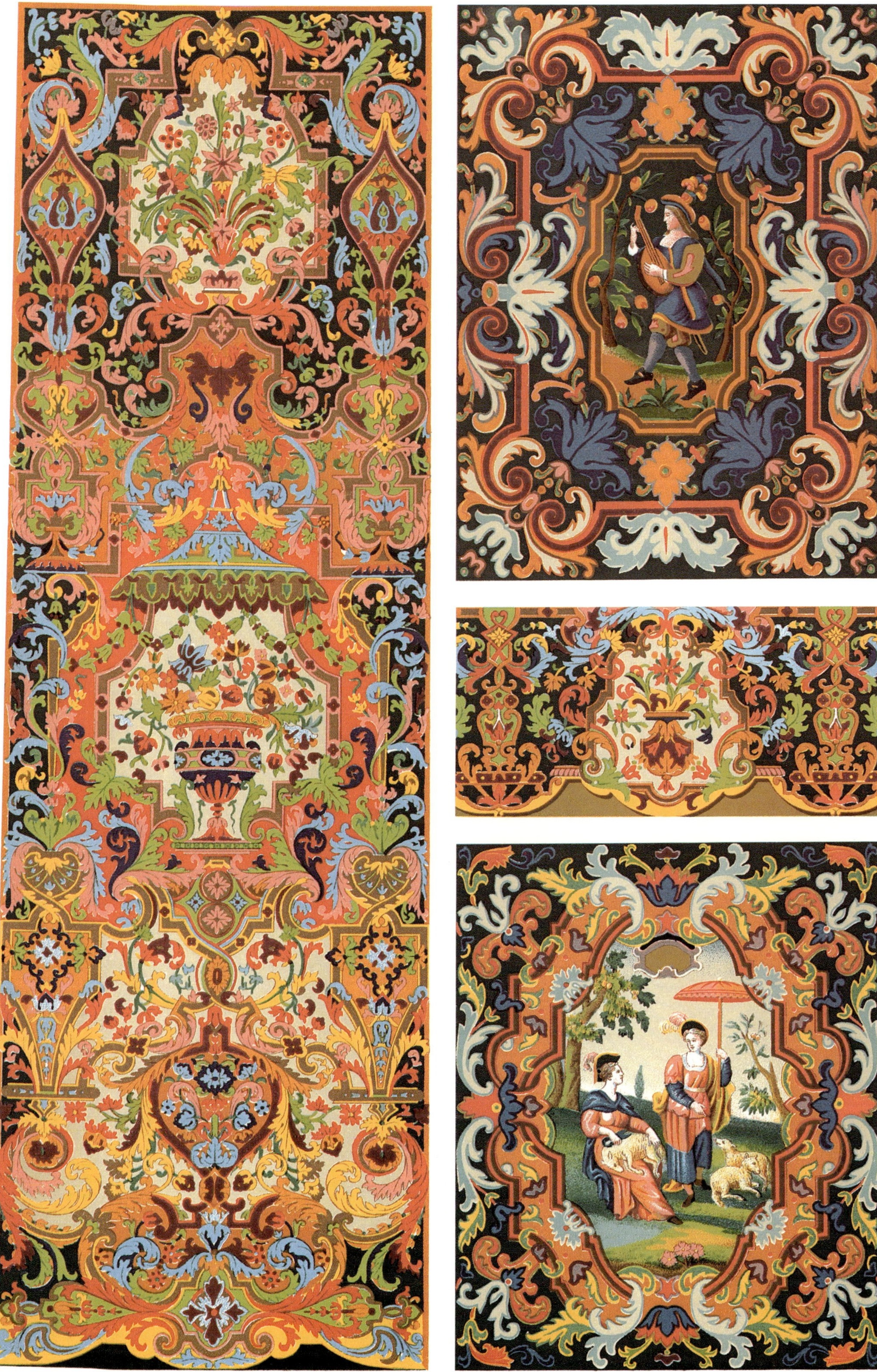

83. Late 17th Century: From French tapestries.

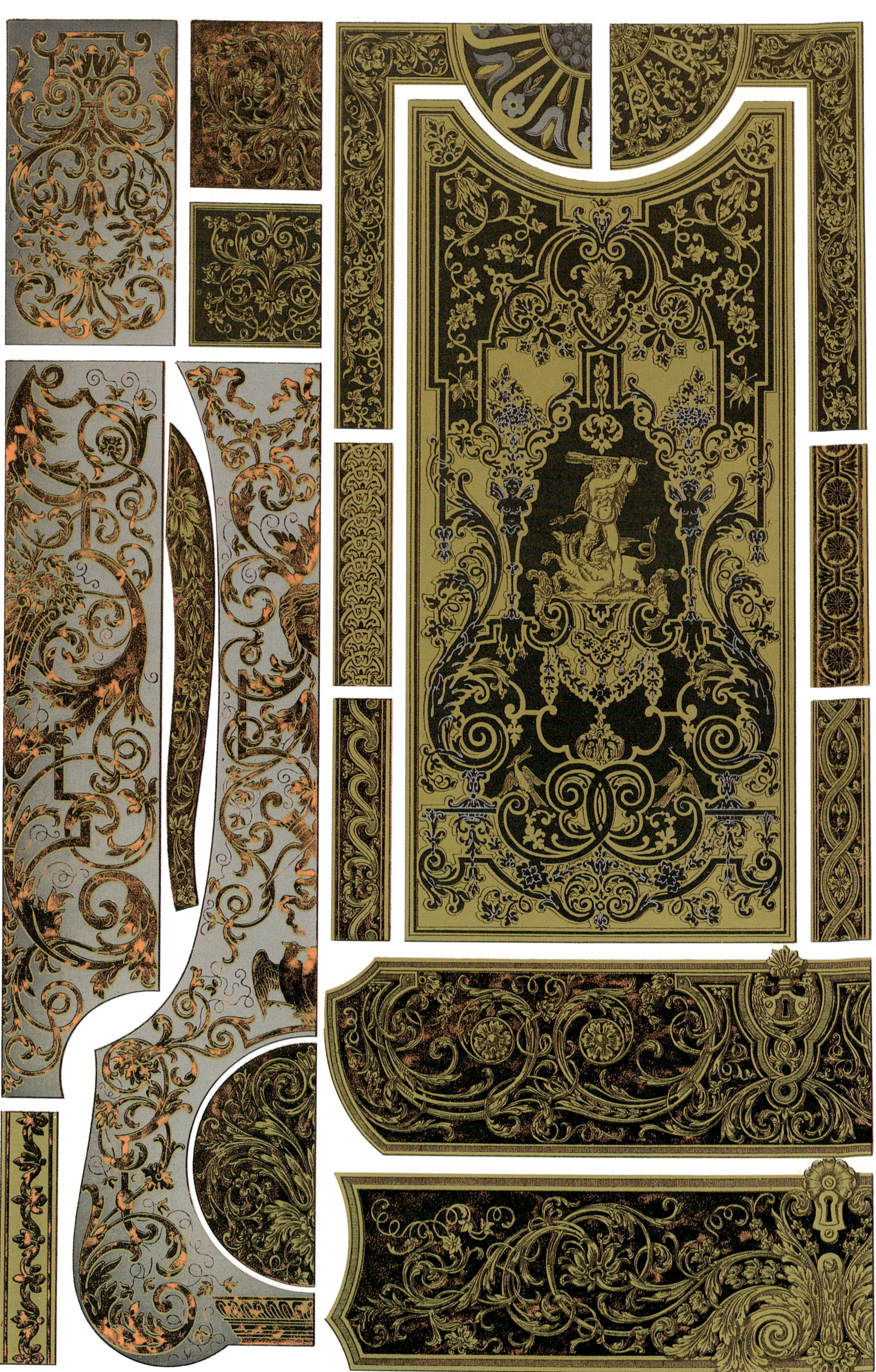

84. 17th & 18th Centuries: From inlaid furniture in the style of A.-C. Boulle.

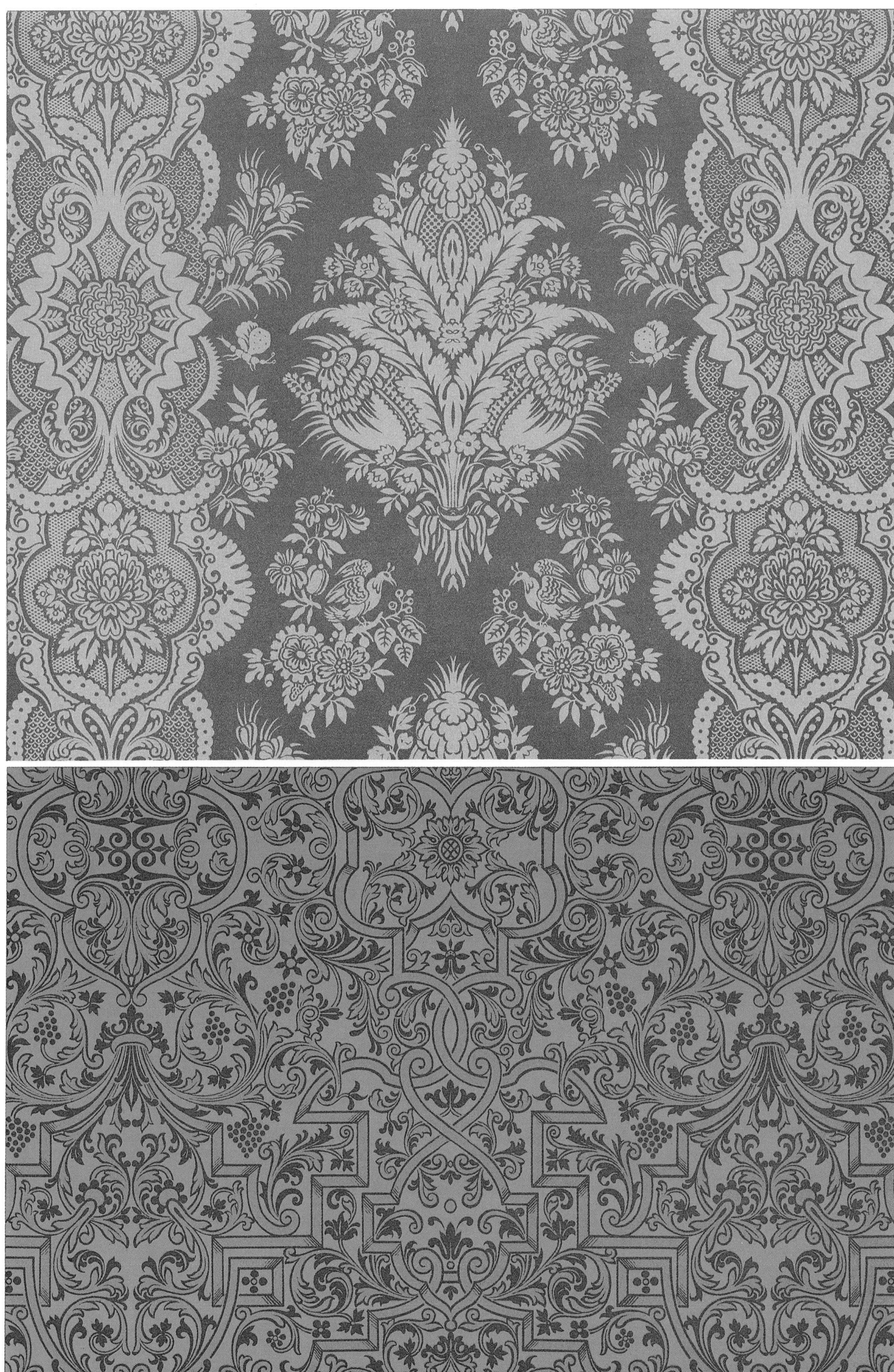

85. Late 17th Century: Silk fabric and stamped book endpaper.

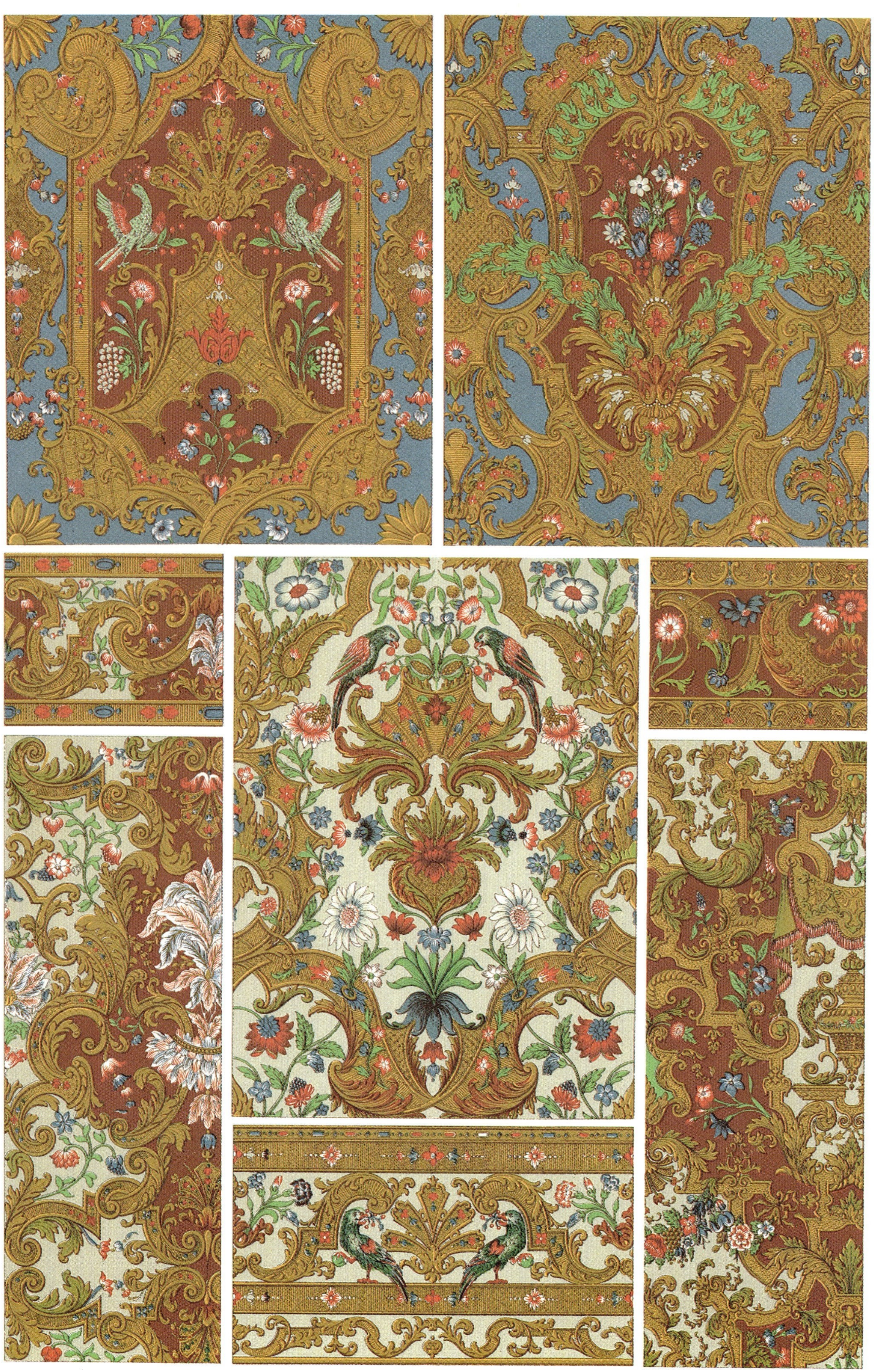

86. 17th & 18th Centuries: From gilt and color-printed leatherwork.

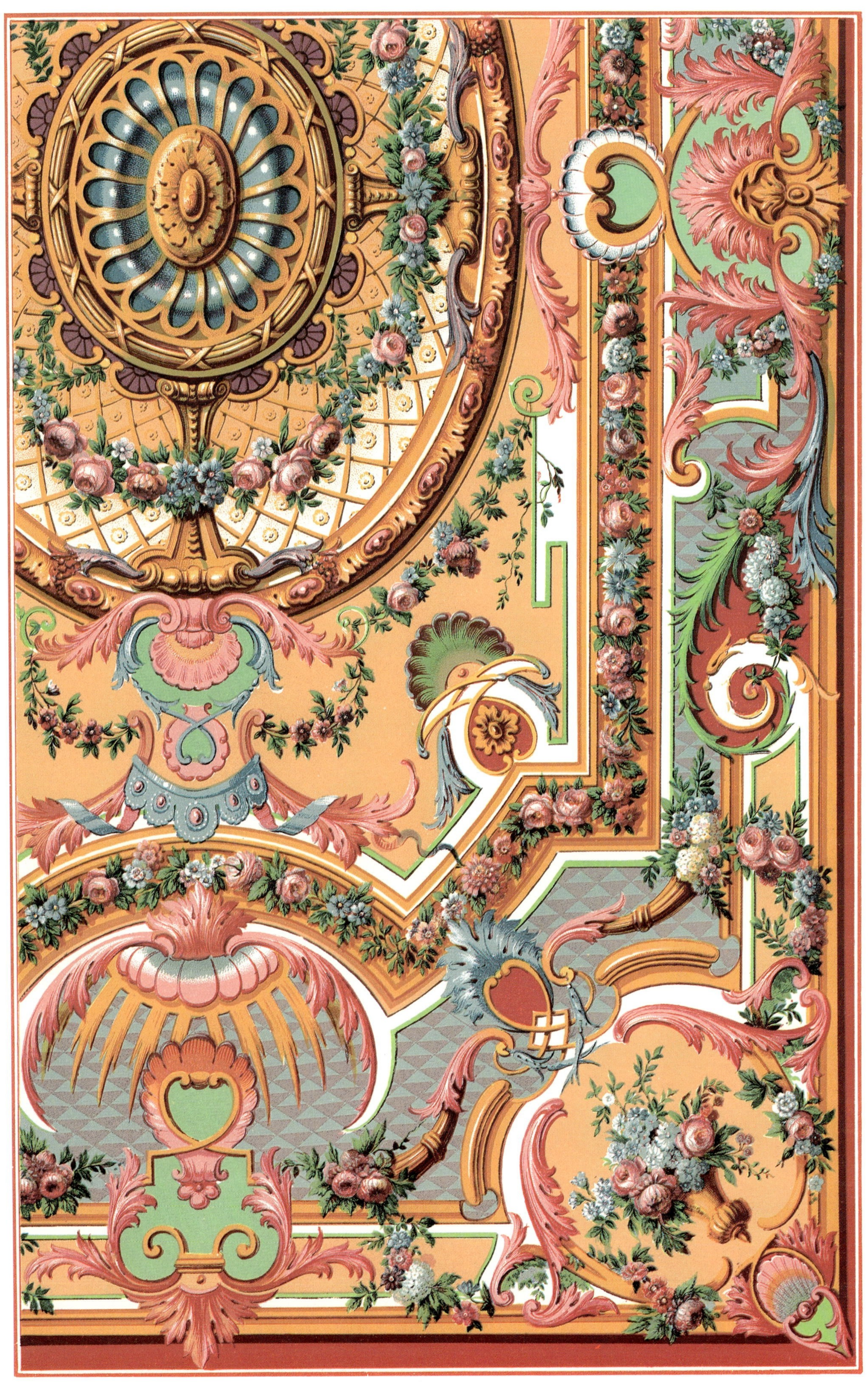

87. 17th/18th Century: Painted Louis XIV carpet design by Robert de Cotte.

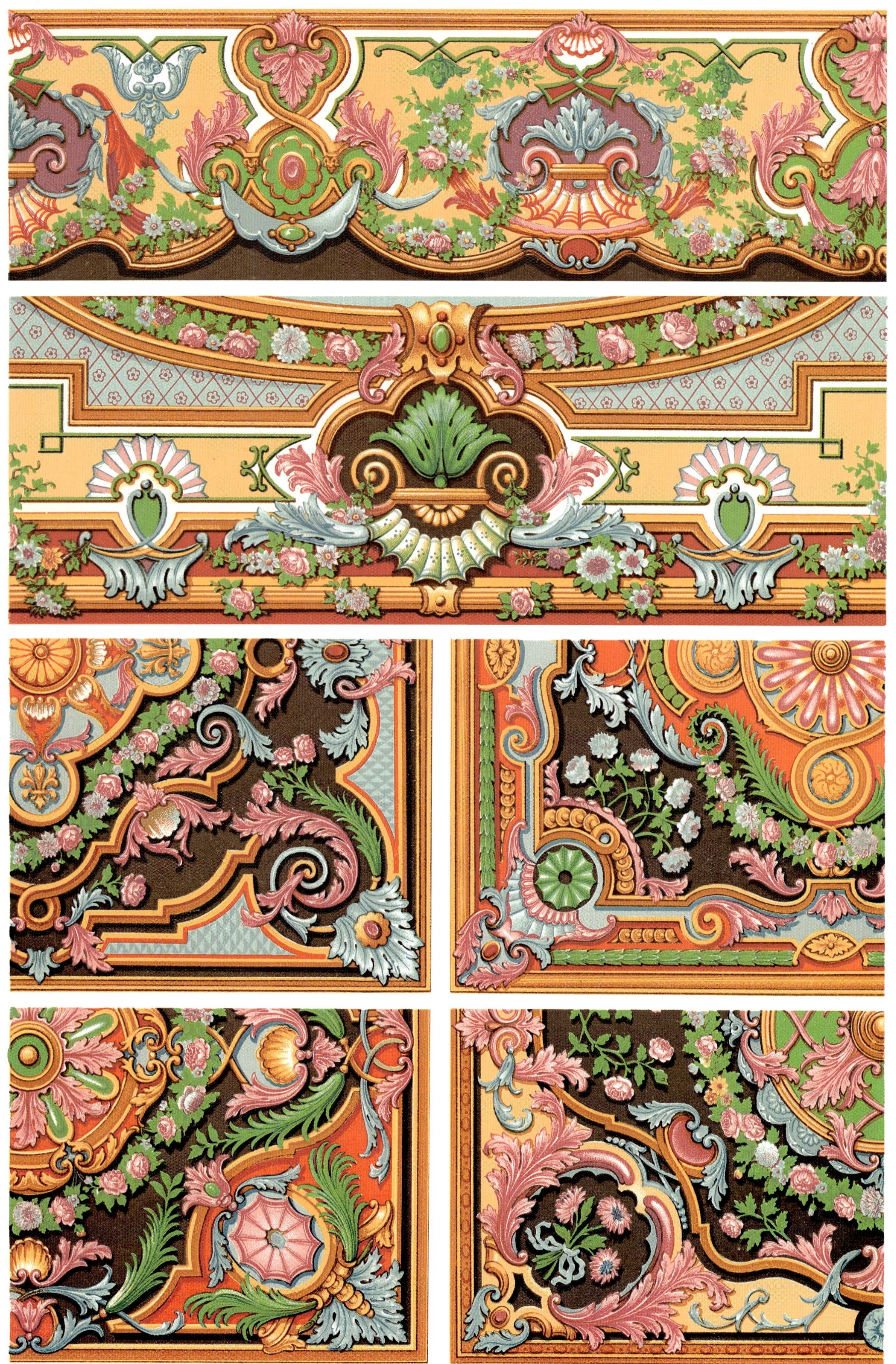

88. 17th/18th Century: Painted tapestry designs by Robert de Cotte and others.

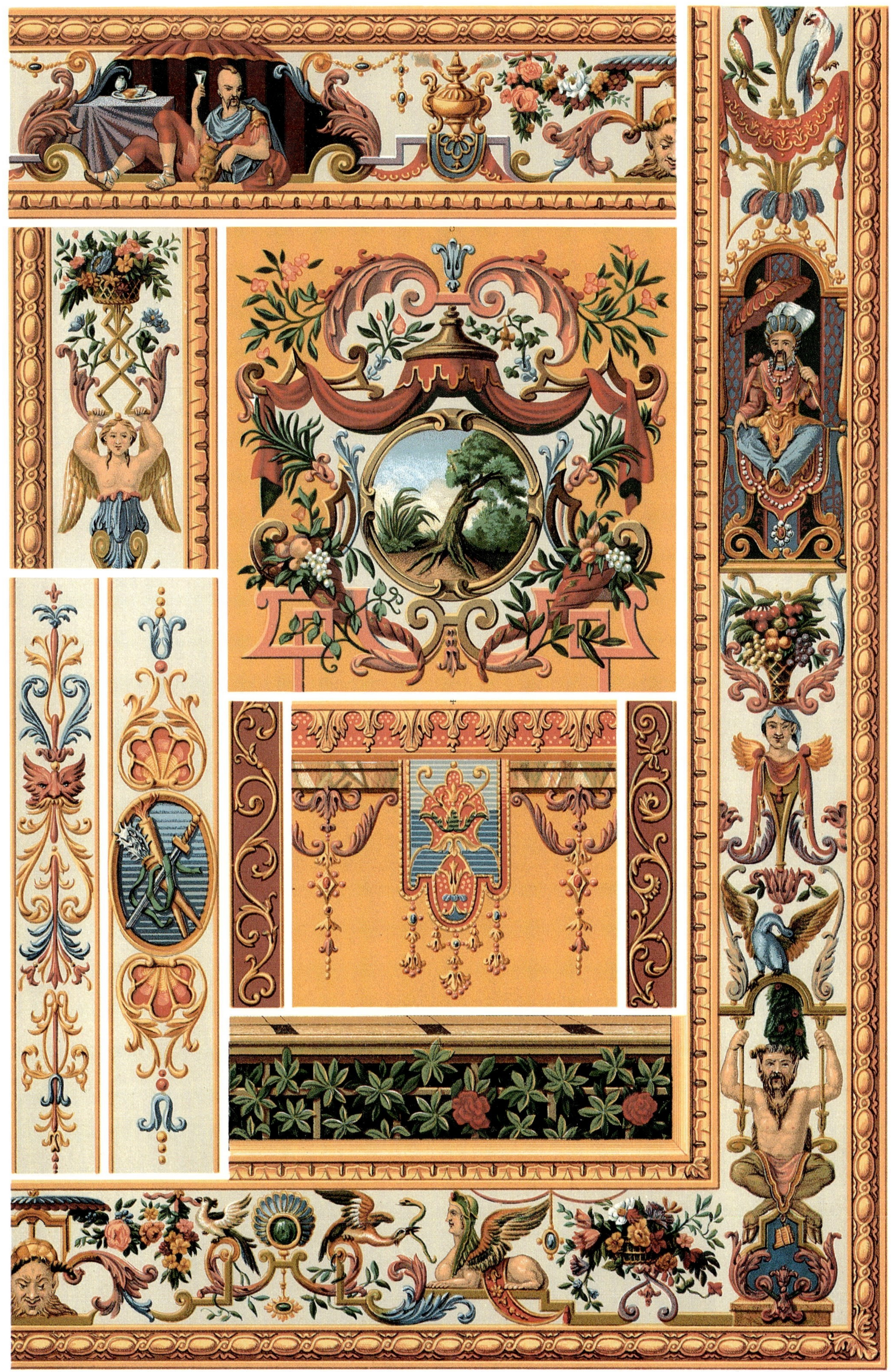

89. 17th & 18th Centuries: From Gobelin tapestries.

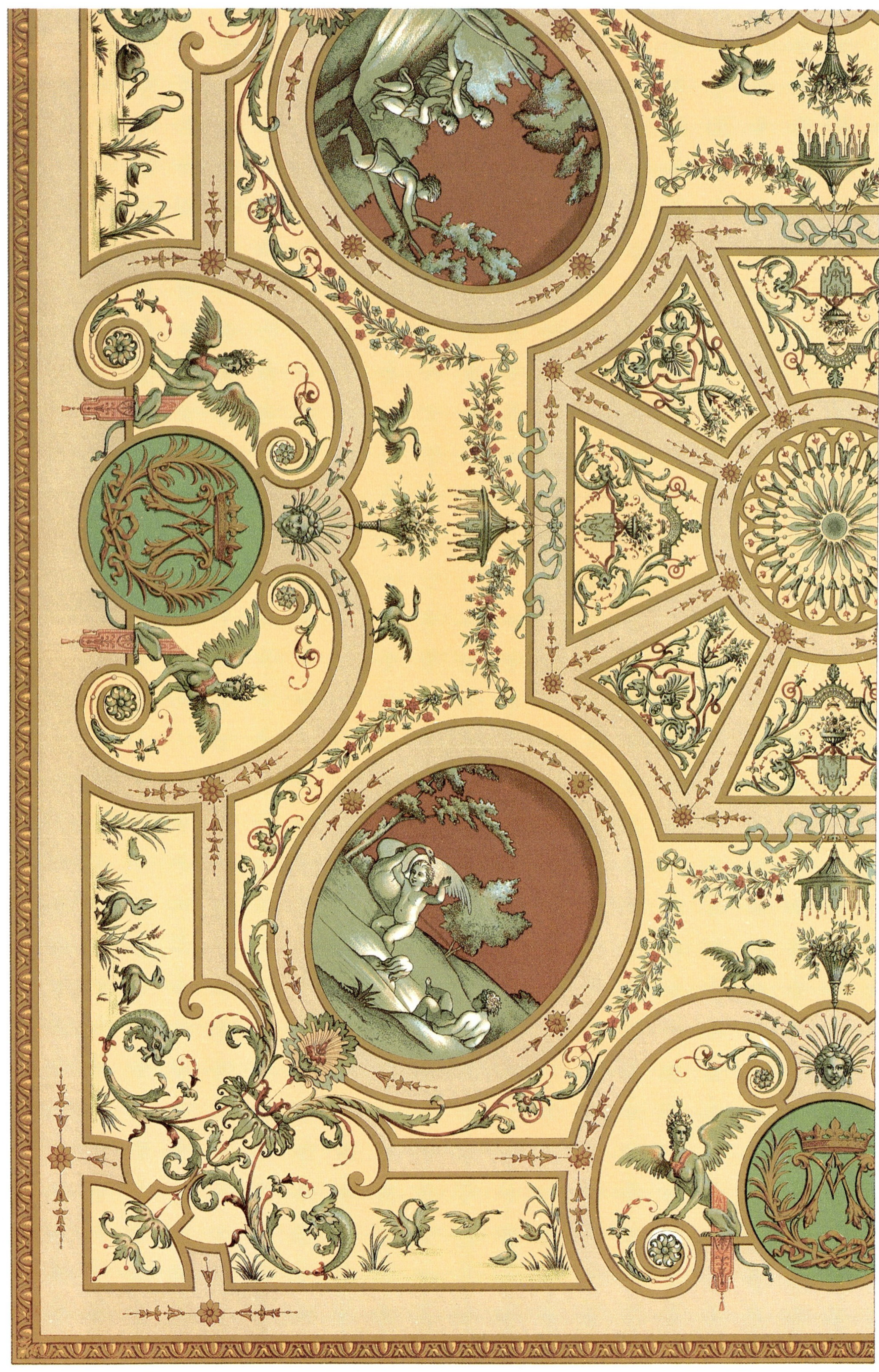

90. Early 18th Century: From a ceiling in a Versailles mansion.

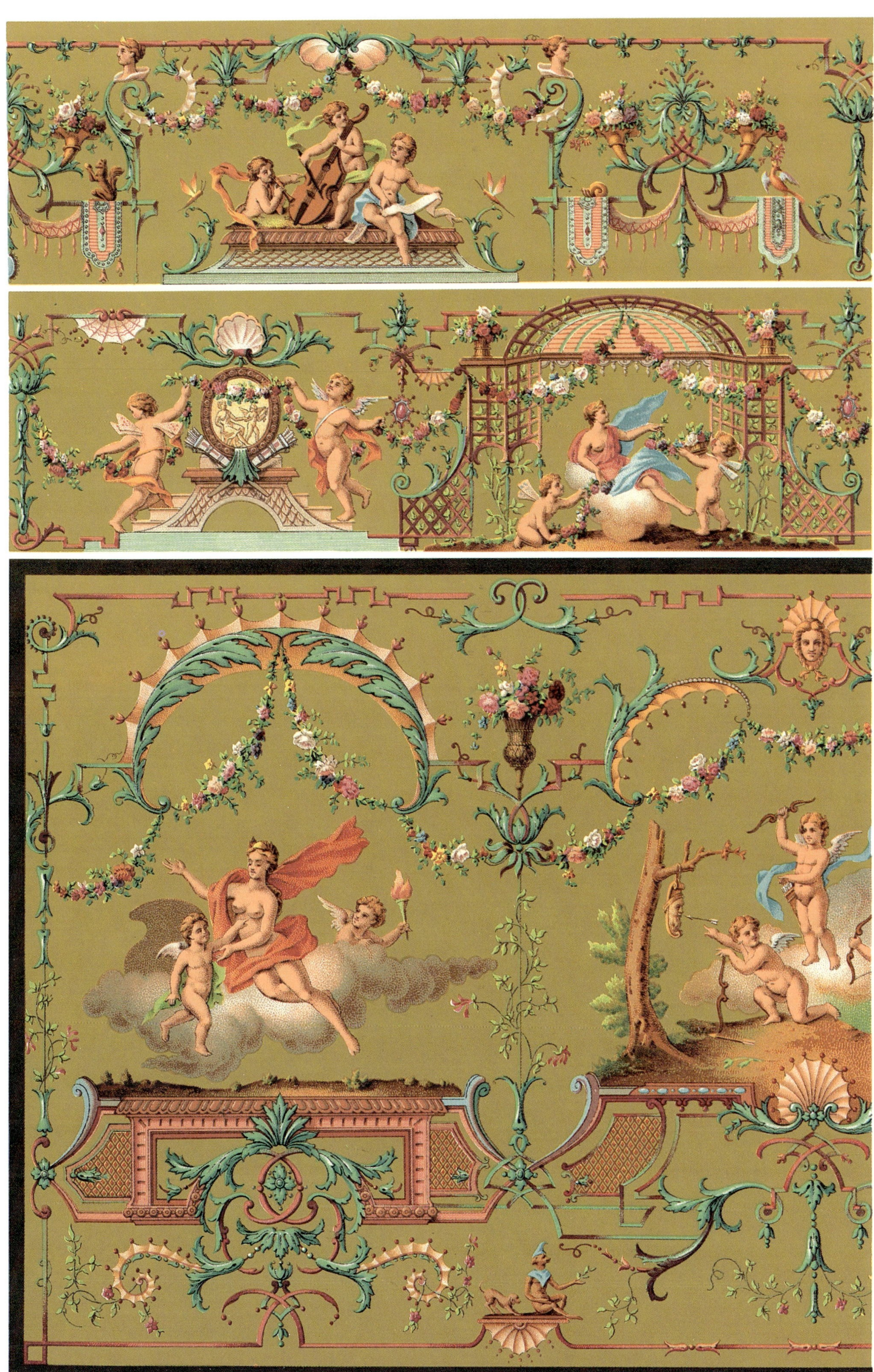

91. Early 18th Century: From a painted French harpsichord.

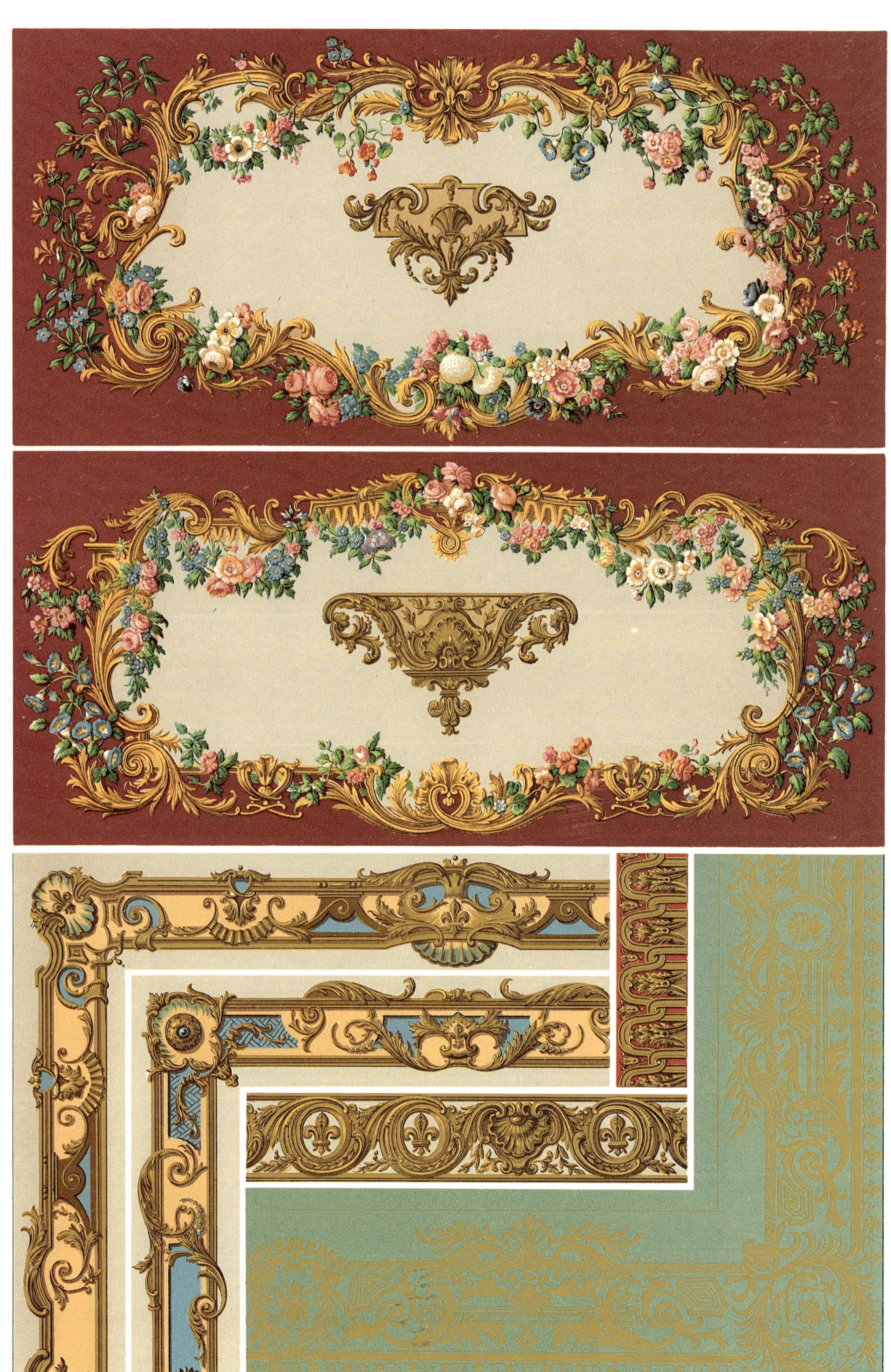

92. 18th Century: From French tapestries, woodwork and a book cover.

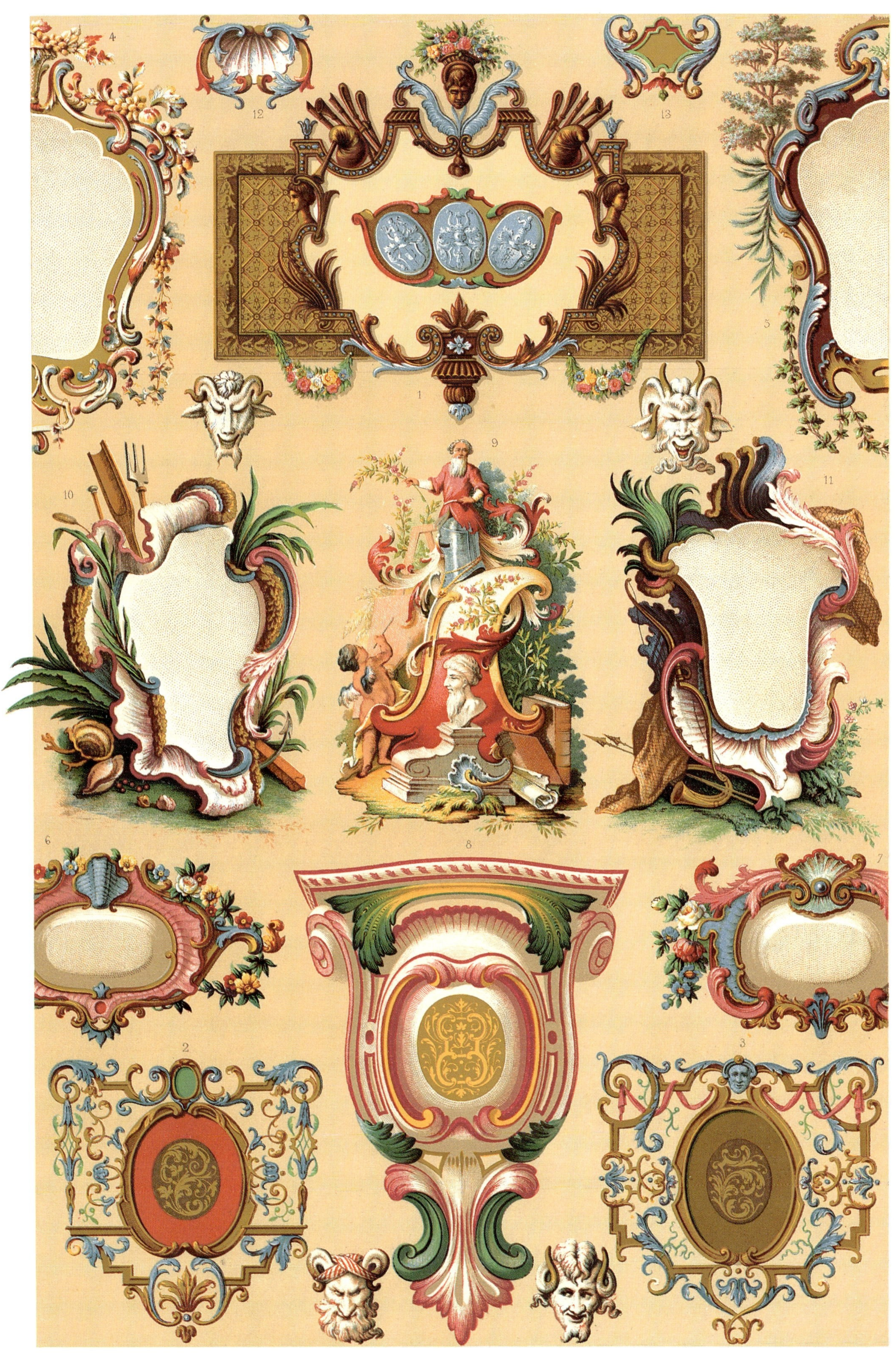

93. 18th Century: Cartouches from various sources, France and Germany.

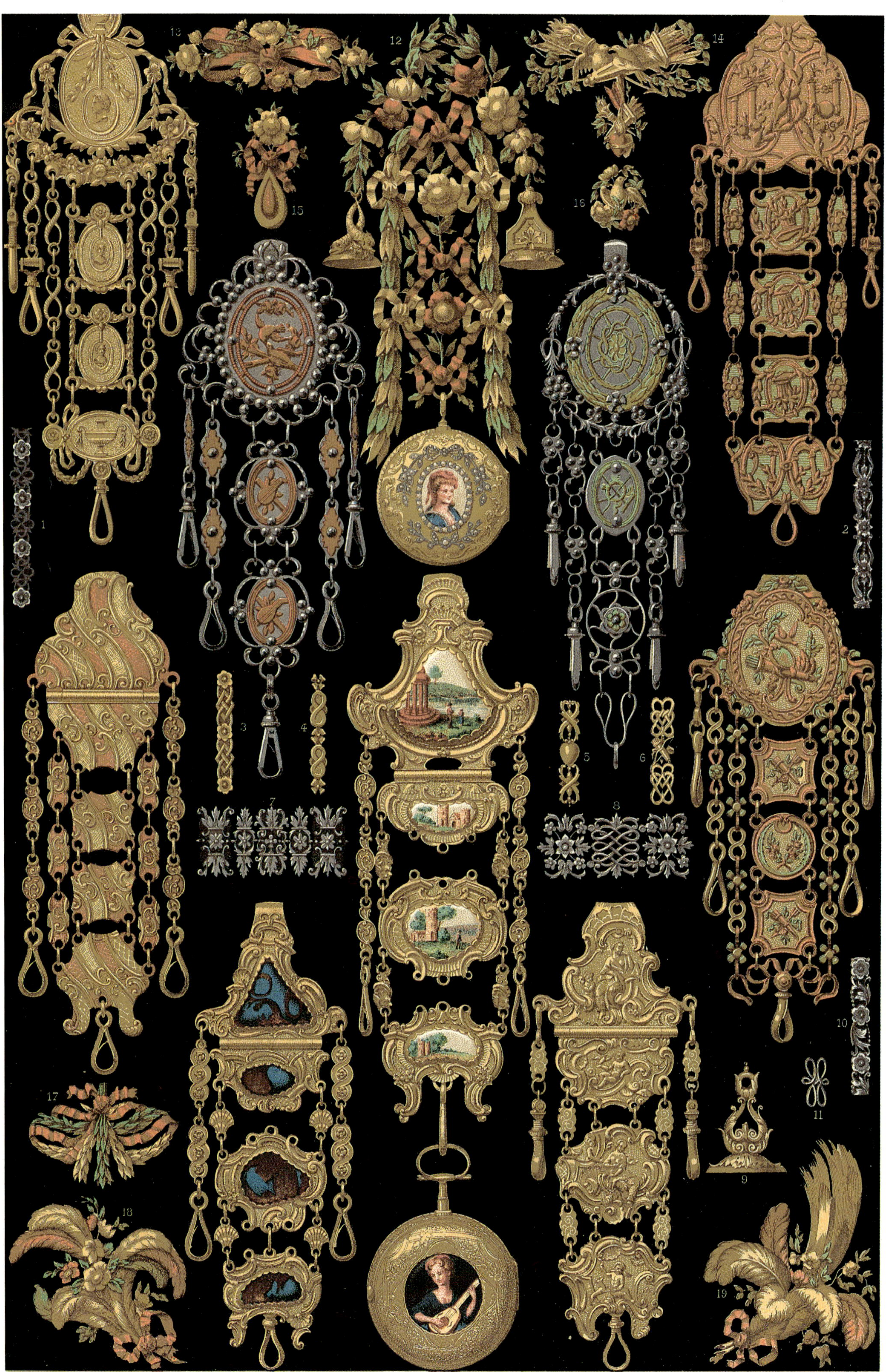

94. 17th and 18th Centuries: French chatelaines.

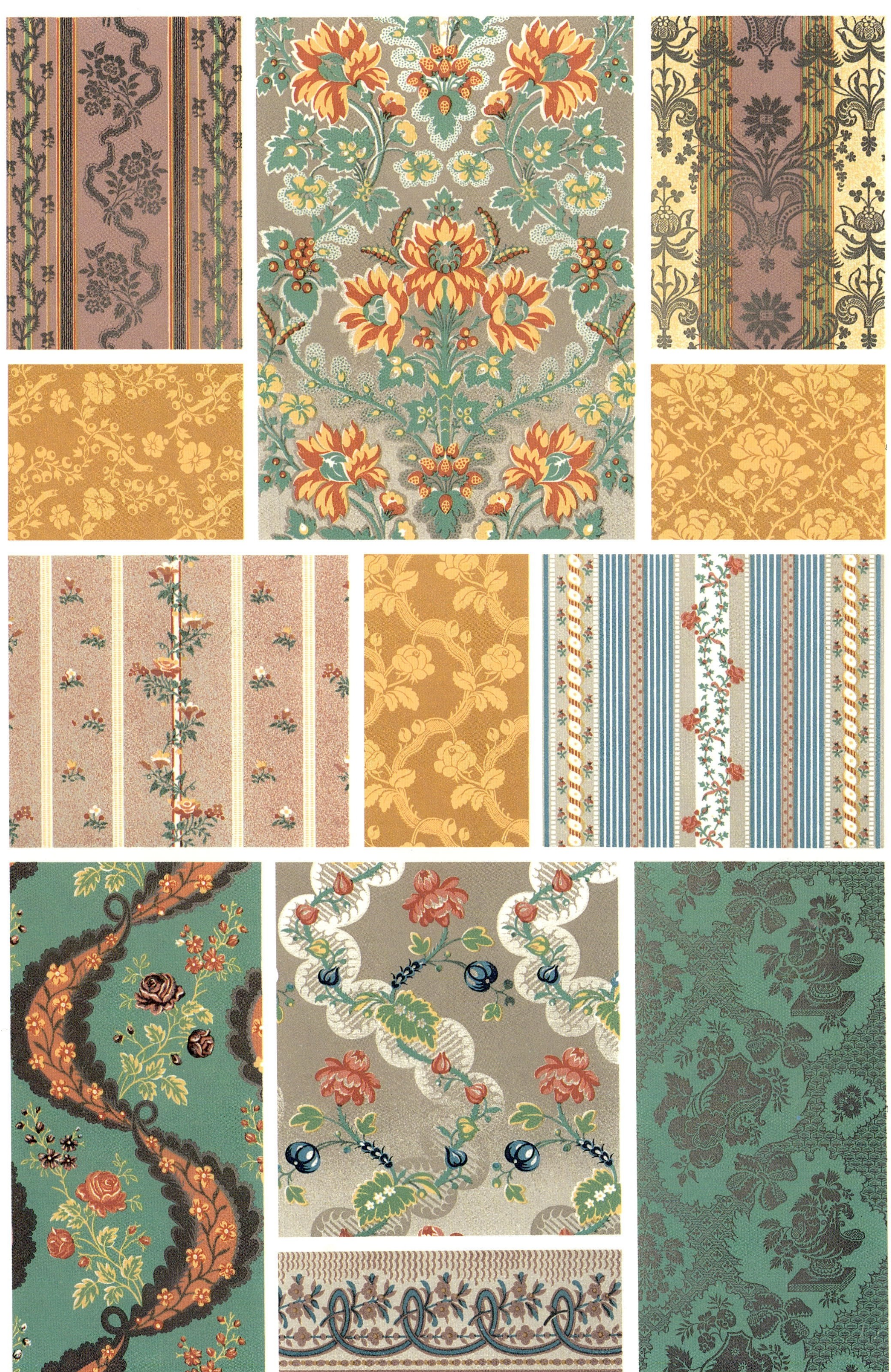

95. 18th Century: French silk fabrics.

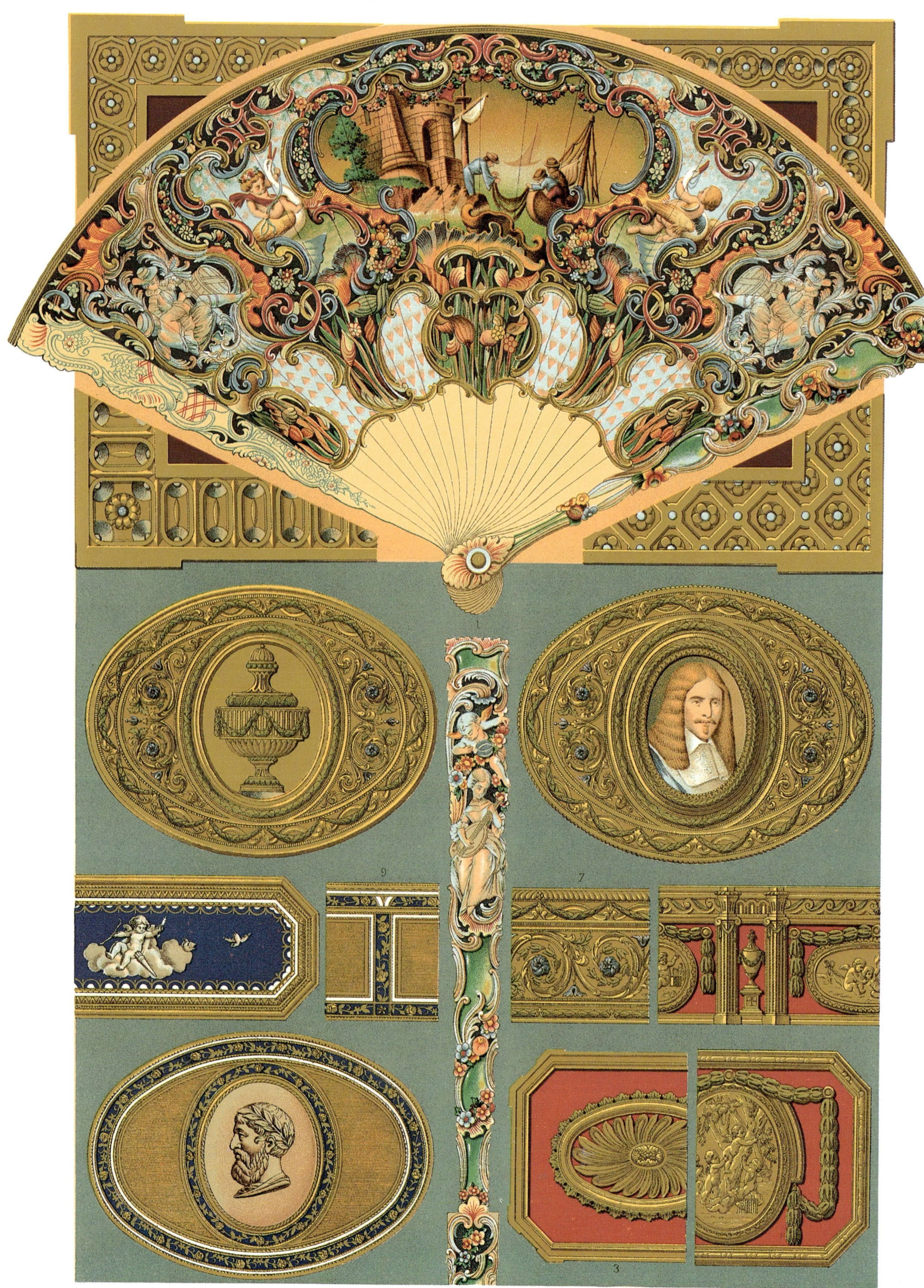

96. 18th Century: Designs from snuffboxes and a fan, and borders (all French).

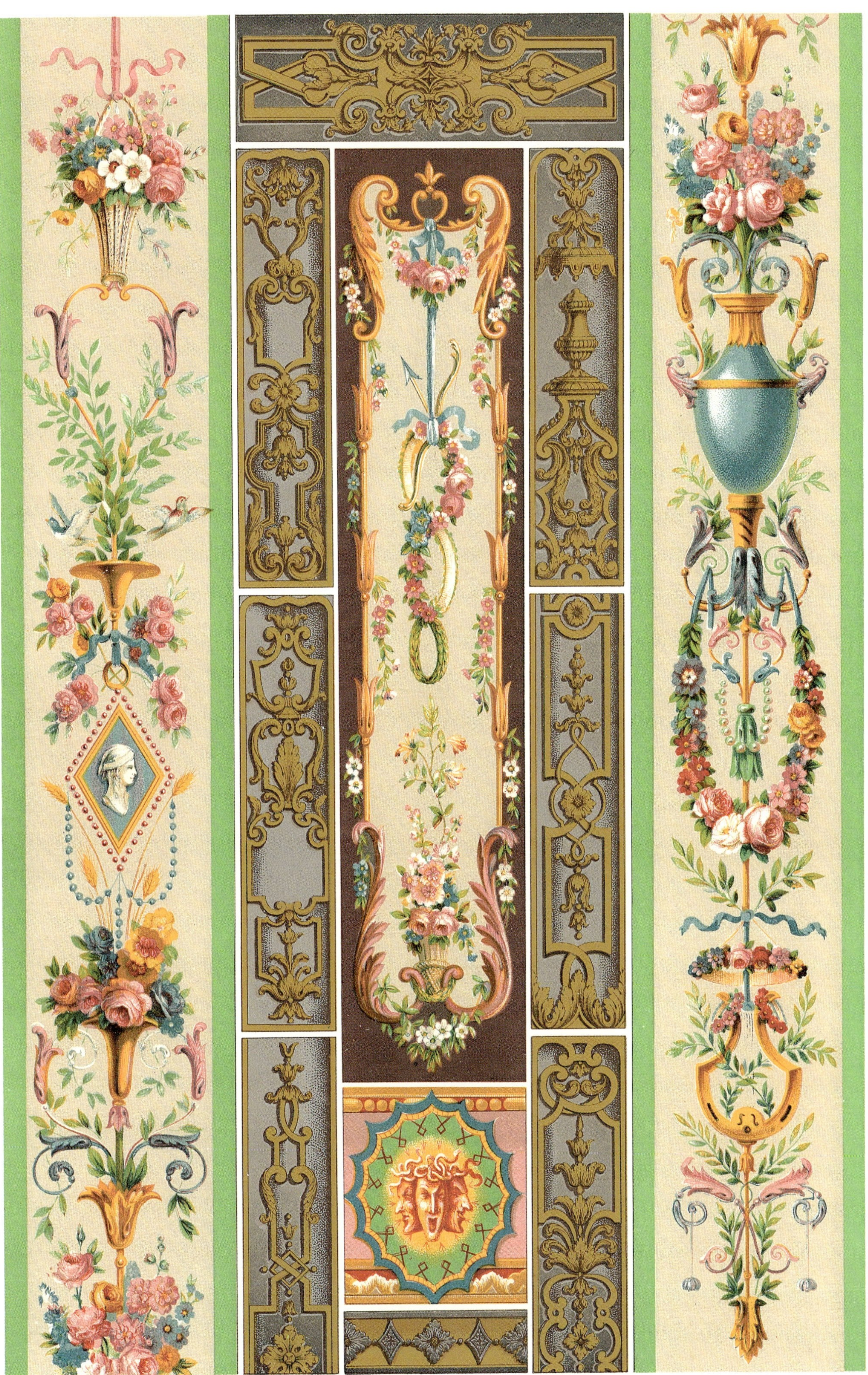

97. 18th Century: From French tapestries.

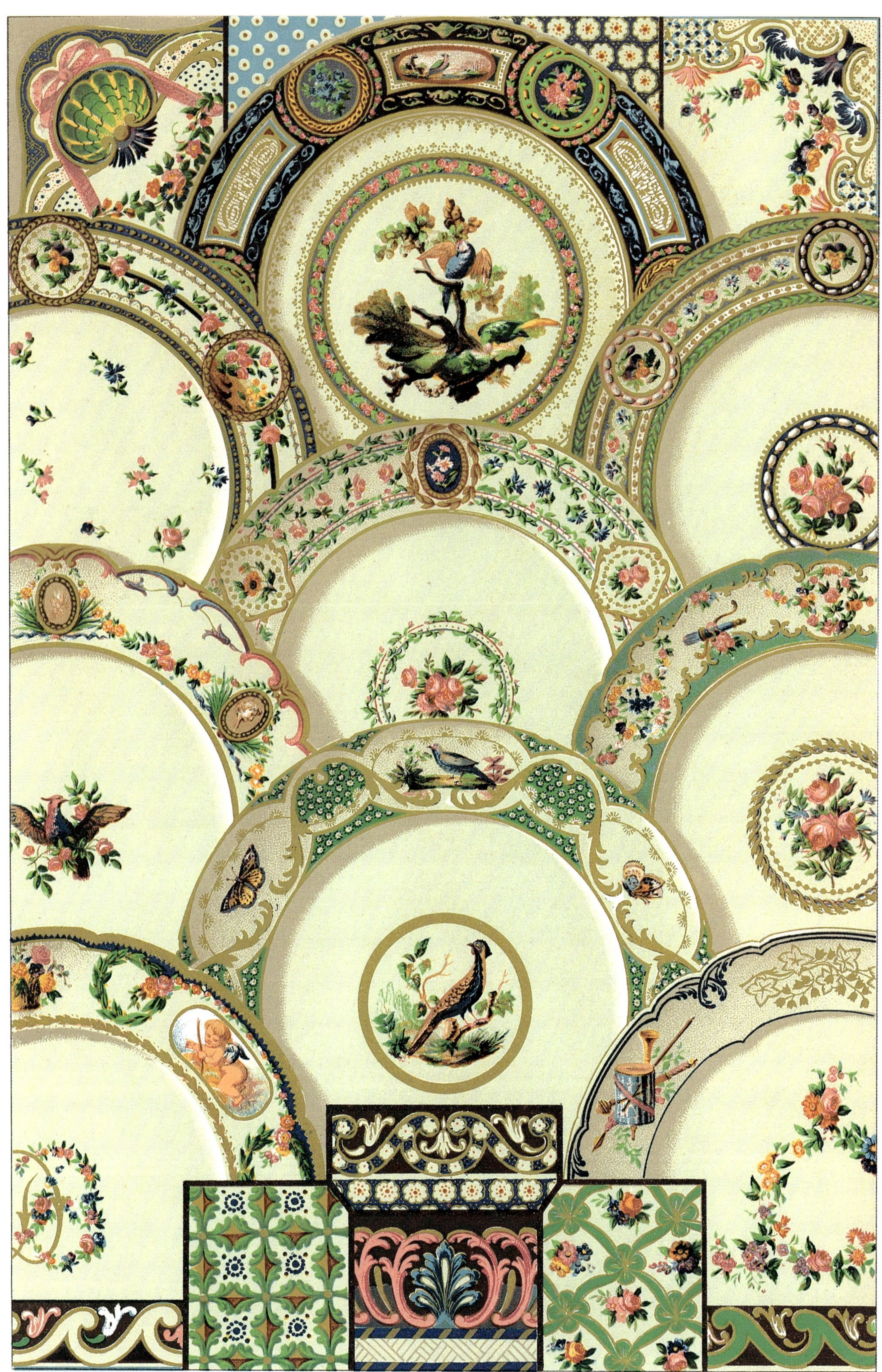

98. 18th Century: From painted Sèvres porcelain.

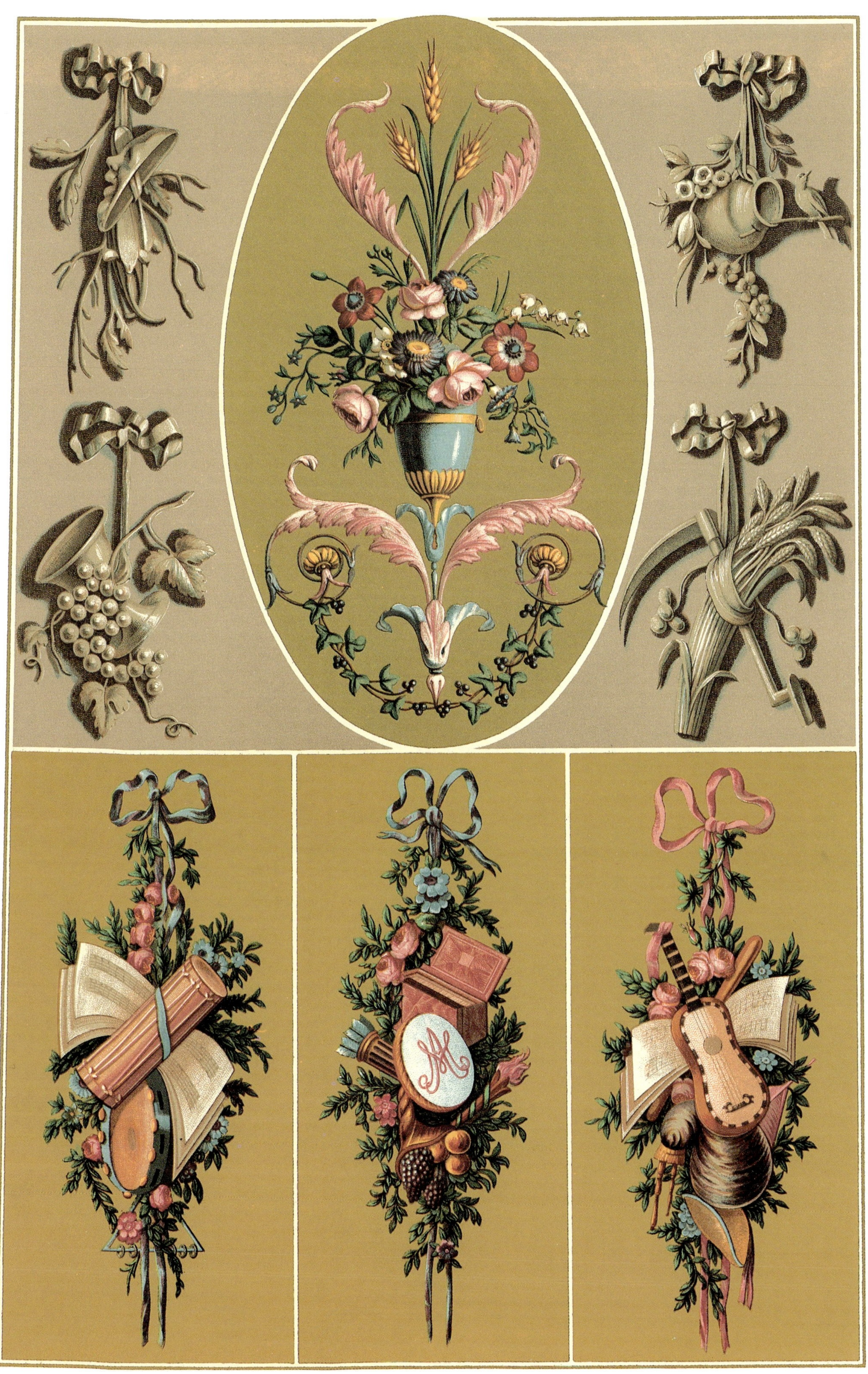

99. 18th Century: Designs from French lacquered woodwork and furniture.

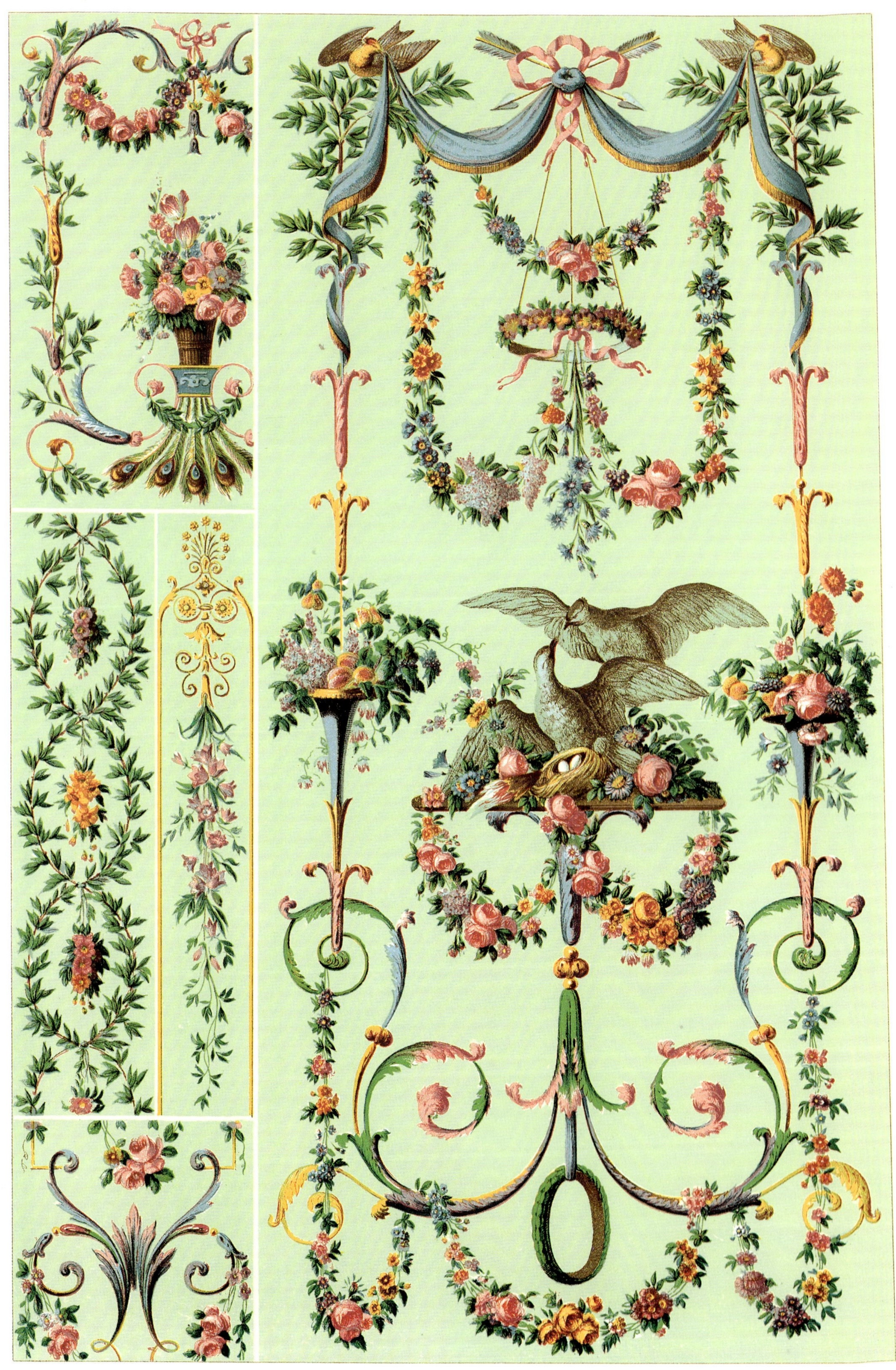

100. 18th Century: Wall painting, from a French mansion, by van Spaendonck.